Learner Autonomy and CALL Environments

Routledge Studies in Computer-Assisted Language Learning

Edited by Carol Chappelle

1. Changing Language Education Through CALL
Edited by Randall P. Donaldson and Margaret A. Haggstrom

2. Errors and Intelligence in Computer-Assisted Language Learning
Parsers and Pedagogues
Trude Heift and Mathias Schulze

3. Learner Autonomy and CALL Environments
Klaus Schwienhorst

Learner Autonomy and CALL Environments

Klaus Schwienhorst

Routledge
Taylor & Francis Group
270 Madison Avenue
New York, NY 10016

Routledge
Taylor & Francis Group
2 Park Square
Milton Park, Abingdon
Oxon OX14 4RN

Routledge is an imprint of Taylor & Francis Group, an Informa business

Printed in the United States of America on acid-free paper
10 9 8 7 6 5 4 3 2 1

International Standard Book Number-13: 978-0-415-36190-3 (Hardcover)

Visit the Taylor & Francis Web site at
http://www.taylorandfrancis.com

and the Routledge Web site at
http://www.routledge.com

Contents

Acknowledgements

This book was written in various countries, and many people have supported it over the years. My first thank you goes to Carol Chapelle, who gave valuable advice throughout the whole process of writing and provided the link to the publisher. A big thank you also goes to David Little, who I was lucky enough to work with for over ten years in Dublin, and who has influenced my thinking enormously and provided the space and time for my thoughts to develop. My colleagues in Dublin have been very helpful, in particular Breffni O'Rourke, who was a great discussion partner over lunch and was always there to point me to interesting new developments. During the sometimes hectic and frankly mad work schedule, many friends showed their understanding and never let me forget that the ideas expressed in this book needed to be grounded in and are relevant for everyday life. Thank you also to my fabulous colleague Peter Kapec in Bonn, who was my Tandem co-organiser during several projects, and Alexandre Borgia, a programming genius from Québec with the rare gift to see the big (pedagogical) picture. My thank you also goes to Claudia Boscolo for inspiration and support in difficult times. Most of all, however, I would like to thank my family: my late father, Heribert, who sadly did not live to see the publication of this book; my mother Rosi who has provided an island of rest whenever I needed one; and my brother Andreas and his girlfriend Petra who constantly reminded me of life beyond academia. They will probably never know how much they helped. It is to my family that I dedicate this book.

Java™, JavaScript™ and all Java™-based trademarks and logos are trademarks or registered trademarks of Sun Microsystems, Inc. in the U.S. and other countries.

Microsoft and Windows are either registered trademarks or trademarks of Microsoft Corporation in the United States and/or other countries.

Moodle is a registered trademark of The Moodle Trust (http://moodle.org).

TopClass is a registered trademark (http://www.wbtsystems.com).

Visual Thesaurus™ (powered by Thinkmap®) ©2004 Thinkmap, Inc. All rights reserved (http://www.thinkmap.com/).

WebCT is based in Lynfield, Massachusetts, U.S.A. (http://www.webct.com).

The use of the Wimba trademark is by permission of Horizon Wimba (http://www.horizonwimba.com/).

Wida is used by permission of Wida Software Ltd. (http://www.wida.co.uk).

Introduction

The title of this book refers to two concepts that pervade much of language learning research and pedagogy today. On the one hand, we have the pedagogical concept of learner autonomy, which — though often misunderstood — has influenced many approaches to language learning for the past decade or two. On the other hand, we have computer-assisted language learning, an expression which by itself does not really say much about pedagogical concepts but rather focuses on the use of computer technology to learn languages. These are concepts on two different levels. Learner autonomy is a concept that refers to a capacity of each learner, while CALL (Computer Assisted Language Leaning) just refers to the use of computers in language learning (whatever the pedagogical approach is). It may be argued that starting with a pedagogical concept, a goal that one would like to achieve, and then choosing the right materials (read: materials that are most likely to fulfil this goal), including technology, would be a plausible way to proceed. In that view, I would outline what the most important features of learner autonomy are, then see how computers can help us achieve these goals. After all, should not our work as teachers and researchers be first and foremost guided by proper pedagogical concepts? Concepts that have arisen out of research in second language acquisition?

Then there is a view, or more often a practice, whereby we start with a (new) technology and see what fantastic things learners can do with it. More often than not, researchers and teachers in this mode refrain from talking about pedagogical principles and concepts. Rather, they suggest that in some way, technology itself will drive learners to do certain things that support their language learning process. Technology, or more specifically, the computer, replaces sound pedagogy. It becomes immaterial, or so it seems, that we often do not know what exactly the computer manages to "do" in the learner, and what role this plays in the overall language learning process, nor how it relates to any pedagogy. Unfortunately, I have seen a substantial number of papers at conferences that were in the latter vein. This technology-focused view often lacks differentiation and is not founded in sound empirical research. That is not to say that many CALL researchers and teachers have not started using computers out of a genuinely perceived need or because of a key experience with that technology, even an epiphany-like experience where they saw clearly what it could be used for, and only much later started thinking about how the technology fit in with their pedagogical goals. I can admit that I was familiar with and fascinated by MOOs (Multi-user domain, Object-Oriented), long before I even knew what learner autonomy was or entailed.

I had been reading and working on James Joyce's *Finnegans Wake*, and there was not one single student or lecturer at my university with whom I could discuss my work. I was also working at the Self-Access Centre at the English Department of the University of Münster, Germany, where I was involved in setting up one of the first computer centres of this kind in Germany, which allowed me to explore what all this new technology had to offer. At some point, through a mailing list, I was made aware of Joyce reading groups that met every week online, in a text-based "live" environment called a MOO. I logged on, and very quickly started talking English to the many users who were connected. I was stunned. Meeting and talking to a native English speaker was still a big challenge and somewhat rare (in spite of a strong British military presence in Münster), and here was an opportunity to do this on a daily basis, whenever I felt like it.

Very soon, I also realised that it was a powerful tool to get things done, to collaborate, to learn. One day I was struggling with a networking issue regarding our computer lab, and logged on to my usual MOO and contacted the first person I met there. Because it was "live", he (or rather, I assumed it was a "he") was able to literally take me through the problem and see for myself which steps I needed to take to solve the issue. I could show him program code and he would comment on it. I got the issue resolved. After a good while, I asked him whether I could help him with anything in return. Probably not, he replied, as he had to finish an assignment for German, and it was on the city of Münster. Also, this assignment had to be done within two hours, as it was already five in the morning where he was, and he had been "surfing" the Internet all night long. I told him that I was both German and actually located in Münster, and told him everything I knew, partly describing what I saw from my office window. At the end of the talk, he finished by saying he needed some time to edit the data (he had recorded our chat in a so-called log).

We were both overwhelmed by the experience and never "met" again after this, but the experience showed me several things that we as researchers still struggle to pin down with objective parameters. As a language learner, I felt challenged, but not overpowered by the intensive demands of L2 input and output. There was a relaxing atmosphere overall. Actually, I did not even feel like a language learner, as I felt totally embedded in an environment and totally focused on real-world tasks. I also realised that in real life, I probably would not have spent two hours talking to a high school student, asking him for advice on work problems, and accepting his expertise. There was an efficiency of communication and collaboration, of mutual support and trust, that allowed us to get quite a few things done and yet enjoying them while we were working on them. In the course of this collaboration, we also learned a lot about the way each of us was going about when we tried to understand or learn something, and how to adapt to each other's working modes. Here was not only a communication tool, but a whole learning space, which allowed me to take notes and record the communication for later analysis; allowed me to communicate very quickly via text; offered tools for presentation, note-taking, and programming; and even allowed me to modify or create these tools!

When I then learnt more about learner autonomy, first by talking to and working with Lienhard Legenhausen and Leni Dam, then by working with David Little, I quickly began to see that this combination of technology and pedagogy might be ideal for language learning. Thus, in a way, I am one of those researchers and teachers who started by becoming fascinated with a particular technology. However, many benefits I recognised in the way I could use this tool also happened to be goals of a learner-autonomy-based pedagogy. My view of CALL technology has therefore never been driven by the technology itself but its affordances and the way these are then exploited in a pedagogical framework of tasks. In other words: what does the technology allow the learner (and teacher) to do in terms of learning (teaching) opportunities, and how will she make use of these affordances within a wider pedagogical framework?

Of course, when we implement a new communication technology, we may find that the communication that is produced with the help of this technology can vary substantially from those communication modes we are familiar with (and that we want our learners to be able to cope with). But this could stem from a number of sources: the activity; the pedagogical set-up; the combination of learners; the unfamiliarity of the learners; to name a few factors. Just with any other communication in the second language, we need to ask whether it is relevant and useful for the learner. In some cases, this might involve very specific communication skills that are — at least at the time of writing — very much focused on one communication technology and are strongly connected to its importance. Consider the case of SMS messaging in the second language. It is of great importance on the learning agenda of many language learners, and deserves inclusion on many language curricula as a skill in itself. On the other hand, it is probably questionable whether the MOO technology in itself will be used as a major communication medium in itself, but the communication in this medium, as I will show later, shares enough features with both speaking and writing to make it a useful tool for language learning.

I would therefore argue that, yes, we do need a sound pedagogical framework, but that we also need to assess critically what each particular technology offers us, both in terms of familiar and unfamiliar features; we might call this with Gibson (1966, 1979) the affordances of certain technologies. In this two-tiered view, we should be careful about making generalised statements about technology such as "all chat programs are..." or "all gap-filling exercises do...", but rather look at the specific features of each program, and how it is embedded in the task and wider pedagogical context. Technologies can be used within different pedagogical concepts. However, it is also the case that some technologies are too inflexible to be adapted to different pedagogical contexts. Sound pedagogy and technology need to work hand in hand. For instance, if a technology provides no choices to a learner who has achieved a high degree of learner autonomy, this learner may not feel that she has ownership of the language learning process any more and become less engaged with the program. If a technology only offers L1 support and interface when the learner is used to communicating in the L2 at all times, the learner might be forced to code-switch between L1 and L2 in a way that is unfamiliar to her and possibly detrimental to the learning process.

I will begin my first chapter with two very concrete scenarios of communication technology in use in the language classroom. I will use these scenarios as a practical reference point throughout to explore the concept of learner autonomy, and also to explain what it is not. One could see learner autonomy, for example, as a capacity, a goal, or a learning/teaching agenda. In any case, learner autonomy serves to develop three different areas in the learner (and also the teacher):

- It tries to support reflection and greater linguistic, metalinguistic, and metacognitive awareness of language and language learning.
- It tries to support a communicator and collaborator, a learner (and teacher) that is able to cope with a variety of communication situations and partners in a second language.
- It tries to support an explorer of and experimenter with language who is willing to develop learning agendas, take charge of her learning, and assume responsibility for it.

The first chapter will look at these three areas in more detail. I will try not so much to present the variety of views that exists in these areas, but rather to synthesise them by referring to the relevant literature. I will use these three areas throughout the book to make it easier for the reader to see parallels between pedagogical theory, CALL developments, and the concrete example of the MOO learning environment. I will close the book by introducing a number of technologies that are being developed by other researcher, but which could contribute usefully to the pedagogy-technology combination that I am proposing.

In the second chapter, I will show how the way we think about CALL technology over the past few decades has merged into a notion of environments rather than tools. In Chapter 3, I will describe in detail how learners in our projects have worked with the MOO, and how a combination of a CALL environment like the MOO with learner autonomy can support learners in becoming more linguistically and metalinguistically aware; how it supports them in becoming better communicators and collaborators; and how it allows them to experiment with language and assume ownership of the learning process. In my final chapter, Chapter 4, I will summarise where MOO tandem still fails to support learner autonomy; what other technological and pedagogical tools we can use; and finally, what the relationship is between CALL environments, a learner-autonomy-based pedagogy, and the language learner.

1 Learner Autonomy

SCENARIO 1

A German and an Irish teacher prepare a tandem telecommunications exchange using a text-based MOO (Multi-user domain, Object-Oriented), running over nine weekly sessions of one hour each, between Irish students learning German and German students learning English. The teachers hand out brief technical explanations, and outlines of tandem principles. Students are to be paired into tandem pairs in the first session, and are then assigned specific tasks to work on.

The first session begins by everybody connecting to the MOO. Students are very lively and engaged, and they feel free to discuss any topic at all, although they know that all the communication is digitally recorded. However, communication is exclusively in English (the stronger L2) and quickly becomes multi-threaded, disconnected. Many students perceive this as chaotic, lose interest and begin to browse the web. Others are not sure what they are supposed to do, or still read the handouts. All the while, the teachers try to pair up students, and assign them to virtual "rooms" where they can work on their own, without success. The balancing act between managing the virtual environment and the physical classroom fails. Students are excited, but their first and lasting impression is one of chaos, disorder, disorientation, and non-guidance. At the end of the session, they still don't know who their partner is.

SCENARIO 2

Both teachers plan another tandem telecommunications exchange using a MOO. Again, it runs over nine weekly sessions of one hour each, between Irish students learning German and German students learning English. This time, the teachers work with previous MOO transcripts in class before the project begins. In groups, students are asked to reflect on tandem principles in practice, becoming aware of opportunities, but also pitfalls during these exchanges. Students are also provided with hands-on introductions to the technology before the project begins. The German students send short introductory e-mails in German and English to the Irish teacher, who, in turn, distributes them among the Irish students. The Irish students then choose their partner themselves. At the beginning of the first MOO session, both teachers and students have lists of tandem pairs, and the virtual rooms they work in. Students know how to get to these rooms. All students have checklists of task frameworks that need to be completed, both online and offline, with deadlines. They also make time to discuss current events, weekend activities, etc. Students know, at least to an extent, how to create virtual objects and share them with their partners. Students also know how to make entries into an online learner diary after each session, and quickly get into a habit of doing so. These entries reveal learning strategies, plans, evaluations, but also just short impressions about L1/L2 differences and learning techniques; anything they feel is worth mentioning. The first session starts smoothly, after 10 minutes all students are working quietly and are absorbed at their computers. They ask their classmates for help, and explore online resources such as dictionaries. Some stay on after the session is over. Students are excited and discuss their partners among themselves. They make plans on how their partners can help them with their projects in class. After four weeks, and at the end of the project, teachers include a review session in class, where students work again in small groups to discuss tandem principles and any problems that came up during the exchange. Reactions are very positive, and students demonstrate a high level of motivation, awareness and engagement in the project.

I have experienced both of these scenarios in my own CALL (Computer Assisted Language Learning) projects, at various points. The reason I am recounting these scenarios here, and indeed the purpose of this first chapter, is to show the need for CALL practitioners to understand the concept of learner autonomy in the full meaning of the word. I will explore three of its central ideas, always in relation to these scenarios. In my first sub-section, I will look at an individual-cognitive view of learning emphasising reflection and awareness as suggested by Kelly in his psychology of personal constructs. In the second sub-section, I will examine a social-interactive view of learning as proposed by Vygotsky. In my third sub-section, I will focus on the view of the learner as an experimenter with authentic target language (TL) materials through the use of exploratory tools in authorable environments. The important issue of teacher autonomy is treated in a separate sub-section. These three views have been discussed, roughly speaking, under the separate headings of "cognitivism", "interactionism", and "constructionism", respectively; however, I will focus on them in this book as necessary components to support a higher goal, that of learner autonomy.

First, however, it might be useful to deal with some "myths" and misconceptions. Learner autonomy does not equal self-access learning. The first denotes a capacity and a goal, the second (in many cases) simply a particular mode of learning; thus these are concepts from different discourses. Learner autonomy is also not a specific teaching method, as it does not describe a specific course of action that determines what happens in the classroom and what learners and teachers have to do. Learner autonomy is also (unfortunately) not necessarily stable, and not necessarily transferred to other contexts. This means that learners might achieve a certain level of autonomy, but then partially allow others to take control of their learning (for example, after moving to a new school). It also means that learners might for example achieve a high level of autonomy in learning English, but are unable to transfer this autonomy to the study of history. Learner autonomy, and here I would agree with David Little (1991:4), is a capacity that each learner has, but also one that needs to be developed. From a learner's and a teacher's perspective, learner autonomy is a constant goal.

In my view, there are three approaches that help us understand what learner autonomy entails in language learning, and these are reflected in the scenarios above. I will expound on those presented in the Introduction. Learner autonomy is a pedagogical concept that denotes a capacity of the learner as well as a pedagogical goal.

- Learners need to become somewhat detached from their own learning; they need to develop linguistic and metalinguistic awareness; they need to be able to critically reflect on their own position as learners. We can summarise this capacity and goal under the heading of reflection.
- Learners need to become communicators and collaborators with other learners, teachers and native speakers when they are learning a second language. They need to understand that actively seeking opportunities for collaboration and interaction will not only help them as language users, but also as language learners who progress through meaningful contact with more knowledgeable learning partners. This capacity and goal can thus be summarised as interaction.
- Learners need to become experimenters with and explorers of language and language learning in a laboratory-like, stress-free environment. They need to understand that they themselves need to take control of and assume responsibility for their learning. They need to plan, monitor, and evaluate their own process of language learning. In summary, this involves experimentation.

These approaches to learner autonomy have also important implications for the role of the teacher, not just the learner.

In the second scenario, my first point is reflected in the use of learner diaries, but also the use of the written language for communication. In our struggle for the latest high-tech CALL tools we might overlook the fact that the written language, and the process of writing itself, plays a hugely important role in developing linguistic and metalinguistic awareness. The second point is reflected in the quite rigid organisational framework of tandem learning, where communication and collaboration become essential to get any work done. In this kind of tandem set-up, it is almost impossible to prevent learners from communicating, but when we look at the two scenarios above, there are huge differences in how they communicate. This involves the way learners adapt their input to each other's proficiency levels, use both languages in equal amounts, etc. My third point is demonstrated in the way that learners were not given any option to shift responsibility to anybody but themselves. They were allowed, but also forced, to make decisions about organising their working partnership and the work themselves. In the second scenario, they could do so because, on the one hand, they operated in an environment that did not have classroom written all over it, but which provided them with tools and resources and allowed them to be creative, playful, funny, honest, angry, upset, etc., and how to express this in a second language. On the other hand, the pedagogical framework for what the learners were doing provided them with a clear framework; thorough introductions to and reviews of the technology; clear descriptions; clear time frame; clear desirables/products at the end of a project cycle; etc. Finally, the role of the teacher should not be neglected. There are important differences between the two scenarios in the way teachers collaborated and discussed the framework; how they prepared the technology for the students and vice versa; how they were able to identify some common ground in their pedagogy; how they intervened in class; how they organised online and offline work; how they analysed learners' work during and after the project; how they discussed and sometimes confronted learners with their work.

When we as teachers conducted our first projects (and maybe other teachers and researchers feel likewise about the first scenario), our dominant question was: "what went wrong?" We had been full of good intentions; we thought we had a pretty good idea of what learner autonomy was; we were familiar with the technology; and we were enthusiastic about the whole project. Yet we were disappointed with the initial results, to say the least, and our disappointment was related to the three approaches outlined above, as well as our role as teacher. Moving from our first to our second scenario, we needed to face the following questions which also determine the structure of this chapter.

- What do we mean when we speak of learner autonomy; why is it a useful concept in language pedagogy; and what is the role of the teacher?
- What are the implications of learner autonomy for the role of the teacher?
- What are practical implementations of learner autonomy in the language classroom?

- In what ways can we implement principles of learner autonomy in computer-assisted language learning (CALL) environments?

These are the central questions, and also sections, at the heart of this chapter. A clear understanding of what learner autonomy is and how it relates to CALL should contribute to a better understanding of why we consider the first scenario in many ways a failure and the second scenario a success. A sound pedagogical concept such as learner autonomy is important when we as teachers or researchers want to implement computer-assisted language learning (CALL) tools.

1.1 LEARNER AUTONOMY — A DEFINITION

The concept of learner autonomy has been around for a few years and even become a buzzword within the context of language learning. Unfortunately, however, it has also been misunderstood in a number of ways. Some have misunderstood it as synonymous with self-access learning. Some, in a similar vein, have assumed it is the same as self-instruction, "leaving the learners alone", letting them decide everything. These notions are not only misleading, but have unfortunately led to a discussion of learner autonomy in terms of a methodology or a particular mode of learning. However, learner autonomy is a pedagogical concept that we should see as a capacity of the learner, and a goal that we as teachers and learners should constantly work towards. Learner autonomy ultimately trusts the learner to make her own decisions, but also assume responsibility for them. However, learners may have lost some of their autonomy (read: capacity for self-determination), for example due to the "spoon-feeding" tendencies of much formal education.

Learner autonomy, in my view, focuses then first and foremost on a learner-centred approach to learning, where learners are encouraged to critically reflect on their learning process and develop a personally meaningful relation to it. Learner autonomy is based on a variety of philosophical, political, pedagogical, and psychological ideas. As a concept in second language acquisition, it emerged in 1979 with Henri Holec's *Autonomy and Foreign Language Learning* (Holec, 1979). Holec defines autonomy as "the ability to assume responsibility for one's own affairs" and, in terms of learning, "the ability to take charge of one's own learning" (Holec, 1979:3). In David Little's words,

> autonomy is a capacity — for detachment, critical reflection, decision-making, and independent action. It presupposes, but also entails, that the learner will develop a particular kind of psychological relation to the process and content of his learning. The capacity for autonomy will

> be displayed both in the way the learner learns and in the way he or she transfers what has been learned to wider contexts. (Little, 1991:4)

This definition still leads recent discussions of learner autonomy (see Benson, 2001:95, also cf. pp. 13, 34, 101, 102; Oxford, 2003). In the model elaborated by Eck, Legenhausen, and Wolff (1994), there are three different learner roles: the intentional learner, who develops an explicit awareness of both affective and metacognitive aspects of learning; the communicator, who continually uses and gradually develops her communicative skills; and the experimenter or researcher, who gradually develops an explicit analytical knowledge of the target language system and some of its socio-cultural context. These also cover the three approaches mentioned earlier in this chapter that I consider essential in the development of learner autonomy: reflection and awareness (the intentional learner); interaction and collaboration (the communicator); and experimentation and active collaboration (the experimenter or researcher). I will look at these in more detail now.

1.1.1 Learner autonomy and reflection

Let us first look at the importance of critical reflection. Why is this an important, if not the most important goal in learner autonomy, and how can we relate this to CALL? When we look back to the two scenarios, and focus on the individual learners' relationship to the second language and to the learning of this second language, we can find distinct differences between the levels of linguistic and metalinguistic awareness in the two projects.

But we might begin by asking why it is important. Why should a learner critically reflect on the learning process and develop linguistic and metalinguistic awareness? In the first scenario, there is very little indication that learners detached themselves from the learning process; that they critically reflected on the learning process; that they compared L1 and L2; that they reevaluated their learning strategies; that they undertook to plan, monitor, and evaluate their learning.

The clinical psychologist Kelly and his personal construct theory have played a major role in definitions of learner autonomy such as that by Little (1991), although Kelly's work has been far more prominent in psychotherapy and counselling than second language pedagogy. Nevertheless, it is very useful in the context of reflection and awareness. In his theory of personal constructs (Kelly, 1955, repr. 1991), Kelly emphasises the importance of reflection and self-awareness for the development of new constructs and their internal hierarchy, and thus learning. Kelly emphasises that man always tries to integrate new constructs within an existing construct system. This is done by increasing the repertory of constructs, altering them for better fits, and subsuming them with superordinate constructs. The incorporation of new and more precise constructs is always measured against the existing system of constructs; when new constructs involve substantial changes to existing substructures, integration can be a difficult or even painful process. The process of construct development can only be effected by the person herself, in a change of her construct system. This is reflected in recent autonomy and learning theory, where "the successful learner is increasingly seen as a person who is able to construct knowledge directly from experience of the world, rather than one who responds well to instruction" (Benson, 2001:19).

Just as in Kelly's context, where it is one of the prime support tasks of the therapist to support the patients in confronting their construct systems, I would argue that one of the prime roles of the teacher in a learner-autonomy-based learning framework is to confront learners with their own linguistic data and their metalinguistic/metacognitive constructs, e.g. their L2 output, their strategies, and their skill levels. Learners often need to be forced to work on these in explicit form, but this is necessary to generate greater self-awareness. The term "force" might sound unusually strong for a concept like learner autonomy, which supposedly is all about unlimited freedom (unfortunately, still a wide-spread misconception). For Leni Dam, one of the exponents and practitioners of learner autonomy principles, there simply was no other choice but to implement learner autonomy principles:

> In order to survive I felt I had to change my usual teacher role. I tried to involve the pupils– or rather I forced them to be involved — in the decisions concerning, for example, the choice of classroom activities and learning materials. I soon realized that giving the learners a share of responsibility for planning and conducting teaching-learning activities caused them to be actively involved and led to better learning. It also increased their capacity to evaluate the learning process. In this way a virtuous circle was created: awareness of *HOW* to learn facilitates and influences *WHAT* is being learned and gives an improved insight into *HOW* to learn. (Dam, 1995:2)

It is central to any understanding of learner autonomy that the learner needs to assume responsibility for her learning process, and this necessarily involves critical reflection, linguistic and metalinguistic awareness. The teacher has the responsibility to create a task framework or a learning environment that lies within the reach of the learner's level of autonomy, but the teacher does not and cannot assume responsibility for a learner's learning processes.

In Kelly's view, changes to the construct system happen most effectively in environments that allow the "use of fresh elements" (Kelly, 1955, repr. 1991:112); experimentation or "trying-on for size" (Kelly, 1955, repr. 1991:113); and the availability of validating data. Learners are more likely to take risks in an environment that does not initially threaten their construct systems than in an environment where every new construct might show up incompatibilities between constructs or even threaten the consistency of superordinate structures. When we look at our two scenarios, we can see whether these features are present. In both examples, learners take charge of the time and the new environment at their disposal. Clearly, this is not seen as an environment that is threatening or supervised by the teacher at all times. However, in the first example they are — for the most part — not autonomous enough to set themselves goals, to determine a task framework, to discuss how they want to conduct the learning partnership, etc. In the second scenario, the teachers made sure that partners and rooms had been selected; that learners knew what the task framework was; that the learners knew how to operate (in) the learning environment comfortably; that they were aware of online diaries, the use of transcripts, and the features of writing in the MOO (such as scrolling). In other words, the pedagogical and technological framework was, on the one hand, within reach of the learner's autonomy; on the other hand, it was also not infringing on the level of autonomy the learner had already reached, i.e. trying to set boundaries where the learner maybe would have wanted to explore a bit further.

"Trying-on for size" does not just refer to the fact that it is mostly language that is being explored, and the learner's position within that target language and its culture (I will return to this in a later section). It may also refer to the fact that learners experiment with their persona, their identity, while learning a second language, and this process may be supported by an environment that allows them to represent themselves independently of sound, video, or photography, i.e. in a more indirect way. We should not forget that language learning ultimately involves developing a new identity in the target language and culture (Byram, 1988:15f.; also see Kramsch, 1998:65ff.), and this is strongly linked to critical reflection.

If we want our learners to assume more control, to become more autonomous, it is important that learners have the necessary tools to reflect on their learning. Kelly refers to these as "validating data". In our second scenario, we can see that learners make use of these tools to a far greater extent. For example, off-line reflective tasks on the MOO transcripts form an integral part of language learning and move from a focus on meaning to a focus on form. Learners use the online diaries much more purposefully than in the first scenario. Preparatory sessions and regular review sessions are introduced to discuss learning strategies and any difficulties explicitly in class. Of course, validating data is equally important to the teacher. For her, it is also essential to know whether the pedagogical framework is just at the right distance, just within reach of the learner's level of autonomy, and the MOO makes all this data easily available.

The issue of reflection on language, language learning, and learning in general has usually been discussed under the heading of awareness. Developing awareness is a central, if not the most important concern of learner autonomy: "the most important aspect of developing learner autonomy is probably a growing awareness of social as well as learning processes, for teachers as well as for learners" (Dam, 1995:80). Through critical self-reflection learners need to go beyond "recipe learning" (awareness as just another tool presented by a transmission teacher) towards a deeper process of "meaning transformation" (Mezirow, 1985:23; also see Benson, 2001:171). This awareness can be expressed in a number of ways. For example, language learners show certain attitudes towards and express certain beliefs about their learning process. Learners adopt certain roles within a learning environment that serve as scaffolds for learning while at the same time protecting core personal constructs. Learners may develop mechanisms for self-regulation, such as planning, monitoring, and evaluating their own learning.

Awareness has been discussed on many levels, and we are still far from terminological consistency in the field (cf. Schwienhorst, 2004a). Masny (1997:105) provides a useful definition of the terms:

> Language awareness has been proposed as an interface mechanism to promote heightened awareness of language forms between the first language (L1) and the target language (TL) and thereby assist second-language (L2) learning. Linguistic awareness or metalinguistic awareness, on the other hand, is an indicator of what learners know about language through reflection on and manipulation of language.

In our two scenarios, there is at least a good potential for greater language awareness by virtue of the pedagogical framework of tandem learning, i.e. the partnerships of learners with complementary L1/L2 combinations. In this way, learners are constantly required to compare L1 and L2 and negotiate meaning with their partner. We know from previous tandem e-mail projects that learners often reflect on issues such as "my partner constantly makes errors when using this construction, I wonder if I am doing the same". Linguistic or metalinguistic awareness has a much more formal and explicit focus, where learners would reflect much more on how they learn languages, what kind of strategies they employ, etc. In this respect, teacher involvement is crucial. However, I think we should not just discuss it in terms of "instructional conversation" (Tharp & Gallimore, 1988), "learner training" (Dickinson, 1992; Esch, 1997), or "learner counselling" (Gremmo & Riley, 1995; Kelly, 1996; Voller, 1997). Teacher involvement also refers to the creation of pedagogical and technological frameworks. It implies that learners have validating data at their disposal, such as records of their communication in the L2; online learner diaries; tools that help them to monitor and evaluate their use of L1 and L2. This is particularly the case in our second scenario, where learners are regularly confronted with what they have worked on. The teacher may remind them to enter comments in their online diary at the end of the session, or the MOO may confront the learner with statistics on language use at the beginning of a session. Of course, the big difference between the MOO and many language classrooms, and many face to face situations, is that all the work, whether communication, collaboration, reflection, or experimentation, is done through the medium of writing. This deserves a closer look.

Gnutzmann (1997:69) has criticised the overemphasis on "instrumental communicative competence in oral communication" in the communicative approach, and even recently it was reported that speaking and listening are a priority in a large number of EU member states (Eurydice, 2005:67-8). Writing and reading not only provide a model for thinking about speech and language (see, for example, studies on illiterates in Scholes & Willis, 1991). Writing and reading also provide an analytical insight into how language is constructed. In second language learning, these two processes can be enhanced, on the one hand, by providing opportunities for learners to constantly compare L1 and L2. On the other hand, we know that the sustained contrastive analysis of both languages in writing supports metalinguistic awareness and thus learner autonomy. In Little's words, "writing makes language visible and at the same time takes it 'off line'" (Little, 2001:12). We can distinguish between two quite distinct views on writing, written text as a product and writing as a process.

In the first sense, written language serves as an "external memory" (Wells, 1981c:242). The permanence of the medium means that text becomes a future learning resource and retrievable for reflective learning activities. This is particularly true for digital writing media such as the MOO, where it is quite easily possible to save all transcripts to a text file. Writing allows "experience to be recorded in a permanent form and so communicated to others who are removed in time and space. It also provides a means for reflecting upon experience — for working out ideas and feelings away from the pressure of face-to-face communication" (Wells, 1981a:1). Wells (1992:122) points out that

> by making a record of text of thought available for reflection, and, if necessary, revision, a written text serves as a 'cognitive amplifier' (Bruner, 1972), allowing the reader or writer to bootstrap his or her own thinking in a more powerful manner than is normally possible in speech

and that in writing

> the individual is made most aware of the symbolising function of language, and of the power that it has to capture experience so that it may be considered, questioned and modified in the interests of increased understanding and future applications. (Wells, 1981c:254)

These views present two great advantages of text that are even more valid in digital text. Writing as a process helps us "think", by writing things down we can more easily plan, monitor, and evaluate what we are doing and organise our thoughts. On the other hand, once we look at the finished product of writing, it becomes something external, something we can analyse, manipulate, re-use, research, and edit, in a variety of ways (Wells, 1981c:244; Olson, 1991). We can summarise by saying that written texts can serve as an interface between two kinds of awareness:

> [O]n the one hand, written texts are a resource that can be drawn on when speaking, so that they support communicative use of the spoken language and thus the development of language awareness in the psycholinguistic sense; and on the other, they provide a focus for the development, via analysis and evaluation, of language awareness as knowledge about the target language. (Little, 1997a:102)

Rather than just serving as a tool for conveying information, written text can be thought of as a cognitive tool (Little, 1999; similar terms that have been used are cognitive amplifier by Bruner, 1972; or thinking device, see Lotman, 1988), "a key resource by which we effectively redescribe our own thoughts in a format which makes them available for a variety of new operations and manipulations" (Clark, 1998:178). It is not surprising that writing plays a major part in pedagogical implementations of learner autonomy principles. Good examples of this can be found in the work of Dam (1995, 2000), Thomsen (2000) and Thomsen and Gabrielsen (1991; also see Little, 1997a; Little, 1997c). Their focus on learner diaries and similar records serves as an external memory, while the creation of posters and other documents in the target language increases metalinguistic awareness. Scharle and Szabó (2000:15–47) also provide a useful catalogue of classroom activities for raising awareness.

The particular features of writing are even more prominent in digital text, and it is no surprise that the word processor has become such a powerful CALL tool in raising learner's awareness (see Dam, Legenhausen, & Wolff, 1990; Milton, Smallwood, & Purchase, 1996). Similarly, the concordancer has become an alternative tool to access and exploit existing texts in new and useful ways for language learning. MOO transcripts are available to be re-used both in word processors and with a concordancer. In addition, the wealth of communication data that can be collected automatically in digital corpora make them important research tools.

In the last decade or so, language learning projects have turned to implementing collaborative writing technologies, and collaborative writing has added a social and pragmatic dimension to the writing process (Murray, 1992). In a medium such as the MOO, writing is the only form of communication available, and even non-verbal communication is expressed verbally, writing becomes the sole focus of attention and the only source of information. This is not to say that interactive writing as in the MOO, does not entail complex interactions between sender, receiver, and context, but whereas in oral communication, meaning is defined by an interplay of speaker, recipient, and context, in writing, to some extent, readers try to infer meaning from the text alone. The use of asynchronous writing environments such as Daedalus InterChange (see, for instance, Slatin, 1992; Colomb & Simutis, 1996; Warschauer, 1996a; Kreeft Peyton, 1999; Hanson-Smith, 1999) and synchronous "chat" environments (Chan, 1996; DiMatteo, 1990; DiMatteo, 1991), which also comprise the MOO environment, for language learning transforms our traditional perceptions of writing and literacy, as they introduce a number of new elements into the writing process or make these more prominent: e.g. authentic audience, environments, and cultural contexts. I will discuss some of these environments in Chapter 2.

In this sub-section, I have started with elements from Kelly's psychology of personal constructs to demonstrate how important the concept of critical reflection and awareness is to my understanding of learner autonomy. I have also explored why writing, maybe contrary to common beliefs which might place more importance on speaking, plays such a vital role in developing a capacity for critical reflection, i.e. learner autonomy. New collaborative writing technologies have introduced social and pragmatic elements into the writing process, and I will look at these in more detail in subsequent sections.

1.1.2 Learner autonomy and interaction

If we look at the definition of learner autonomy by Little (1991) cited in the introduction to this section, it would be easy to misinterpret the concept of autonomy as a solely individual-cognitive process of independence and self-determination. However, in practical terms the two scenarios are dominated not by individual but collaborative work. Learners would probably see the MOO tandem work first and foremost as collaboration. Especially in the second scenario, learners are not only communicating, but negotiating, correcting, modifying, and giving feedback. In this section, I will explore the collaborative element in learner autonomy and its meaning for CALL in more detail.

In child development, there is a clear interplay between self-determination and the interaction with the environment, and this also applies to a more social and educational view (Newell, 1990:20). In Little's (1991:5) words:

> The developmental learning that unimpaired small children undergo takes place in interaction with parents, brothers and sisters, grandparents, family friends, neighbours and so on. Education, whether institutionalised or not, is likewise an interactive, social process. For most of us, important learning experiences are likely to be remembered at least

partly in terms of our relationships with one or more other learners or with a teacher.

Both independence, as explored in the previous section, and interdependence are thus equally important for the development of autonomy.

The work of the Soviet psychologist Vygotsky has moved more and more into the centre of the discussion about learner autonomy and second language acquisition and has also been influential in our MOO projects. Vygotsky (1978, 1986) argues that "higher cognitive functions (those that are unique to humans) are internalized from social interaction, which is shaped by language" (Little, 1999:80). Vygotsky's emphasis on social relationships in the development of mental abilities and thus also learning underlines the importance of peer support for any form of learning. Central to his theory is the idea of

> the zone of proximal development. It is the distance between the actual developmental level as determined by independent problem solving and the level of potential development as determined through problem solving under adult guidance or in collaboration with more capable peers. (Vygotsky, 1978:86)

For second language acquisition, then, the Vygotskian approach stresses the need for a collaborative learning environment where learners are enabled and encouraged to interact with and support one another, a public space characterised by interaction and collaboration (also see Nunan, 1992:3). As regards our two scenarios, one might argue that learners were interacting in both cases, in the sense of communicating. However, the pedagogical and technological framework of the first scenario did not enable learners to interact in the sense of inter-action, of adjusting to each other, of collaborating. Interaction in a space with around 50 to 60 people, without the ability to signal to each other when somebody wants to communicate or not, is extremely difficult, even impossible. In the second scenario, this was reduced to 1+1 partnerships, in dedicated rooms, which reduced the multiplicity of communication demands and allowed interaction. Not only interaction, but also collaboration, as students knew how to share virtual objects such as documents, exchange them, and work on them together. Learners in 1+1 partnerships are also better able to adjust to each other's levels of language proficiency, an important step to make any interaction between native speaker and non-native speaker successful.

In this context, Bruner and others (Bruner & Ratner, 1978; Ninio & Bruner, 1978) have proposed the notion of scaffolding, which describes the activities of the more knowledgeable peer in Vygotsky's ZPD. Arising from the role of adults or parents in child development as described by Bruner, Cambourne (1988) sees scaffolding as a conversation to help learners, first by focusing on the learner's conception, second by extending or challenging this conception, third by refocusing and encouraging clarification, and fourth by redirecting the learner by offering new possibilities for consideration (also see Fosnot, 1996a:21). The focus on learners' conceptions, similar to Kelly's approach described earlier, is in my view vital for the success of scaffolding, not only between teacher and learner, but also between learners in peer support, or in a MOO tandem project where it is a vital component for success.

Scaffolding in tandem learning does not place all responsibility on the more knowledgeable partner, i.e. the native speaker. Equally, the non-native learner has something to bring to the learning process. There are at least two types of knowledge the learner already possesses when beginning a second language: "knowledge of how conversation works and knowledge of the world which [the learner] can share with the native speaker of his target language. Even as a beginner, therefore, the learner of a foreign language has quite a lot of usable knowledge" (Devitt, 1986:17; also see Devitt, 1989:7). The interaction between what Barnes (1976:81) has called "school knowledge" ("the knowledge which someone else presents to us") and "action knowledge" ("that view of the world on which our actions are based") forms therefore an important part of scaffolding and of the learning process in general.

Corrective feedback can, similarly to scaffolding, provide more than mere correction: An

> important consequence of feedback is that by comparing the verbal formulation actually transmitted with the initial meaning intention, a speaker has the opportunity to become more aware of his own thoughts and to modify and develop them. This is even more true of writing, where there is greater opportunity for correction and revision. (Wells, 1981b:62)

Corrective feedback, particularly written feedback, can therefore work towards the development of greater language and linguistic awareness. Wells seems to have been writing about this with the MOO system in mind. Again, we see the strong link between interaction, reflection, and the medium of writing.

I have not yet discussed the reasons why communication in the target language is such an important aspect of language learning, although this has become an accepted tenet. Many teachers and researchers will be familiar with the phrase "language learning is language use" (Ellis, 1985). This has been at the core of the communicative approach, although, as mentioned before, this was often at the expense of written communication (also see Wolff, 2000:111).

It is essential for the language learner to interact with and in the target language as much as possible. In order to develop the learners' control of the target language system, we need to foster what Krashen (1981:1) has called "meaningful interaction in the target language — natural communication — in which speakers are concerned not with the form of their utterances but with the messages they are conveying and understanding" (also see Little & Grant, 1986). Although the interaction with authentic resources, which I will discuss in my next sub-section, is certainly important, learners need social interaction with peers or native speakers: "passive input, such as that provided by television, is not sufficient for language acquisition to take place; acquisition requires person-to-person interaction, for example, between parent and child." (Johnston, 1999:57; also see Debski, 2003:138).

For Little et al. (1989:2), language learning is fostered by contexts rich in opportunities for interaction in and with the target language. When social interaction is meaningful to the learner, it becomes psychological interaction; TL input is psychologically processed so that it interlocks with and modifies the learner's existing knowledge (Little, Devitt, & Singleton, 1989:5). In Dam's (1990) view collaboration is the mode of interaction most apt to promote learner autonomy. When we move from a teacher-centred to a learner-centred classroom, it is "not just useful but necessary to underline this change in roles by changing the focus from the teacher and the blackboard to the learners themselves" (Dam, 1995:42; also see Scharle & Szabó, 2000:80–100, for class activities supporting this role change). Group work and collaboration, in this respect, facilitate the move towards learner-centredness. In her classroom, the students work in groups, deciding on content and structuring it. Dam herself sets the initial boundaries. Learners (and teachers) have to keep a log of their work in a diary. Apart from individual diaries, learner groups present posters to the class, containing the work that they have done in groups. After group work, learners compare notes, evaluating what went well or not so well in the session, what they want to improve, and how they want to proceed. At the end of each session, groups will share more general problems and issues that have arisen in group work (for other collaborative activities in the autonomous classroom, see Scharle & Szabó, 2000:66-73). Naturally, the roles of learners and teachers change in this context. Dam reports on the "octopus syndrome" (Dam, 1995:26), the traditional teacher role as sole provider of information who in a learner-centred context can easily be overwhelmed by the support she has to provide. She therefore enlists some learners as assistants or "helpers". These can give assistance in the form of peer-tutoring and group work in general. I will expand on the role of the teacher in a subsequent sub-section.

When we look at the two scenarios, we can again note substantial differences. I noted that communication was also present in the first scenario, but maybe not so much interaction as in the second scenario. The second scenario also contains various other signs of collaboration such as scaffolding and corrective feedback. It is interesting to note that in the first scenario, with absolute freedom of choice, learners were unable to conduct meaningful topic-focused communication. In the second scenario, on the other hand, they were forced to a 1+1 communication scenario; they were given frameworks and support for various topics (from which they would then eventually depart as they assumed more autonomy); they focused primarily on meaning, on "getting the message across" to an authentic audience, and the amount of interaction they generated in the target language was far beyond what they would create in a normal classroom session. We can sum up with Wolff (1994:8):

> The importance of group work in language learning has been stressed both in second language acquisition research (peer corrections are more efficient than teacher corrections) and in social psychology (the face-saving nature of group work). It has also become clear, however, that group work is efficient only when the tasks the group has to fulfil are authentic.

If we adopt a view of developmental learning as a "symbiotic relation between the individual-cognitive and the social-interactive", then "appropriately focussed interaction between learners is likely to be the best way of stimulating the cognitive growth of individual learners" (Little, 1999:83). Again, I would like to refer to the "technology" of writing. When used for personally meaningful interaction among peers, writing also externalises learners' processes and forces learners to confront these processes in negotiation that might otherwise have remained implicit and unexamined (Little & Ushioda, 1998:48). Interactive writing, as in e-mail projects (Appel, 1997, 1999; Little et al., 1999) and in some composition tasks in the MOO, "acts as a scaffold for composition writing, which is more cognitively demanding, since the writer has to produce text without the support of an interlocutor and to create a situation to represent to himself" (Appel, 1999:11). Here, interactive writing externalises and increases awareness of otherwise hidden strategies and can thus prepare for more complex compositional tasks by transforming issues of editing, structuring, etc. into a collaborative activity (also cf. Abrams, 2001).

A social-interactive view of learner autonomy is closely linked to an individual-cognitive view. Starting with a Vygotskian framework of child development and the ZPD, I explored how interaction and collaboration are essential ingredients of the autonomous language classroom, and thus also for any CALL environment. We should not forget that CALL environments, especially in a second language context, allow many learners for the first time to communicate with native speakers in the target language community. I examined various related concepts such as scaffolding, corrective feedback, and the role of interaction in learner autonomy, and explored how these were realised to a varying degree in the two MOO scenarios from the beginning of this chapter, focusing not only on the importance of interaction from a socio-pragmatic perspective, but also its role in developing metacognitive skills.

1.1.3 Learner autonomy and experimentation

In the first scenario, any observer would agree that learners were certainly free to determine what they wanted to do; nevertheless we would also say that in terms of real autonomy, i.e. taking control and assuming responsibility, learners still had much to learn.

Why do we find that the learners in the second scenario displayed much more autonomous behaviour than the learners in the first, although there were more "restrictions"? Again, even the question goes back to a central misunderstanding about learner autonomy. Just because a learner can do whatever she wants, she may not necessarily be able to plan, monitor, and evaluate her learning and reflect on her learning. She may also not make use of the opportunities that the learning environment offers. Part of this problem lies with the level of autonomy achieved by the learner. Part, however, also lies with the teacher/designer/researcher who has failed or succeeded to bring these learning opportunities within reach of the learner. In this sub-section, I would like to focus on the responsibility and control of the learner.

I would argue that the language learner, apart from being supported to become more aware of the language learning process by processes of reflection and using language in interaction and collaboration with other learners and the teacher, needs to be put into a position where she can experiment not only with other people's language learning materials but also with her own. Wolff (1994:8) has made the point that "[L]anguage learning must be seen as a process of creative construction and that there are severe constraints on the teachability of language" (also see Hyltenstam & Pienemann, 1985). Many studies of successful language learners point to the fact that, through exploration, they were able to find the most successful strategies that work for them as individuals. Learners will only experiment, in my experience, if, on the one hand, they have easy-to-use tools and materials for experimentation. This could refer to large databases of authentic materials, and search tools to find personally relevant material. On the other hand, they also need a pedagogical framework that brings these materials and tools within reach of their autonomy, so that they see at least part of them as personally meaningful and relevant. The notions of experimentation and active participation have found their way into second language pedagogy by way of several concepts that some readers may be more familiar with: authenticity, activity theory, constructivism, constructionism, and situated learning.

Authenticity

The use of authentic material has been discussed both within the communicative approach as well as in relation to learner autonomy. McGarry (1995:3) has noted that authenticity is an important element in promoting learner autonomy, for two reasons. On the one hand, "[w]hen students are working on topics of interest to them, they are likely to adopt a more positive attitude to the task in hand, because their interest in the subject makes the task more enjoyable or more meaningful"; this is supported by research from psychological and psycholinguistic research (Little, Devitt, & Singleton, 1989:5; Little & Singleton, 1988:1). On the other hand,

> when texts are chosen which allow students to exploit, to a significant extent, their own existing knowledge of the subject and of discourse structures, the students may be more willing to attempt the use of inferencing and other strategies for unlocking the meaning of the text. (McGarry, 1995:4)

Authentic materials have been defined as "materials which have not been prepared for language teaching" (Dickinson, 1987:68), and an authentic text as

> (i) the record of any communicative act in speech or writing that was originally performed in fulfillment of some personal or social function and not in order to provide illustrative material for language teaching, and — by extension — (ii) any communicative event that can easily become such a record, for example radio and television broadcasts and certain forms of electronic communication. (Little, 1997b:225; also see Little, 1989:23).

More recently, the concept of authenticity has been extended from materials to audience (Johnston, 1999:60) and task (Chapelle, 1999:103).

In our two scenarios, authenticity was present in a variety of meanings. Learners were exposed to and themselves produced authentic target language input. Learners in the second scenario discussed any topic in the target language they considered relevant from their own perspective, and over the years, MOO tandem partners have discussed fairly sensitive topics, such as experiences with soft and hard drugs; sexual orientation; or criminal activities. The frameworks that we created as teachers were adopted from the project tasks that we use in the institution-wide language programmes here at Trinity College Dublin. That means that students are given a format such as "debate", but the topic is up to them to decide. In this way, learners are able to fill frameworks with topics that might go into all possible directions, according to their individual interests, while at the same time providing a common focus for the whole group.

Sometimes, however, authenticity was achieved without much of a structure. I remember one afternoon in late November, when the German teacher who I was talking to during the MOO project mentioned that it was slowly starting to snow in Germany, for the first time that winter. Within a few minutes, the news had spread to all partnerships, and we later saw in the transcripts that they subsequently exploited possibly everything that could have anything to do with snow. Building snowmen; the art of making and throwing snowballs; stories around sleighs; then Christmas with or without snow; snow in the mountains; glaciers; the Alps; Canada; Scotland; avalanches; mountaineering; etc., etc. A few snowflakes in Germany triggered off one of the most intensive examples of authenticity I have ever experienced. Everything was related to the learners' experience, and no two partnerships discussed the same issues, but somehow they all started with a few snowflakes.

Subsequently, we found that exploiting the "here and now" is vital in live communication systems such as a MOO, and learners should be given the freedom to work with the topics of their choice within frameworks that allow for this choice. Of course, learners can exploit and have exploited a sheer unlimited variety of Internet resources while communicating with their MOO tandem partner. The provision of a great variety of authentic materials alone, however, does not lead to more authenticity in the classroom, more personally meaningful interaction, and thus more autonomous language users and learners. The term authenticity needs to go further.

Chapelle (1999) has identified five different features for analysing the authenticity of a second language task, and within each feature, there are several questions that can help us define the task's authenticity. These categories are goals, "what the learner is trying to accomplish in the task" (Chapelle, 1999:102); process, "what the learners are engaged in while completing the task" (ibid.:103); topic, "some content other than the linguistic forms of the target language" (ibid.:103); and location and duration, "where each participant works on the task and within what time period" (ibid.:103). Chapelle's categories provide a useful catalogue of features to assess the authenticity of classroom tasks and make clear that the issue of authenticity needs to go beyond materials. In conclusion, we can say that authenticity involves not only materials, but all aspects of the language learning process. If students are using authentic materials, but are then given a task that is far removed from "natural communication" with the target language community, a task that is not content-oriented, and heavily restricted in terms of location and duration, we can hardly call this an authentic task (Lee, 1996:171). Project work, as mentioned in our scenarios, has been shown to be quite useful to realise authenticity (McGarry, 1995:33; also see Little, Devitt, & Singleton, 1989; Devitt, 1986; Dam, 1995).

There is also a more cognitive function of authenticity. We need to "transform learners from the role of *consumers* to the role of producers, exercising some level of control and influence over the centre facilities" (Littlejohn, 1997:190). Littlejohn sees the design of exercises for other learners as one means of involving learners. Another option is the data-driven learning model of Johns (Johns, 1988, 1991; also see Rautenhaus, 1996) which stresses "the value of the corpus in revealing recurrent patterns" (Aston, 1997:208; also see Cheng, Warren, & Xun-feng, 2003, for a discussion of corpus linguistics in language learning) . In this sense, materials become what Sturtridge (1982) has called "learning materials" as opposed to "practice materials" when they fulfil a more cognitive function of providing linguistic information as well as mechanisms for independent learning "such as how to set learning goals, decide on what to do with materials and carry out self-assessment" (Lee, 1996:196). I shall now examine this cognitive function of authentic materials in more detail.

Activity theory

Activity theory has been developed over the course of the past 70 years, mainly in the former Soviet Union. Beginning with Vygotsky, activity theory has striven to provide a framework in which a unity between consciousness and activity is achieved:

> Activity theorists argue that consciousness is not a set of discrete disembodied cognitive acts (decision making, classification, remembering), and certainly it is not the brain; rather consciousness is located in everyday practice: you are what you do. And what you do is firmly and inextricably embedded in the social matrix of which every person is an organic part. This social matrix is composed of people and artifacts. (Nardi, 1996a:7)

Similarly, van Lier (2000:246) argues that perceptual and social activities of the language learner "do not just facilitate learning, they are learning in some fundamental way" (see also Basturkmen & Lewis, 2002:33; Bødker, 1991; Leont'ev, 1978, 1981; Wertsch, 1981).

Activity theory proposes to involve learners in experimentation and participation. Bellamy emphasises two points: first, learners should be constructing artefacts and share them with their culture (Bellamy, 1996:130; Hung & Wong, 2000:35). Second, "learning situations should feature collaboration among people with all levels of expertise, adults and children" (Bellamy, 1996:130), thus involving a variety of different interaction and collaboration partners to support the Vygotskian ZPD. The development of consciousness (in Vygotsky's terms) or awareness (as discussed in subsection 1.1.1) is contained in the mediated activity with people and environments. In this educational context, the teacher becomes a facilitator (Bellamy, 1996:142).

Particular importance is placed on artefacts "as crucial mediators of human experience" (Nardi, 1996b:xi, 1996a:10). Artefacts "could be in the form of presentations, written documents, progress reports, models, pictures, etc." (Hung & Wong, 2000:35). The idea behind the interaction with artefacts is that

> humans can control their own behavior — not 'from the inside', on the basis of biological urges, but 'from the outside', using and creating artifacts. This perspective is not only optimistic concerning human self-determination. It is an invitation to serious study of artifacts as integral and inseparable components of human functioning. (Engeström, 1991:12)

This optimism regarding self-determination also underlies the whole concept of learner autonomy.

Our second scenario fulfils both the demands of an activity with artefacts as well as people. Through the technological framework of the MOO, using suitable tasks as scaffolding, learners were enabled to create and experiment not only with virtual tools, but (by virtue of writing) with language itself, which became an analysable and manipulable object. Transcripts record each individual's experience in the MOO (although these are not time-coded, which might be a useful feature that could be implemented quite easily). Because the MOO is open-source software, I can give learners access to all levels of re-constructing the environment, something they are unable to do with most commercial software. They can assemble and build those tools and resources they as individual learners consider useful for their learning process. Through the pedagogical framework of tandem learning, learners were exposed to and actively involved in communication with a wide range of target language speakers and more or less knowledgeable peers. In addition, much educational software provides neither the means for evaluation and research, such as user tracking, for designers (Raeithel & Velichkovsky, 1996:203), nor records for the learner/user to monitor and evaluate her learning process (Chapelle, 2001:173). In our MOO scenarios, this has in principle been possible at all times.

In section 1.1.1, I referred to Kelly's theory of personal constructs. Kelly (1955, repr. 1991:112-115) makes the point that if materials and classrooms are considered to be separate entities from personal experience and the immediate application of what is learned, they will not affect overall personal constructs. Individuals must be enabled to construct their own private learning spaces according to their needs and fill them with personally meaningful learning materials. A similar concept has been developed under the name of constructivism as a model for learning and, more recently, instructional design, and provides a useful additional perspective on experimentation.

Constructivism

The foundations for constructivism have been mainly associated with the works of Piaget (1950, 1952) and Vygotsky (1978, 1986). Some researchers have argued that constructivism corresponds to learner autonomy as a major approach to issues of knowledge and learning in humanities and the sciences (Benson, 1997:18).

Piaget (1977) describes human development as a dynamic process of self-regulated behaviour, or equilibration, involving processes of assimilation and accommodation. Assimilation is "the organization of experience with one's own logical structures or understandings. It is the individual's self-assertive tendency, a tendency to view the world through one's own constructs in order to preserve one's autonomy as a part within a whole system" (Fosnot, 1996a:13). However, as Kelly noted, some constructs need to change in order to avoid disequilibrium between personal constructs and new experience. This process is called accommodation: "Accommodation is comprised of reflective, integrative behavior that serves to change one's own self and explicate the object in order for us to function with cognitive equilibrium in relation to it" (Fosnot, 1996a:13).

We can distinguish between similar processes in Vygotsky's concept of child development (Vygotsky, 1986:146ff.), where spontaneous and scientific concepts meet in the ZPD (Fosnot, 1996a:18; Ewing, Dowling, & Coutts, 1999:7–11). Both Piaget's and Vygotsky's models are problematic: Piaget has been interpreted as clinging to "a residual naive realism. Constructions for him were representations of an autonomous real world to which the growing child had to fit or 'accommodate' (Bruner, 1986:98; von Glasersfeld, 1996:3); and Vygotsky similarly might be interpreted as saying that there is some objective truth in scientific concepts that can be transferred to the child/learner (Fosnot, 1996a:21). This is, however, not the case. We constantly refer "to objects that constitute the organism's experiential world, not things in themselves that have an independent existence" (von Glasersfeld, 1996:4).

According to Bruner (1986:95), the core of constructivism "is that contrary to common sense there is no unique 'real world' that pre-exists and is independent of human mental activity and human symbolic language; that what we call the world is a product of some mind whose symbolic procedures construct the world". This process of creative construction of the world "involves the transformation of worlds and world versions already made" (Bruner, 1986:97); success is measured as "predictive efficiency", in Kelly's terms (Kelly, 1955, repr. 1991:9; von Glasersfeld, 1996:4). This definition does not result in total individualism, however, as in any community, constructions are discussed "until new, temporary, 'taken-as-shared' meanings are consensually agreed upon as viable. (Fosnot, 1996a:28; Cobb, Yackel, & Wood, 1992). A constructivist view

> suggests an approach to teaching that gives learners the opportunity for concrete, contextually meaningful experience through which they can search for patterns, raise their own questions, and construct their own models, concepts, and strategies. The classroom in this model is seen as a minisociety, a community of learners engaged in activity, discourse, and reflection. (Fosnot, 1996b:ix)

While there are more extreme interpretations of constructivism (see, for example, von Glasersfeld, 1984, 1987, 1989; and Bauersfeld, 1988:39; Schoenfeld, 1987; Brown, Collins, & Duguid, 1989; Greeno, 1991), many views would hold that constructivism has an individual-cognitive and a social-interactive component. Just as in activity theory, the teacher's role becomes more one of facilitator, and the "learners take on more ownership of the ideas" (Fosnot, 1996b:ix).

Constructivist learning environments should have the following characteristics: learners should be active; the introduction of multiple perspectives is valued as necessary for the learning process; collaborative learning is preferred to competitive learning; learners are encouraged to take control of the learning process; and the environment provides "authentic, real-world learning experiences" (Carr, Jonassen, Litzinger, & Marra, 1998:8). Activities should also be recursive (Willis, 2000:9). Recursion is related to grounded theory research (hypotheses are formed and then tested, if new data provides interesting viewpoints, new hypotheses are tested) and presents an iterative process of data analysis and theoretical analysis, with an ongoing verification of hypotheses throughout the learning process. Examples of this recursive process in CALL are word processing (Dam, Legenhausen, & Wolff, 1990; Milton, Smallwood, & Purchase, 1996) and data-driven learning (Johns, 1988, 1991; Aston, 1997), especially when students are encouraged to analyse their own texts, their own production, in the target language. Our second scenario fulfils these demands well. In the combination of tandem tasks and MOO environment learners were often given as much freedom as they were capable of handling at their level of autonomy. Learners need to feel in control of the learning process; only then can they assume responsibility over their learning. As the two scenarios show, this does not mean complete freedom or a lack of framework. In fact, I would argue that it is precisely a well-adapted framework of technology and pedagogy that allows learners to take control. Learners are also involved in recursive processes of hypothesis-testing, an important ingredient of a learning situation supporting learner autonomy (Little, 1991:17).

The contributions of constructivism to the concept of learner autonomy are considerable. Constructivism does not accept the traditional view of teaching as knowledge transfer, because learning is perceived as individual meaning-making. Increasingly, constructivist views have assumed a more social-interactive view of learning, where meanings and knowledge are developed through interactions between teacher and learner and among learners. I will briefly look at two learning models that are both based on constructivist ideas: constructionism and situated learning theory.

Constructionism

If we go back to Kelly's theory of personal constructs mentioned in section 1.1.1, we can see that Kelly also saw the concept of experimentation, of "trying on for size" (Kelly, 1955, repr. 1991:113) as crucial in the learning process. His views, therefore, not only share similarities with constructivism, as argued in the foregoing paragraphs, but also with Levi-Strauss's concept of bricolage (Levi-Strauss, 1968), and Bettelheim's (1987) notion of *Spielraum* (which means free scope, plenty of room to experiment with things, rather than "a place to play"), of tinkering around with new ideas in a stress-reduced environment. This concept was further evolved in the learning theory of constructionism by Papert (1990, 1991, 1993). Papert sees constructionism as an extension of constructivism:

> We understand 'constructionism' as including, but going beyond, what Piaget would call 'constructivism'. The word with v expresses the theory that knowledge is built by the learner, not supplied by the teacher. The word with the n expresses the further idea that this happens especially felicitously when the learner is engaged in the construction of something external or at least shareable [...] a sand castle, a machine, a computer program, a book. This leads us to a model of using a cycle of internalization of what is outside, then externalization of what is inside. (Papert, 1991:3)

This certainly echoes the notion and function of artefacts in activity theory. However, in addition constructionists have maintained that building, designing, and playing have intrinsic motivational effects on learning (Goldman-Segall, 1992:259; Malone, Lepper, Miyake, & Cohen, 1987; Bruner, 1966; Bruner, 1986).

There are two major perspectives here: on the one hand we have the learner as *bricoleur*, who is "guided by the work as it proceeds rather than staying with a pre-established plan"; on the other hand we have the idea of the "direct exploration" of ideas with physical objects (Papert, 1999): "Constructionism places a high priority on *making projects personal.* It asserts that students (and teachers) who make *personal connections* with their projects invariably do the most creative work — and learn the most from their experiences" (Resnick, 1991).

The inclusion of participation in the learning environment is also central to constructionism. Bruckman and Resnick (1995) have criticised so-called interactive multimedia design by saying that

> [i]f this technology is 'interactive,' it is in the limited sense that most hypertext systems are interactive: there are multiple paths through the material, and the system has a limited ability to react to the user. However, the ways in which the system reacts are designed by the artists and engineers who constructed it and not by the users.

They argue that "users need to be the creators and not merely consumers of virtual worlds" (ibid.). In the context of language learning, learners need to be transformed "from the role of *consumers* to the role of producers, exercising some level of control and influence" (Littlejohn, 1997:190). The term "agency" as defined by Murray (1997:128) seems more useful than "interactivity" which has become too vague and pervasive. Agency "goes beyond both participation and activity", in that learners can choose their actions freely and in that their effects are related to the learners' intentions. It is encouraging to see the concept of agency becoming more widely discussed in both learner autonomy (Oxford, 2003) and CALL literature (Kramsch, A'Ness, & Lam, 2000; Debski, 2003:138). Learners must be enabled to make CALL environments their own; otherwise they will remain extraneous to them. The MOO fulfils this requirement in both our scenarios (though it may be argued whether the user interface could be improved); the pedagogy and technology become not just paths through a material, but constitute a framework that supports and challenges learners to take their autonomy a step further. CALL design in general must not only allow learners to produce materials in the target language, but must also provide structures so that the learner's creation and other authentic materials become cognitive tools, tools that enable the learner to reflect on the learning process and on the target language.

The major contribution of constructionism to learner autonomy is maybe that it emphasises the creative construction of artefacts. Little, in his work on learner autonomy, has repeatedly emphasised the importance of learners devising their own learning materials; the learners "experience the learning they are engaged on as their own, and this enables them to achieve to a remarkable degree the autonomy that characterizes the fluent language user" (Little, 1991:31; also cf. Dam, 1995:6; Wolff, 1994:16). This calls for learning environments such as the MOO that are flexible enough for learners to experiment in and make them their own. For an example of constructionist learning, see sub-section 3.4.1.

Situated learning

The last learning model I would like to discuss is the concept of situated cognition or situated learning, another extension of constructivism. Bruner (1986:127) suggests that discovery learning or learning by invention is embedded in a communal context:

> I have come increasingly to recognize that most learning in most settings is a communal activity, a sharing of the culture. It is not just that the child must make his knowledge his own, but that he must make it his own in a community of those who share his sense of belonging to a culture. It is this that leads me to emphasize not only discovery and invention but the importance of negotiating and sharing — in a word, of joint culture creating as an object of schooling and as an appropriate step en route to becoming a member of the adult society in which one lives out one's life.

Situated learning models focus on this relationship between creative construction and activities in a community of practice. The beginnings of situated learning theory are generally associated with the works of Brown, Collins, Duguid and Newman (Brown, 1985; Collins, Brown, & Newman, 1989; Brown, Collins, & Duguid, 1989), and Lave and Wenger (Lave & Wenger, 1991; Lave, 1991), although many theorists cite Vygotsky's work as a foundation (Hay, 1996b:205). These models have been interpreted as having a slightly behaviourist undercurrent, as some theorists emphasise the role of the situation in determining the reaction. In this view "[p]eople 'orient to a situation' rather than proactively generating activity rich with meaning reflective of their interests, intentions, and prior knowledge" (Nardi, 1996c:81); "knowledge is contextually situated and is fundamentally influenced by the activity, context, and culture in which it is used" (McLellan, 1996:6; Brown, Collins, & Duguid, 1989:19; Carr, Jonassen, Litzinger, & Marra, 1998:6).

Brown et al. (1996:31–32) refer to indexicality to demonstrate that the contents of a shared environment contribute significantly to communication. In Halliday's words, a "text is embedded in a context of *situation*" (Halliday, 1978:122). This can be shown in two areas: vocabulary acquisition in L2 and conversations at a distance. Miller and Gildea (1987) have shown that vocabulary acquisition depends on the context, on extralinguistic help, such as indexicality or deixis: words like *I*, *here*, *now*, *next*, *tomorrow*, *afterwards*, *this*. These words are not only context-sensitive, but context-dependent (Brown, Collins, & Duguid, 1996:31). Indexicality also becomes an issue when we try to hold conversations at a distance, within a medium such as the telephone. Over time, conversation partners need to find ways to situate reference in other ways than they would by using indexical words (Rubin, 1980). If we try to replace indexical words with descriptions, conversation and attention markedly change. In some situations, the indexical term cannot be replaced (Perry, 1979; also see Boyle, 2000:587). Indexicality is impossible without a shared mental environment; in other words, we cannot use words such as *here* and *there* without an implicit or explicit agreement between communication partners about the frame of reference. As language learners, we will have serious deficits in the vocabulary acquisition and the use of indexicality if there is no way to practice them in an authentic target language environment. Our scenarios provide examples for an environment that allows for this type of practice, and I will return to the notion of a shared mental environment in sub-section 3.4.3.

Situated educational practice tries to avoid decontextualized, oversimplified instruction (see Cognition and Technology Group at Vanderbilt, 1993). We can distinguish between four different purposes of situated learning. First, the purposes and applications of learning are accentuated. Second, learning is seen as using and constructing knowledge rather than just receiving it. Third, as students are involved in several different contexts, they learn how to apply their knowledge. Fourth, the multiple contexts of learning support the abstraction of knowledge, which means that learners see knowledge both embedded in use and independent of context. This enables them to transfer and adapt knowledge to new problems and domains (Brown, Collins, & Duguid, 1996; also see Warschauer, 1996c).

The situated learning model also encourages us to think that "different types of instructional materials afford different kinds of learning activities" (Cognition and Technology Group at Vanderbilt, 1996:126). My colleague O'Rourke and I have explored this interplay between technology and pedagogy (O'Rourke & Schwienhorst, 2003; Schwienhorst, 2002b) and argued that it is useful to look at the various affordances of learning tools and materials. We cannot ignore the fact that certain technologies do or do not allow us to implement certain communication scenarios, and that they are related to their situatedness not only in a spacial, but also and more importantly, a socio-cultural context. I will return to this concept, Gibson's (1966, 1979) theory of affordances, in Chapter 2.

Situated learning goes beyond the creation of artefacts to embed them in a community of practice (see Hay, 1996a:91–94, for a critical discussion of constructionism and situated learning). It reminds us not only of the situatedness of learning, but also of language, which is reflected in the indexicality of language, both in vocabulary acquisition and telecommunications projects. Learners should also be encouraged to experiment with various roles. This not only entails the demand for a variety of environments, but also the demand for quickly changing interaction scenarios and technologies. Learners and teachers are involved in a fluctuating context of interaction modes in the language classroom. Group work changes to individual work, to learner-teacher exchange, to large group scenarios, to pair work, etc. These options only exist in very few CMC tools, certainly not in many video conferencing settings, but are a crucial requirement for language learning environments (see Hughes & Hewson, 1998:49). Our MOO scenarios, again, are closer to learning environments that allow situated learning. Learners are free to create artefacts at any level (i.e. using existing artefacts to programming completely new objects); they can change roles very quickly and experiment with new ones, an essential step for every language learner; they can make use of the situated nature of language, i.e.

using language as if they are sharing a communal mental environment with speakers that are actually thousands of miles away.

1.2 THE ROLE OF THE TEACHER IN LEARNER AUTONOMY

The role of the teacher is crucial for any pedagogical approach based on learner autonomy. We can see in the two scenarios that the mere provision of freedom and a sheer limitless availability of material will not support, in itself, learner autonomy. Both the pedagogical framework and the learning environment (and/or its technology) need to be brought within reach of the learner's autonomy, so that the learner will pick up and connect to resources and tools that help her language learning process. However, a teacher can only support learner autonomy if she has benefited from teacher education that is structured along the same principles. Thus, I briefly look at these two aspects of teacher autonomy, (1) the role of the teacher in language classrooms based on learner autonomy principles, and (2) the principles that should guide teacher education based on learner autonomy.

The role of the teacher in learner-autonomy-based pedagogies has therefore a central role in judging how much autonomy a learner is ready for, or in other words, how much of a pedagogical framework is necessary to support the learner. In our first scenario, one of the basic reasons why we would consider this (and similar projects) project a failure is precisely this. The opportunities or affordances that learners were presented with in the first scenario of the MOO tandem project were far too demanding compared to the learners' level of autonomy that they had reached. To present another example from our daily practice at the Centre for Language and Communication Studies (CLCS) foreign language modules: learners are required to do several group projects during the year. If I tell them: "ok, the next project is a debate or a public hearing", they will get to work immediately, form groups, decide on topics, search for authentic materials, etc. They are able to make decisions within the given framework. If I were to tell them: "ok, it is completely up to you what you want to do as a project", the result would likely be confusion, long discussions that lead nowhere, and dissatisfaction. Although they can make more decisions, have more freedom, learners are often unable to plan, monitor, and evaluate learning when there is no structure and no concrete goals or deliverables. If I were to tell them: "ok, the project is a debate on recycling, and I have selected these two authentic texts and made a glossary of vocabulary for you", it is likely that the project would also be dissatisfactory, as learners may feel too much restricted in their decisions and the teacher may actually infringe on the learners' autonomy. In areas such as topic selection and material selection where many learners (at least in my experience) are well able to make decisions, it would mean that somebody else takes the decision away from them. My colleague O'Rourke and I have discussed the delicate balance between the pedagogical framework and the individual level of autonomy in more detail elsewhere (O'Rourke & Schwienhorst, 2003; Schwienhorst, 2002b).

I have previously argued at various points before (see pages 13, 24, 33) that the position of the teacher changes when we implement learner autonomy in the language classroom. In my view, the key role of the teacher in a classroom based on learner autonomy principles is to bring the learning environment (which comprises physical learning tools like dictionaries; peers; native speakers; technology; but also cognitive tools that the learner has developed for herself) within reach of the learner's current level of learner autonomy. This new role is reflected in our initial scenarios. First, we largely failed to see that the learning environment was too far removed from the learners' autonomy to be perceived as a learning opportunity or to employ already developed concepts. More technical help and a sound pedagogical framework in the second scenario led to "optimal flow", where learners perceived the situation they were in as difficult but ultimately "doable" (see Csikszentmihalyi, 1991; Csikszentmihalyi & Csikszentmihalyi, 1988).

Voller (1997) sees three different roles of the teacher: facilitator, counsellor, and resource. In Holec's (1985:184–186) view, the teacher as facilitator has the function to give psycho-social and technical support. Psycho-social support involves the personal qualities of the facilitator, the capacity for motivating learners, and the ability to raise learners' awareness. Technical support includes helping learners to plan and carry out their independent language learning, helping learners to evaluate themselves, and helping learners in general to acquire the skills and knowledge needed to implement the above (also see Wright, 1987; Ryan, 1997). A second role of the teacher is as a counsellor, as someone who can "provide information and answer questions about self-access resources and how best to use them" (Voller, 1997:104). Variously, this role has been discussed as counselling (Kelly, 1996:105), "instructional conversation" (Tharp & Gallimore, 1988), or learner training (see Esch, 1997:174; Ellis & Sinclair, 1989:1; see also Entwistle, 1987; Dickinson, 1992). A third function of the teacher is that of resource: This means that the teacher brings her own creativity and experiences, particularly those of learning and language learning, into the classroom. I would interpret this role as being able to share "action knowledge", personally meaningful experiences regarding language learning and learning in general. This entails an ability for improvisation and creative design. In Wolff's words, "[t]he creativity of the teacher becomes more important than his knowledge about the language" (Wolff, 1994:14). An impressive example of such an approach to teaching is described by Falbel (1989) in his account of the Danish Friskolen model. In such an approach, the teacher becomes a researcher and learner herself (Breen & Candlin, 1980; also cf. the concept of action research, see Benson, 2001:181–183; Little, 1997d:128).

Dam (1995:80) has contributed substantially to this new teacher role. In her language classroom, one of the key elements is awareness (also see Tort-Moloney, 1997:16–17; McGrath, 2000:104) and socially determined responsibility. Within a framework of basic principles, classroom activities are jointly negotiated and elaborated by the teacher and the students (see Little, 1995:180). Teachers need to use similar tools as learners such as diaries, contracts, etc. to increase their awareness of the teaching process. The whole process of planning, monitoring, and evaluation becomes an ongoing dialogue between teacher and learners, and thus involves group, peer, and self-assessment. It makes sense to apply these principles to teacher education.

Little suggests that "[we] must provide trainee teachers with the skills to develop autonomy in the learners who will be given into their charge, but we must also give them a first-hand experience of learner autonomy in their training." (Little, 1995:179–180). On the one hand, therefore, teacher education needs to develop a creative and flexible capacity to provide options to the learner; teachers need to be consistent in negotiated decisions; they need to develop a creative and flexible approach to the integration of learner autonomy principles within the framework of the context they are working in (e.g social, institutional, physical); they need to develop interactional skills to cope with a variety of negotiation scenarios; and also become, of course, a skilled target language speaker and expert. Especially this final point also means, on the other hand, that principles of learner autonomy need to be experienced first-hand in teacher education: aims, content, tasks, and assessment are just some of the issues that need to be negotiated (see Tort-Moloney, 1997:51; Tharp & Gallimore, 1988; Benson, 2000). We as teachers in our scenarios experienced that our negotiations before, during, and after projects, within the very same learning environment that our learners used, provided us with deeper insights into learner autonomy. These detailed negotiations not only made us work better as one unit, but also contributed to the pedagogical framework within which we as individual teachers were able to move.

In this sub-section, I have looked at teacher autonomy as a complementary concept to learner autonomy. Drawing on several sources, I have discussed three major roles of the autonomous teacher in the classroom, on the one hand, and the role of teacher autonomy in teacher education, on the other hand. I have argued that many elements of teacher autonomy can be adapted to teacher training. Unless future teachers experience teacher autonomy in teacher training, most of them will not make its principles their own.

1.3 IMPLEMENTING LEARNER AUTONOMY — TANDEM LEARNING

In the previous sections, I introduced some principles of learner and teacher autonomy. I noted that that we need to support the learner to become more detached and more reflective; more communicative and collaborative; and more experimental and participatory. One pedagogical implementation of these principles has been tandem learning, which has also been the framework for our initial scenarios and the empirical research that follows in Chapter 3. In this sub-section I will show how the principles of learner autonomy translate into an actual pedagogical framework, and what the opportunities and pitfalls are.

Tandem learning has extended the concept of learner autonomy to a dynamic exchange between language learners and native speaker experts sharing a complementary combination of languages. Early Tandem learning developed as face-to-face meetings between two learners with different L1s learning each other's mother tongue. Learners teamed up with a native speaker, such as an exchange student, and learned each other's language while being supported by a framework of counselling sessions, collaborative tasks and activities, etc. (see Dalwood, 1977; Henner-Stanchina, 1985; Murphey, 1987; Little, 1988; Müller, Schneider, & Wertenschlag, 1988). The eTandem Network in Bochum, Germany, has supported and organised exchanges of this kind since 1994 in a Lingua-funded project, now with more than a dozen languages in a variety of bilingual combinations.

The principles of tandem learning do not directly map unto the three areas of reflection, interaction, and experimentation, as outlined in section 1.1. While these three are essential capacities and goals for each language learner on her way to learner autonomy, the principles of tandem learning can be largely seen as prescriptive "operating procedures" in a specific context (one-to-one learning partnerships between learners with complementary L1/L2 combinations) to ensure that these capacities and goals are realised. After all, in tandem learning both learners are at various points learners who need to communicate as much as possible in the target language but also native speaker experts who need to provide as much authentic input as possible. In order to keep these two roles balanced, some ground rules need to be established.

The first rule is reciprocity. Each partner must benefit equally from the partnership, and can expect to receive as much help as s/he gives. Each partner depends on contributions from his/her partner to make the partnership successful. This involves compromise and commitment, honesty and courtesy. The second principle, linked with reciprocity, is bilingualism, which requires that each student should use the same amount of L1 and L2 in each message. This equal balance of L1 and L2 is not only vital for the training of receptive and productive skills. Research by Appel (1997,

1999) has shown that the quantitative relation between L1 and L2 content in e-mails has repercussions for the success of a tandem partnership. The process of correcting the partner's output was reported to lead to increased awareness of L1 structures. The third principle is learner autonomy. Each learner is responsible for his/her own learning process and must determine learning objectives and methods to achieve these. As both learners are in a partnership, there is also mutual responsibility to make the partnership as rich and beneficial to each partner as possible.

At the Centre for Language and Communication Studies (CLCS) at Trinity College, Dublin, we have organised tandem partnerships since 1995, with mixed results. We found that the official channels of the eTandem Network, the tandem dating agency and the forums, were perceived as inadequate by many students. We therefore started to organise tandem partnerships ourselves. E-mail projects are relatively easy to organise, because of the asynchronous nature of the medium, but usually far from easy to monitor and sustain. The teacher's role as a dispenser of knowledge disappears almost completely in tandem learning. Bilingualism may be in danger if one partner is far more proficient in the target language than the other. Regular awareness-raising activities such as questionnaires or mock-exchanges that are discussed in class can also help (Little et al., 1999). A departure from the principles of reciprocity and bilingualism often results in a one-sided relationship, and in many cases signals the end of a partnership.

The evaluation of projects in electronic media has obvious advantages. An e-mail environment such as that developed by Appel and Mullen (2000) will automatically collect all e-mail data, and facilitates the quantitative and qualitative analysis of data. Part of this evaluation process can and should take place in class. Students need to be confronted with their own learning in such a way that they reflect on it, become aware of the underlying processes, and define new goals for themselves.

In our first e-mail tandem project at CLCS (Little et al., 1999), we followed a content-based qualitative approach with a questionnaire that was sent out twice to our students, once during the term and once at the end. Questionnaires were discussed in groups in class, thus making them part of the awareness-raising process. They showed that content-driven discourse leads to larger cross-cultural awareness and relates directly to learners' personal experiences (also see Schwienhorst, 2003). Learners valued their partnership because it allowed them to use the language and at the same time observe it in use (communicative purpose), which resulted in greater encouragement, increased confidence, and risk-taking. Students reported becoming more aware of similarities and differences between the two languages. Learners did not see correction and feedback as too important, but access to everyday authentic language, personal interaction, a focus on their own needs, the fact that it was a mutual partnership, and its speed and convenience.

In our analysis of the linguistic data in e-mail tandem we found that students followed the principle of bilingualism throughout their exchanges (90% of all e-mails were bilingual). In terms of language register, we found that, like other researchers (Warschauer, 1996a; Dam, Legenhausen, & Wolff, 1990; Murray, 1985; Wilkins, 1991; Reinman, 1995), e-mail discourse uses discourse fillers and non-standard punctuation. We also found that students explicitly tried to co-ordinate their exchanges by using tandem-related metatalk to discuss error correction, topics, attitudes to tandem learning, linguistic content, or the technical operation of the partnership. Our findings in error correction were that students used a wide variety of conventions. In several cases students were able to discover deficits, and in comparatively few cases they were able to generalise across language systems, or generalise across their interlanguage. Their use of meta-language and their corrections were often inaccurate, and there was hardly any "recycling" of corrections.

We found that some organisational difficulties remain (Little & Ushioda, 1997). Pedagogical frameworks need to be created that integrate e-mail into a course. The affective data of our research suggests that students found these exchanges congenial and different from other language learning contexts, in that they themselves had personal ownership of the content and process of learning. The linguistic data suggests that they understood the principle of bilingualism, but that meta-talk and error correction still needed to be improved.

Let us summarise a number of potential benefits, but also pitfalls and problems of tandem learning. One of the problems is that tandem learning may at first seem like just another penfriendship; student work may become unfocused, unbalanced, and trivial. Indeed, even recent CALL papers have called e-mail tandems "keypalships" (Vilmi, 1999), a term I would avoid. Tandem learning requires commitment and discipline to become an effective tool in the language learning process.

Then there is the fact that tandem learning, at least within the context of e-mail, is an exclusively written medium. This may prove difficult for learners who have been learning the target language mainly within a classroom where more emphasis was placed on oral than on written communication. Within e-mail as an asynchronous and thus non-reciprocal written medium, they have the added problem of not being able to negotiate meaning or provide scaffolding in the way they could in synchronous media like the telephone (Little, 1998). On the other hand, the written medium is ideal for awareness-raising activities, as I mentioned earlier in this chapter, and thus has some advantages for tandem learning (Little, 1997c).

The potential benefits of tandem learning are manifold. Every learner is partnered with a native speaker of his or her target language who is not only fully acquainted with the language but also with the target language culture. The topics of discussion can be agreed on and are thus potentially much more meaningful than much classroom discourse. Working arrangements can be agreed on with the partner. The fact that both partners depend on each other and are on the same level as learners and experts can increase motivation and puts both in similar positions. Both learners possess a record of all the e-mails which can be worked on later for further learning or evaluation (Little, 1998). All these are advantages of tandem learning that have persuaded us to refine our approach and transfer it to other computer-assisted media.

1.4 FROM CALL TOOLS TO THE NOTION OF LEARNING ENVIRONMENTS

In sub-section 1.1, I have defined the concept of learner autonomy, looked at three of its vital ingredients and showed how the resulting pedagogical demands have been realised in various degrees in our telecommunications projects. I have also tried to define the new role of the teacher within a learner-autonomy-based pedagogy. In the previous sub-section, I have looked at the concept of tandem learning which has developed from face-to-face collaboration to computer-mediated collaboration. I will end this first chapter with a look at learner autonomy and computer-assisted language learning, and the relationship between language pedagogy and technology in general. Computer-assisted language learning research has moved from isolated tools to the notion of learning environments. The way these environments have been defined has much in common with elements of the two scenarios above, and learner autonomy principles in general.

The integration of technology into language learning in general can be traced back to the 1960s and 1970s. As learner autonomy has only been discussed since the late 1980s, or early 1990s, at best, it is not surprising that the body of research on learner autonomy and technology is comparatively small, even within the general computer-assisted language learning (CALL) research. Thus, various learner autonomy principles have more often found their way implicitly rather than explicitly into CALL literature, and even recent and respected overviews of CALL history (such as those in Bax, 2003; Levy, 1997; Chapelle, 2001; Warschauer, 1996b; Warschauer & Healey, 1998; Warschauer, 2000; Beatty, 2003) hardly ever mention learner autonomy explicitly.

Over the years, CALL has moved away from seeing the computer as a tutor to seeing it as a tool or even a (communication) medium. This parallels the development in teaching methodology from the audiolingual method to the communicative approach and beyond. Fixed media such as CD-ROMs have lost some of their appeal in the light of the Internet revolution. Increasingly, Internet communication tools and learning environments now take centre stage in CALL research and development. In this process, technology and pedagogy support each other and promise to have a serious impact on language learning (cf. Garrett, 1997), although I would question recent arguments that CALL will reach a stage of "normalisation" (Bax, 2003) where it becomes invisible in the language learning classroom. We should keep in mind that exercises on screen differ from exercises on paper, and video conferencing is just as different from face-to-face communication as e-mail. Maybe we should ask how CALL is supporting the learner in her struggle for learner autonomy, and this is a two-way process; technology can work as an "amplifier" for pedagogy, and vice versa.

Let us take, for example, the fact that the communication in our scenarios takes place exclusively in writing. Writing is used quite extensively in learner-autonomy-based classrooms (see Little, 1997c; Aase, Fenner, Little, & Trebbi, 2000; Little, 2001), as it naturally supports processes of awareness more than oral speech; in that sense, we might say that our pedagogical concept seemed to recommend the technological tool, even in our first scenario. However, by the time we reached our second scenario, we had understood (and made use of) the fact that it was also digital written synchronous communication. The availability of transcripts of spontaneous authentic conversation meant that we were challenged to find a use for them within learner autonomy; a challenge that would hardly occur in a non-CALL learning environment as transcripts would be almost impossible to create. We are simply unprepared as teachers and learners to have a transcript of a communication we have just had. Indeed, after many years of MOO projects, I have often found myself in situations in Spain, Italy, or France, where — after a face-to-face discussion in an unknown dialect, for instance — I have often wished I had a transcript; after all, our phonological working memory is limited (Baddeley, Gathercolea, & Papagno, 1998; Jefferies, Ralph, & Baddeley, 2004; Chun & Payne, 2004; Perani, 2005). In that sense, technological features developed and have continued to develop what we could do pedagogically in the language classroom.

There are some indications that we can currently see a paradigm change in CALL design in the light of learner autonomy. Recent CALL literature moves away from the notion of tool towards the notion of environment or virtual community of learners. This environment is influenced by, but also influences itself the underlying pedagogy:

> we conceive of technology as support for a total environment for learning rather than as a single tool or a source of information only. Our premise is that using technology can change not only *how* teachers teach but *what* they can teach — in the most positive sense — and whom they can teach: Technology reaches out to the most distant learners in the most isolated places and offers a hitherto undreamed-of richness of experience. (Egbert & Hanson-Smith, 1999:ix)

and Little argues that "it is possible to think of a 'virtual' target language community, available to language learners anywhere in the world" (Little,

1997b:235). Thus, if there is a trend towards globally accessible computer-assisted language learning environments, then we need to think how these can best work with a framework of learner autonomy. In my definition, learner autonomy centres on supporting learners in three major areas: reflection, interaction, and experimentation, and in the next chapter I will explore what technology has to offer in this respect.

In this sub-section, I have made the point that CALL tools have gradually begun to develop into CALL environments. In the way that many CALL programs have stopped imitating or speeding up physical learning tools, and instead tried to explore ways of supporting learner autonomy, many approaches to the use of technology in the language learning classroom would also now argue that technology is not just a tool to realise a certain pedagogy, but has itself certain qualities that influence the way we think about pedagogy. In our next chapter, I will focus more on the technology side of things. What are the tools in CALL environments, and the MOO environment in particular, that support learner autonomy?

1.5 SUMMARY

In this chapter, I have defined the concept of learner autonomy by using two very different classroom scenarios and three different perspectives: an individual-cognitive view of the learner as intentional learner, a social-interactive view of the learner as communicator, and an experimental-participatory view of the learner as researcher. In this last view, activity theory, constructivism, constructionism, and situated learning theory have been discussed as additional learning models. They not only underline many learner autonomy principles, but have added useful principles for the design of learning environments. As the role of the teacher has been frequently misinterpreted, I have also discussed teacher autonomy in a separate sub-section. Finally, I turned my attention to the relationship of pedagogy and technology, and argued that a move from CALL tools to environments goes hand in hand with a move from a pedagogy-centred view to a view that emphasises more the interrelatedness of pedagogy and technology.

2 Towards Integrated CALL Environments for Learner Autonomy — The MOO

In the previous chapter I defined the concept of learner autonomy as it relates to the application of technology in the language classroom. I have looked in more detail at three of its major points, reflection, interaction, and experimentation, to emphasise the need for a learner-autonomy-based pedagogy in CALL. I concluded that while a sound pedagogical framework is necessary, we also need to consider the particular features of technology, and that therefore pedagogy and technology are interrelated. In this chapter, I will look in more detail at CALL environments, and how the three areas of reflection, interaction, and experimentation can best be supported in them.

I had indicated a shift in CALL research and development on several levels. Recent overviews of CALL speak of a shift towards "Integrated CALL" (Bax, 2003). The way I understand this shift is that we are now moving towards CALL environments that integrate not only various media (the aim of "interactive multimedia"), but a variety of CALL tools that are interlinked within a coherent pedagogical framework such as learner autonomy. This does not mean that we should be aiming towards a "one size fits all" solution, but rather modular systems that integrate — from a learner's perspective — tools for reflection, communication, and experimentation/participation, and — from a teacher's/researcher's perspective — tools that store and analyse learners' interlanguage and provide detailed data for empirical analyses (for instance, within a framework of action research).

These integrated CALL tools have all too often been called environments, often with a "virtual" attached to it, or "virtual communities", or "virtual realities", etc. Just as "Artificial Intelligence" (AI) or "Interactive Multimedia", however, these terms have often been used indiscriminately, without any background knowledge of their development in the field (or related areas). One might well argue that "virtual" and "environments" have gone the way of all over-hyped terminology and should be assigned to computer history — unless we seriously evaluate them for the purposes of CALL. But why should we, do we not have enough paradigms for the future of CALL? I would argue that in order to work towards "integrated

CALL", we need to understand what makes learners reflect on language learning, what makes them communicate, and what makes them experiment and participate in language learning, how all this can be done most effectively, and, most importantly, how these areas are interlinked. This is were we need to focus on language learning *environments*, and I hope to show that also the term "virtual" has significance here.

In the first sub-section I will look at the implications of the concepts "virtual" and "environments" for CALL, while in the second section I will describe the text-based virtual environment called MOO (Multi-user domain, Object-Oriented), which is probably the most widely used virtual environment in CALL to date, and the implications of its features for reflection, interaction, and experimentation/participation, as well as for teachers and researchers as a data collection and analysis tool.

2.1 VIRTUAL ENVIRONMENTS

When we discuss the term "virtual environments", and its components, "virtual" and "environments", we are very quickly reminded of the absurdities of similar terminologies such as "interactive multimedia", which have become a prime example of how new terminology through generalisation has lost almost all of its meaning for useful discourse in CALL. The term, "virtual", has been extensively overused, even in CALL alone, thus "the oxymoron 'virtual reality' and its cousin 'immersive virtual reality' have all but disappeared from the lexicons of researchers. Scholars now speak of virtual environments without confounding 'reality' and 'virtual'" (Blascovich, 2002:128). Nevertheless, it is useful to look back at some of the definitions of virtual reality and its synonym, cyberspace, and I will try to use the term virtual reality or VR when it was used by the respective authors/researchers.

Gibson, in his influential quotation from *Neuromancer*, describes cyberspace as a

> consensual hallucination experienced daily by billions of legitimate operators, in every nation, by children being taught mathematical concepts...A graphic representation of data abstracted from the banks of every computer in the human system. Unthinkable complexity. Lines of light ranged in the nonspace of the mind, clusters and constellations of data. (Gibson, 1984:67)

According to Veronica Pantelidis, "VR has been defined as a highly interactive, computer-based, multimedia environment in which the user becomes a participant with the computer in a 'virtually real' world" (Pantelidis, 1993:23). Carr concludes that "all [definitions] are concerned with the stimulation of human perceptual experience to create an impression of something which is not really there" (Carr, 1995:5).

Just as "artificial intelligence", or "interactive multimedia", "virtual reality" became the new mantra in the early to mid 1990s. We can certainly extract some common traits from these definitions: VR should imply multiple users, should involve a multisensory transfer of information, should present a computer-generated space that is perceived as real, and could replace the current point-and-click interface. Over a decade on, CALL environments that have realised these features are emerging, although human-computer interaction has hardly progressed since the implementation of screen, keyboard, and mouse, and speakers and microphone. We might well ask: do we need to progress beyond these tools for the context of CALL? And do we need virtual elements in CALL?

The term environment can be understood as referring to the following contexts:

> The phrase 'CALL and the environment', theme of the 1995 Exeter CALL conference, is richly ambiguous in the context of our work, where 'environment' means four things. In the broad view of a language teacher, the environment is the web of classroom, text and laboratory activities into which a CALL system connects and integrates. To a cognitive scientist, the CALL system itself can be an environment for a human mind engaged in a learning process. An even more localized view of an environment is as a microworld: a collection of graphically presented objects with associated properties and actions, in an interactive learning environment. Finally, to a computer scientist, an environment is a suite of integrated software tools placed at the disposal of a developer. All four of these interpretations- the pedagogical, cognitive, microworld and development- are important for our conversational system for foreign language learning. (Schoelles & Hamburger, 1996:213–214)

The first of these contexts refers to the important argument that all CALL systems need to be integrated into an existing pedagogical framework and existing classroom work. The second refers to general CALL systems that learners become involved in. The third environment is the more "virtual" aspect of a spatial representation of interactive learning tools, whereas the fourth aspect refers to the programming environment of a software developer. Of course, an important aspect of any language learning environment is missing: meaningful interaction, between learners and their peers, learners and teachers, and learners and native speakers. Not surprisingly, Schoelles and Hamburger's FLUENT system was an intelligent tutoring system using NLP (see Hamburger & Hashim, 1992; Hamburger, 1995). Apart from this omission, we can also identify and re-interpret some of these aspects in the light of aspects of learner autonomy I focused on in section 1: the strong teacher role in integrating CALL in existing frameworks; the importance of learners becoming involved or absorbed in CALL systems and assembling meaningful learning tools within a spatial metaphor, and the notion of CALL environments as programming environments, as areas of participation and experimentation for teachers as well as learners.

For an overview of graphical virtual environments, see for example Schwienhorst (2000b), Schroeder (2002), and Costa (2003). In a recent article (Schwienhorst, 2002c), I have given a more detailed overview of high-tech and fully immersive virtual reality applications in language learning so I will only mention a few applications here. Very little empirical research has been conducted on these tools, and the pedagogical basis of these applications is often more than questionable, similar to related areas in intelligent tutoring systems (for criticism, see Oxford, 1995). There are certain parallels between Zengo Sayu, a Japanese environment presented by Rose (1996) and Rose and Billinghurst (1995), Zohrab's recreation of Greek and Roman environments (1996), Kaplan et al.'s Military Language Tutor (MILT, Kaplan, Sabol, Wisher, & Seidel, 1998; Holland, Kaplan, & Sabol, 1999; Sams, 1995; Kaplan & Holland, 1995), and Trueman's QuickTime® VR developments (Trueman, 1996). Their pedagogical framework and their notion of feedback are often too simplistic, and the view of AI in providing feedback is too naive and optimistic. I do not wish to devalue the efficiency of automatic feedback altogether: especially research by Heift (2001, 2002) and Pujolà (2001) has provided some valuable results. Nevertheless, AI is in many cases unable to provide the explicitness and appropriateness of feedback that learners need (Egbert, Chao, & Hanson-Smith, 1999:5).A recent addition to implementations of VR in language learning is presented by Svensson (2003), who emphasises the learner-controlled nature and opportunities for social and cultural interaction in VEs.

In the following three sections, I will look at how we can support learner autonomy through CALL environments, focusing in turn on the three perspectives outlined in section 1.1. What features do CALL environments need to support reflection; interaction; and experimentation?

2.1.1 Towards CALL environments that support reflection

I would like to consider three aspects in a discussion of reflection in CALL environments: the importance of the medium of writing; the importance of learner representation in CALL systems; and the interplay between learner, learner representation and interface. First, the medium of writing still has some major advantages over other media such as audio or video in terms of reflective potential. Learner diaries that are stored on the web are easily accessible and searchable by learners and also researchers (if given permission). Collaborative writing tools allow for continuous editing and re-editing of texts, and some CALL environments allow learners to post notices, posters, or other information resources in virtual environments. In principle, these written artefacts can, of course, be much easier retrieved and made available than audio or video resources, for example selectively through concordancing tasks. Only recently have we seen similarly effective developments for audio concordancing, such as the publicly accessible databases by the Institut für Deutsche Sprache at http://www.ids.de and video concordancing, such as the impressive Multimedia Adult English Learner Corpus (MAELC) at Portland State University (see Reder, Harris, & Setzler, 2003). They are also potentially much more accessible and flexible than printed materials. As a process, interactive writing as in the MOO can also support reflection, in that it can lead to processes of language and metalinguistic awareness such as "noticing" (O'Rourke, 2005).

Second, CALL environments offer some interesting opportunities for reflection on learning environments and learner identities. In a learning environment such as the MOO, learners cannot just participate in creating their own learning environment, but they can also create an online representation of themselves. I would argue that, in this respect, the MOO has advantages over video conferencing systems, with their inherent tendency to identify speaker with representation. This discussion has only in recent years, albeit sporadically, found its way into CALL research (see, for example, Tammelin, 1998, 2003; Schwienhorst, 2004a). Virtual reality studies that assess self-presence or self-awareness have focused on the relationship between the self and its representation in VR, often referred to as avatar:

> [I]n almost any virtual environment system with any significant level of embodiment, there are three bodies present: the objective body, the virtual body, and the body schemata. [...] The objective body is the physical, observable, and measurable body of the user. The virtual body is the representation of the user's body inside the virtual environment. The body schema is the user's mental or internal representation of his or her body. (Biocca, 1997)

Biocca's category of self-presence has important consequences for the support of learner awareness as outlined in section 1. Rather than trying to pursue photo-realistic representation (such as in video conferencing), a virtual character could serve not only as a scaffold, but also an experimental "other" for learners, allowing for the detachment that is crucial to encourage processes of awareness. In addition, the interaction with the environment could contribute significantly to the creation of a stress-reduced laboratory-like learning environment as described by Kelly (1955, repr. 1991:112–116). Ridley (1997:58) has described the importance of experimenting with various learner roles for awareness, as the "self-concept is multi-faceted and dynamic, in that it is constantly shifting". By adopting a virtual self, language learners can experiment with different concepts/roles of self and explore their identity in the target language and its community.

Third, we need to look at how the learner is supported in reflective processes by the environment. When learners have the opportunity to be active agents in the learning environment, when they don't simply digest prepared material, they are far more likely to use the artefacts they create as cognitive tools, as tools that go beyond the requirements of the exercise or task and actually become instruments to think about certain larger contexts of grammar, pronunciation, etc. This means that CALL environments should be, in principle, extremely open in the functionality and tools they offer the learner, and these tools should have a tendency towards meta-tools, e.g. a tool that allows the learner to generate exercises; making a learner more into a designer or agent (for a discussion of agency, see Murray, 1997:128; also Stone, 1995:11; Oxford, 2003; Kramsch, A'Ness, & Lam, 2000; and Debski, 2003:138).

Of course, this has to go hand in hand with a pedagogical framework. In our language modules at the CLCS, we have for the past few years implemented a project where students select an authentic text of their choice in the target language and use this text to create a coherent cycle of exercises, including preparatory exercises about the topic; exercises focused on the text itself; and production exercises beyond the focus of the text. As a four-week project, our students exchange their exercises at some point with peers, solve other students' exercises, but the focus is not so much on the actual exercises, but the additional knowledge they acquire about a variety of language learning issues on a meta-level: how do I focus on a particular study area? How do the exercises relate to the learner proficiency level? How do I make study periods interesting? Maybe most of all, this project leads them away from their traditional (and sometimes fossilised) learning methods to explore new avenues for learning. In good CALL environments, it is easier to support the development towards awareness than in the classroom, as the learner can adapt the tools and the environment to her needs, and move away from rote learning towards greater awareness of learning methods, styles, proficiency levels, etc. I will demonstrate this idea in sub-section 3.4.1.

In summary, when we consider the importance of reflection in CALL environments, I would argue that we need to (1) acknowledge the importance of writing as a medium that has unquestionable advantages in supporting reflective processes, not only as an artefact for future work, but also as a process; (2) recognise that virtual, i.e. computer-generated and mediated, learner identities can support processes of detachment and thus reflection; and (3) work towards learning tools and environments that offer more learning opportunities on a meta-level.

2.1.2 Towards CALL environments that support interaction

Interaction has been, at least since Swain's "comprehensible output" hypothesis (Swain, 1985) and Ellis's tenet "language learning is language use" (Ellis, 1985), one of the central means and goals of language learning. Target language use plays not just a central role in communicative language learning, but also in learner autonomy, where the exclusive use of the target language, together with collaborative learning modes, is seen as a necessary condition for language learning.

When I discussed interaction and collaboration in the context of learner autonomy in the first chapter, I argued for meaningful interaction, scaffolding, rich contexts, stress-free environments, and interactive writing. These arguments are also true for computer-mediated communication (CMC). However, CMC has at least a large potential to fulfil these demands better than the physical classroom.

First, one feature of computer-assisted learning environments is that they can provide a large number of communication partners all over the world, from a large variety of speaker groups, in a wide variety of modes, with various purposes, and in various settings. I could e-mail a web site to alert them to technical problems; use SMS text messaging to confirm a lunch date; use text-chat to talk to German football fans; use audio to leave a voice-mail message on a public notice board; use audio conferencing in a virtual environment, on a virtual character, to practice pronunciation; or have a video conferencing session with an Australian businessman, while collaborating with him in real time on a spreadsheet document. However, it may be more difficult to find ongoing, reliable communication partners as in physical learning environments, and learners may not experience the kind of scaffolding they need. This is where strong organisational and pedagogical frameworks are required, such as tandem learning. Due to the mediated nature of CMC, we can also hypothesise that CMC will result in a more stress-reduced atmosphere, where learners are more willing to interact than in the physical classroom.

Second, the fact that CMC takes place through the computer and is "mediated" also means that we need to think what effect this has on the learning environment that learners are faced with, and how learners perceive themselves in it. Apart from the question of verbal and nonverbal communication and their "mediation", we also mediate identities; identities that are linked to shared mental spaces (see my discussion of situated learning in the previous chapter). An expression such as "Hi, I didn't think you'd make it here in time" assumes a common understanding of the references "I", "you", "here", and also "in time" (in time for what?). Language, as I mentioned before, is often strongly situated in particular contexts, and these are difficult to simulate in the language classroom. One point that we should therefore discuss is how space and identity can be mediated via computer networks; whether we choose CMC tools that emphasise mediation (virtual characters and environments, e.g. the MOO) or non-mediation (e.g. video conferencing).

In many communication media, interaction is bound to be only partly successful, due to the maintaining of the distinct locations of participants and thus their essential difference in reference models. The obvious drawback for most traditional forms of telecommunications is what Short et al. have labelled the "coffee and biscuits problem" (1976:140). They cannot be offered to the other party in a teleconference, because "no matter how elegant the telecommunications system is, the two parties are still in different places and this precludes certain types of activities" (Short, Williams, & Christie, 1976:143). This problem occurs independently of the mode that is chosen: "Faultless two-way audio and video link-ups [in distance education] are not automatically equivalent to a mental and affective connectedness" (Zhang & Fulford, 1994), and Short et al. have rightly remarked that "there is a very obvious barrier between the two parties communicating, no matter how 'transparent' that barrier may be" (Short, Williams, & Christie, 1976:140). As I have noted in my discussion of situated learning in section 1, this affects collaboration as well as communication between parties involved in a telecommunications activity. We should ask, for example, whether it is more beneficial to emphasise separateness of space (as for example in video conferencing) or bring users/learners together in a virtual space; whether we give the illusion of identity of character and representation (as in video conferencing) or have a virtual character that might behave differently from the physical self.

Third, both our initial scenarios used interactive writing, and by definition, all CMC is mediated, i.e., not face-to-face. What are the features of interactive writing and CMC in general and how does this affect interaction? At first glance, we might think that the first and foremost demand on any communication media is to try and emulate face-to-face communication. The notion behind this is that the more verbal and non-verbal information we can transmit, the more effective or useful or "natural" our communication will be. However, the last two decades have seen a revision of this idea, not only because of research and development in CMC, but also because of developments in the mobile communications market. Instead of focusing on one "ideal" medium, we seem to invent an ever greater variety of communication tools that combine text, visuals, sound, virtual environments, virtual characters, etc. A great surprise is that in spite of advanced video technology, text-based communication tools such as SMS or e-mail dominate both Internet and mobile communication networks. A number of these tools require us to learn completely new skills in our first, and even more so, our second language. One example is SMS text messaging, which has variously been described as a decline in literacy skills (Johnston, 2003; n.a., 2003) or simply a new literacy that needs to be learned (Lee, 2002).

The lack of non-verbal cues is probably the most commonly perceived problem in all forms of telecommunications. This is particularly obvious in audio conferencing and text-based conferencing, but video conferencing is also affected. While the medium may suggest that there is hardly any difference between face-to-face and video conferencing, there are differences on a number of levels. Depending on the set-up of the video system, these can include a whole range of non-verbal cues, such as back channels, facial expressions and gestures, redundancies, referential language, etc. (for a critical view of video conferencing, see Egido, 1988; Heath & Luff, 1991; also see Wang, 2004). According to Birdwhistell (1970), there are two groups of non-verbal cues, those used for integrational and those used for informational purposes. While the first purpose includes behaviour that "keeps the system in operation, regulates the interaction process, cross-references particular messages to comprehensibility in a particular context and relates the particular context to the larger contexts of which the interaction is but a special situation" (Birdwhistell, quoted in Short, Williams, & Christie, 1976:44), the second is directly concerned with the transmission of information to another person, e.g. a nod to signal agreement.

Short et al. (1976) have persuasively argued against some of the myths surrounding the importance of non-verbal cues. First, the notion that reduced cues will lead to reduced efficiency is questionable when we think about negotiations. In these situations, the audio-only channel may well be preferred to a face-to-face situation (Christie, 1972). Second, the notion that we can compare the functions of certain cues and their presence or absence, we can predict the effects on interaction, is invalid for a number of reasons. Non-verbal cues are not transmitted in isolation; the awareness of reduced non-verbal cues may lead to modification of behaviour; non-verbal cues are not invariant in their meaning across situations; and we do not know enough about the relationship between the use of the visual cues and the outcome of the interaction.

Short et al. suggested that when interpersonal exchange, as in some media, is reduced, "attention must focus instead on the cues which are available — the verbal channel containing the interparty, task-oriented, cognitive material" (Short, Williams, & Christie, 1976:65). They focused on the term of social presence, which was defined as "the degree of salience of the other person in the interaction and the consequent salience of the interpersonal relationships" (ibid.). Social presence theory shifted the focus from the actual parameters of the medium to the user's synthetic perception of it. I think Short et al.'s shift towards the users' perceptions of the medium is important. The user/learner will look at the particular features of a communication medium and then communicate depending on the pedagogical context; thereby making use of pressures, potentials, and affordances that she perceives (Schwienhorst, 2002b; O'Rourke & Schwienhorst, 2003). The effects of experience may prove that users may become used to a new medium and learn to use it more effectively over time. The generation effect may show that some media may open the way for new activities or even new types of communication not previously envisaged or thought possible.

A particular distinction has often been drawn between task-based collaboration and interpersonal interaction. While task-related communication in CMC is in many cases viewed as favourable, Walther (1996:3–4) reports that interpersonal communication (as described by Short et al.) is the area where CMC is seen by some theorists and researchers as deficient because it provides too little social information (Dubrovsky, Kiesler, & Sethna, 1991:119). However, Walther (1992; also see Gunawardena, 1995:154) also reports a longitudinal effect for interpersonal communication: "users learn to adapt their verbal behavior to the restrictions of the textual medium; over time, such interaction may adapt to more customary interpersonal levels" (see Walther, 1996:9; also see Rice & Love, 1987). The view that interpersonal communication in CMC may be slower but just as potent over time, is summarised in Walther's (1994:465) Social Information Processing Perspective (SIPP, also see Herring, 1999). Walther also noted that "whatever subtle social context cues or personality cues do appear in CMC take on particularly great value" (Walther, 1996:18), an observation that took shape as the Social Individuation/ Deindividuation model (SIDE, see Walther, 1997:346). Walther even speculated that "[a]nother beneficiary of the lack of physical cues for the CMC sender may be in increased cognitive resources devoted to message construction" (Walther, 1996:22). Walther has also spoken about the possibility that CMC assumes a hyperpersonal dimension by exceeding face-to-face interpersonal communication (Walther, 1996:5). This notion has remarkable parallels with Biocca's concept of "hyperpresence" in virtual reality research (Biocca, 1997):

> it may be possible to develop a medium in which one feels **greater** 'access to the intelligence, intentions, and sensory impressions of another' than is possible in the most intimate, face-to-face communication. (Biocca, 1997)

In summary, I think it is pointless to argue for an ideal CMC communication tool; it does not exist, just as there is no ideal interaction tool in non-mediated communication. We have always used various communication media side by side, in different situations, and new media have been integrated with existing ones (Murray, 2000:405). In this sub-section, I have emphasised that interaction through CMC can be supported in a number of ways. First, we need to provide learners with reliable native speaker interaction partners, though thereby not neglecting the importance of peer work and learner-teacher work. Second, we need to recognise that, apart from the communication tools that we have at our disposal to express ourselves, interaction is always situated, bound to speakers and environments. It is therefore vital to consider the importance of presence in CMC environments to see whether and how virtual identities and virtual environments influence interaction through CMC. Third, interaction within each medium will tend to develop its own rules, and cues missing from one medium may not play an important role in another medium; alternatives may be gradually cultured within a community. The important thing is that our learners have the choice between various communication modes (e.g. synchronous vs. asynchronous) and contexts (one-to-one, one-to-group, etc.).

2.1.3 Towards CALL environments that support experimentation

When we think about learning environments that can support experimentation and participation as outlined in 1.1.3, we have to concede that learners' abilities to experiment and participate in the physical language classroom are usually far from ideal. Realities that learners and teachers are faced with include: classrooms that are not dedicated to language learning; non-permanent classrooms (i.e., classrooms that are used by other subjects/classes); a lack of pedagogical and authentic materials that are readily accessible; a lack of materials for learner production (i.e., posters, video cameras, etc.). In more dedicated language learning environments, as described by Dam (1995), learners have access to authentic resources and dictionaries, and a variety of materials that they can use to accomplish personally meaningful tasks. How can we transfer this flexibility to the computer-generated environment? How can these environments become even more effective learning spaces for experimentation and participation, without repeating the mistakes and restrictions of the physical classroom?

A few areas seem important to me: we need to consider the functionality that CALL environments offer; the interface that allows access to this functionality; and of course the pedagogical framework that connects the learning environment and the learner. Chapelle (2001:27n.) has noted that CALL has been influenced very little by human-computer interaction research (also see Levy, 1997, Chapter 3). I think this is a serious drawback. All too often have I seen CALL software that has fundamental flaws in either its functionality or its interface, let alone its pedagogical structure (if there is any discernible pedagogy).

I have discussed previously the notion that language is situated and that it very much depends on the environment that it takes place in. So far, many mediated communication media, such as the telephone, were based on the premise that both communicators were based in different locations. However, since the early 1990s and the creation of virtual environments, we have begun to see alternative contexts for communication. These include CALL environments that work by representing communicators in one, albeit virtual, computer-generated environment. In previous articles, I have argued that the notion of virtual environments for CALL has not just an important influence on how the learner perceives herself and her new identity in the target language community; and how the communication becomes situated; CALL environments as a form of virtual reality can also enhance experimentation and participation (Schwienhorst, 2002c, 2002d).

Several factors influence the learner's ability to experiment with language. First, the resources may not be there; second, the functionality may differ; and third, access to both may be restricted and/or unclear. Let us look at each problem in turn. We can say that the Internet has, without doubt, become the most important language learning resource for many learners. It offers sheer unlimited access to a large variety of language resources, in many different styles, registers, media, and other contexts. Search engines are continually facilitating the search for particular language resources, and working with search engines has become an important literacy skill in itself. On top of all the "static" resources, learners can also contribute in a number of ways, e.g. by taking part in forums and web quests; communicating with native speakers; or setting up web sites themselves. As a resource, the Internet has brought learners much closer to target language communities and their users. With the amount of resources at the learners' disposal, it is no surprise that the functionality of these resources varies significantly. While one online newspaper may offer the whole archive online, searchable with Boolean operators, others may not have a search function at all, and only offer a selection of excerpts. One online dictionary may allow me to search for lexical derivatives or synonyms; others would just allow an alphabetical browse function to access their entries. The third important area I mentioned is access to these resources.

One problem is that not every language classroom has a computer, let alone one for every learner. This automatically restricts severely what the individual learner can access. Provided every learner has a networked computer, it is likely that they have the same operating system, that they have the same interface based on a windows-metaphor. This interface is largely accepted as the status quo, and yet, many computer users experience frustration with current user interfaces (see Klein, 1999; Picard & Klein, 2002; Tractinsky, 2004). It seems plausible that some obstacles in experimentation with resources lie within the interface yet we seem to have very little research on CALL software that deals with interface issues.

Three interface metaphors that we find in online environments seem particularly important: conversational, direct manipulation, and hypertext interfaces. First, some environments allow for direct communication, using natural language processing (NLP). Recent tests conducted by the BBC (1998, 1999), for instance, show that even comparatively crude implementations of artificial intelligence (AI) such as pattern matching and activation networks seem sufficient for a user to enter into a conversational dialogue with a computer. It seems that believability is far more important than creating a model of how the human mind works (Bates, 1994). Some of the most successful implementations of conversational interfaces, like the large-scale BBC research, have been in text-based environments. Particularly the technology of programmable agents and bots, i.e. small programs that behave and communicate like real users (see Foner, 1993; Nardi, 1996a; Dautenhahn, Ogden, & Quick, 2002; Gerhard, Moore, & Hobbs, 2004), appears to be promising for language learning.

Second, direct manipulation interfaces entail "(1) continuous representation of the objects of interest, (2) physical actions instead of complicated syntax, and (3) rapid, incremental, reversible operations with immediate visual feedback" (Brennan, 1990:393; also see Shneiderman, 1982; Hutchins, Hollan, & Norman, 1986; Heeter, 1991). Direct manipulation interfaces enable users to act as in the physical world, with expectable results. While this notion is more prominent in three-dimensional VR interfaces, I argue that text-based virtual reality can also enhance experimentation and participation. If a learner accepts the learning environment as a (virtual) classroom, she expects tools such as blackboards; (links to) dictionaries; posters; etc. She also expects to be able to manipulate them; change them to a certain degree, move them around, etc. These expectations are based on Gibson's theory of affordances (Gibson, 1979:128), which claims that when we perceive an object, we perceive what that object affords. The theory of affordances does not contradict activity theory where "human beings actively create the meaning of the objects in the process of interaction with the environment" (Kaptelinin, 1996:56). Human beings certainly arrive with expectations of object behaviour in their encounters with the environment, but will modify their expectations once they encounter difficulties or inconsistencies with their previous constructs. In Gibson's words, an affordance "points two ways, to the environment and to the observer" (Gibson, 1979:141). The theory of affordances has been widely applied by interface designers in virtual environments and ties in observer, physical environment, and virtual environment (Biocca, 1997). On the one hand, direct manipulation in virtual environments allows learners the familiarity of object expectations in the form of perception-action coupling (Neisser, 1976; Smets, Stappers, Overbeeke, & Mast, 1995), i.e. objects behave as in the physical world; on the other hand, it unlocks the potential of vast learning resources on the Internet.

Third, hypertext and hypermedia have become another important metaphor for interacting with Internet resources, but it is questionable whether they can cope with large data sources. Originally developed by Nelson (1965), hypertext aims "to permit fast and easy access to vast quantities of information by establishing multidimensional links among related items" (Gygi, 1990:279; also see Bailey, 1990). Gygi, however, sees the problem of "spatial and conceptual disorientation" (Gygi, 1990:279). Especially when resources become very large, their management through hypertext becomes difficult (ibid.:284). Nevertheless, hypertext has become the dominating interface metaphor on the Internet.

The three interfaces I mentioned above are not mutually exclusive (Schwienhorst, 2002d). When users/learners are involved in a learning environment, or activity, they are "involved" in the environment/activity in various degrees. This involvement, or immersion (Palmer, 1995; Quarrick, 1989; Lombard & Ditton, 1997), is an important pre-requisite for successful experimentation in language learning. It provides, among other things, a focus on the task at hand; an exclusion of distracting influences; a concentration of learners, learning resources, and tools. In this context, the concept of presence is discussed in almost the same terms as "flow" in motivation (see Fontaine, 1993; Csikszentmihalyi, 1978, 1991; Csikszentmihalyi & Csikszentmihalyi, 1988). Interaction and real agency in CALL environments can generate immersion and involvement in the experimental activity the language learner should be engaged in:

> The rewards generated by intrinsic motivation are usually defined in terms of positive feelings, such as enjoyment, pleasure, satisfaction, self-indulgence. Since these rewards arise directly from involvement in an activity, they create a self-sustaining pattern of motivation that leads to voluntary persistence at the activity. (Ushioda, 1996:20; also see Csikszentmihalyi, 1978:213)

In this subsection, I have looked at features in CALL environments that support and encourage experimentation and participation. I made the point that resources and tools must be available to the learner, and that they need to involve a useful functionality. Both resources and functionality are, however, compromised if the interface with which the user organises and accesses these resources does not encourage experimentation. To this end, I argued that a stronger focus on conversational, direct manipulation, and hypertext interfaces should be considered in the design of CALL environments. These are not mutually exclusive, but, as has been shown, can be combined. In order to experiment with and participate in CALL environments, learners certainly need resources and appropriate tools, and access to make these tools into meta-tools (e.g. from a cloze test to a cloze-test-generator and beyond). They also need functionality to access these resources and tools. One of the biggest technological challenges (I am not discussing the pedagogical framework here), however, lies in the interface: if the interface to these resources does not encourage experimentation and participation, learners will remain passive consumers of whatever language diet is presented to them.

2.1.4 CALL environments and the role of the teacher

In section 1.1.4, I had emphasised that learner autonomy necessarily — and dramatically — changes the role of the teacher in the language classroom. The teacher, just as the learner, needs to consider carefully which CALL technologies are most likely to support learner autonomy, and how to combine them with classroom activities (the concept of blended learning has recently become more important in instructional design, see Henning & Van der Westhuizen, 2004; Vaughan & Garrison, 2005). The interplay between pedagogical and technological frameworks is crucial.

There are several features of CALL environments that support the role of the autonomous teacher, if we see the teacher's role as facilitator, counsellor, and resource (Voller, 1997).The teacher as facilitator might use or develop CALL systems that automatically remind learners of their own targets and plans when necessary, or evaluate their progress in the form of computerised, peer, or teacher feedback. As a counsellor in CALL environments, the teacher can communicate with learners independently of space and time. Text-based communication, but also digital versions of counselling tools such as the ELP, learner diaries, and posters, have the advantage that they are much easier to be retrieved and re-used as a future learning resource, for example in tutorial sessions. As a resource, the teacher might often be consulted for technical help, but she can also remain much more in the background than in the physical classroom. In the physical classroom, the teacher, if only for insurance purposes, is almost always present and has to be, and this can have an intimidation effect on the learners, such as: not to use the L2, not to engage in tasks, or not to focus on peers. In CALL environments, the teacher has — potentially — the opportunity to adhere to her duties of supervision and to collect learner data, while at the same time almost disappearing from the field of view of the learners until they need her as a resource. In my view, this is an important difference to the physical classroom, and an opportunity only rarely exploited. The teacher can become an observer until her help is requested or until she sees the need to become involved.

I have maintained before that in teacher autonomy, teachers also need to become researchers. One of the general features of CALL environments is that they can provide the teacher with a wealth of information about learners: their interlanguage; learning styles; preferred resources and tools; to name just a few areas. This entails that at any stage, and to any extent, the teacher has access to a large variety of data in the CALL environment. However, this is more often the case in either open-source or proprietary CALL environments. The large commercially-produced middle ground of easy-to-use software packages often does not take account of teacher and learner autonomy, and many software producers were completely uncooperative as regards the introduction of research tools, unable to provide such mechanisms, or unwilling to allow access to others to integrate them. The freedom to experiment and exchange ideas is one of the great strengths of open-source software, not just for teachers, but also for learners. Teachers and researchers should demand the integration of research tools into CALL software as a norm, rather than as a fortunate exception. This has been reiterated by various researchers in the field, such as Chapelle (2001:173). She has provided a useful catalogue of demands for future CALL software which very much emphasises the role of the teacher as researcher. In detail, these functions are:

- "A means for estimating task difficulty", a function for designers to select the appropriate level of tasks for intended learners and provide feedback for task development
- "Functions for analysis of learners' linguistic output" (ibid.:171) in order to "assess task authenticity, assign point values and collect diagnostic data for language assessment, and gather learner data for research"
- "Functions for analyzing the language of objects" (ibid.:172); for example, it may be possible "to analyze video in a way that is useful for task construction. These analyses need to be accessible as functions within a set of authoring tools so that the author can select a video from existing electronic sources, and have the function return useful information about its contents."
- "A means of organizing and creating objects", for example, changing text into a cloze test.
- "A means for gathering process-oriented data" (ibid.:173); here, Chapelle refers to the need "to explore context-appropriate, process-oriented assessment of learner characteristics. To do so requires a means for gathering and storing data about learners' working processes in CASLA tasks."
- "A structure for learner models"; it may be that learner models from research on intelligent tutoring systems might be "equally or more valuable for assessment of language ability"
- "A means for authoring learning conditions" (ibid.:174); this implies that "software should provide a means for the author to make salient key linguistic characteristics of the target language input that learners receive", such as highlight input on screen, but also that authoring tools should "provide a means for offering modifications of linguistic input to learners", such as repetition, simplification, or the help of reference materials
- "A means for delivering CASLA [Computer-assisted Second Language Acquisition] via a familiar interface" (ibid.:175); one explanation for the lack of replicable results because "the platforms for implementing CASLA have constantly changed". Chapelle argues here for the standardisation and modularisation of CALL software, and Web-based browsers as the standard delivery tool. This is vital not only for research but also for the education of future CALL developers and users.

It makes sense, of course, to apply the very same principles to teacher education and teacher training. If teachers do not have first-hand experience of CALL environments — and I do not refer to one-hour introductory sessions, but long-term use of these tools — we cannot expect them to use these technologies comfortably and knowledgeably, or to convince learners of the usefulness of these tools. I will illustrate this in my next sub-section.

In this subsection, I have discussed some features that are valuable for CALL environments. I have maintained that Voller's distinction of the teacher as facilitator, counsellor, and resource, also holds true for CALL environments. However, the role of researcher also moves more and more into the foreground: we need to demand that CALL environments provide us with detailed research tools so that we as teachers can plan, monitor, and evaluate our work; and enable us to make changes to the environment that are appropriate for the pedagogical framework on which our teaching is based. This may involve programming and implementing new features and mechanisms that have not been envisaged by the original designers, and thus points towards open-source software.

In this section I looked at the features of CALL software and argued that more and more we are developing towards CALL environments that support learner-autonomy-based pedagogies. My major arguments are as follows (cf. Schwienhorst, 2002d:205):

- CALL environments allow for greater self-awareness and encourage learners to experiment with different roles through the use of virtual representations, thereby reducing the affective filter.
- CALL environments may go beyond face-to-face communication in the way they can enhance linguistic and cognitive awareness of the learning process, especially through the medium of writing.
- CALL environments support interaction by locating participants in a shared environment, thus allowing for a common linguistic reference point.
- CALL environments enhance conversation management and group work by allowing for collaboration in a variety of rapidly changing group work scenarios.
- CALL environments with their underlying spatial metaphors are a more natural way of organizing information resources than an interface that relies solely on the use of buttons and/or menu bars.
- CALL environments enable learners to collaborate on resources in real time.
- CALL environments encourage and enable learners to actively participate in the creation and organization of their learning environment.
- CALL environments provide an ideal support for the teacher as facilitator, counsellor, and resource; in addition, they provide the teacher with a large number of research tools.

In the next section, I will look at how these features translate into the MOO, one example of a text-based CALL environment.

2.2 THE MOO AS A TEXT-BASED VIRTUAL ENVIRONMENT

CALL environments have to be measured against the principles and theories set forth in my previous section where I gave a detailed overview of several concepts I consider relevant to a discussion of CALL. This section will now look in detail at one system that my colleagues and I have used and modified at the Centre for Language and Communication Studies (CLCS), Trinity College Dublin. In the following sub-sections, I will look at the tools that the MOO offers to language learners and teachers for the four areas outlined in my previous section: tools for reflection, interaction, and experimentation and participation from the learner's perspective, and teacher autonomy from the teacher's and researcher's perspectives.

The historical development of MOOs has been described elsewhere in great detail (Schwienhorst, 2000b; Aarseth, 1997). From text-based adventure games popular in the mid-1970s to the highly complex enCore database (Holmevik & Haynes, 2000; Haynes & Holmevik, 1998), which is constantly updated and expanded (while still being available as an open-source software), MOOs have developed towards user-friendly and highly effective educational platforms for collaborative work. The MOO is basically a client-server application (for more information on the MOO programming structure, see Haynes & Holmevik, 1998; Holmevik & Haynes, 2000; Schwienhorst, 2000b). This means that the MOO is running on one machine (the server) and all its users access it from their respective machines (the clients). The MOO architecture is built around three components: the MOO server program, the MOO database and the MOO client program.

As the MOO is an object-oriented environment, it means that "most everything on the MOO (including your character) is an object and has a unique object number assigned to it. At another level, however, object-oriented describes the programming environment from which a MOO is built and by which MOO users can extend it" (Barrios & Wilkes-Gibbs, 1998:68). The MOO "database is organised as a hierarchy of *objects* that are interconnected through a mechanism called *inheritance*" (Holmevik & Blanchard, 1998:125). This means that any extension to the MOO database does not have to be programmed from scratch, but can be built by extending or modifying the functionality of existing objects, whose features the new object "inherits", like a template or blueprint. Let us look at one such hierarchy (taken from Holmevik & Blanchard, 1998:125) (see Figure 2.1)

Users are also organised in a hierarchy, where guests are non-permanent and administrators have access to all parts of the MOO database. Builders and Programmers have the permission to create new objects within the MOO and program new ones.

The MOO system offers multi-platform, individually customisable access to sophisticated tools through a combination of text and hypertext

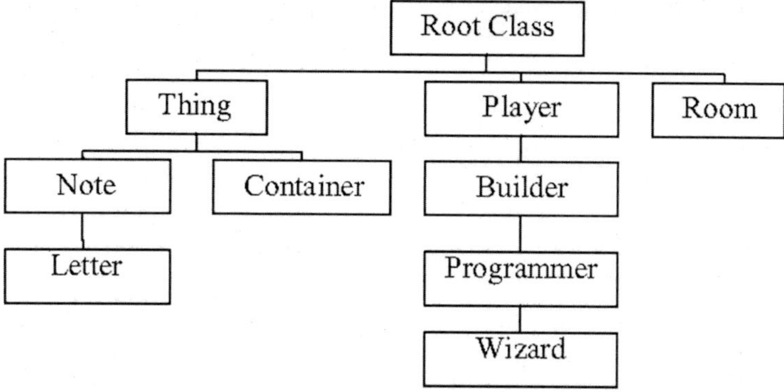

Figure 2.1 Simplified view of a basic top level object hierarchy

interfaces. The organisation of the MOO as a de facto open-source development, using a framework of more or less clearly defined programming tools and openly accessible programs, has led to extensive support networks between MOO users that greatly facilitate the expansion of the MOO technology. These support networks have made enCore probably the favourite MOO database for educational purposes and have recently (2005) lead to the foundation of the enCore Consortium (http://encore-consortium.org/).

2.2.1 Reflection in the MOO

The fact that many subject areas, such as writing, or language learning, are largely mastered through active processes of comprehension and production within a textual medium, as I maintained in chapter 1, only confirms that the MOO medium may well prove more than adequate to the task at hand. The textual medium, as described by Di Matteo (1991), may also enhance reflective and meta-linguistic processes:

> The writing of speech makes visible a compositional activity that disturbs the intentionality of our own language use. It alerts us to the difference of utterance meaning and sentence meaning. Rather than mere message senders, writers in real time also feel like receivers of their own messages.

In parallel with my general section on reflection in CALL environments (sub-section 2.1.1), I will now give examples of how reflective processes can be supported in the MOO.

First, the tools that Dam (1995) has used in her autonomous classrooms are largely present in MOOs. The notebook function allows learners to keep learner diaries that they can revise, edit, and save. These notebooks are only available to the individual learner, but also, at any time, to the teacher/researcher as a research tool. As regards an equivalent of posters, the MOO offers learners (provided they have been made builders or programmers by the MOO administrator) to not only create certain artefacts that they can display to other learners, but they can also create whole online environments such as room descriptions in writing or with multimedia content, hyperlinks to external web resources, etc. Thus, learners have even more opportunities to use writing in many facets for reflective work. We have also developed a shared whiteboard facility at the CLCS that allows learners to collaborate more easily on texts in real time.

In the MOO, learners are represented as objects (from a programming perspective). As such, they can be modified, or customised, as any other object. Although the learner is initially only represented in text and hypertext, she can add multimedia elements to the online persona. One can assume that the written channel provides much more scope for self-awareness and reflection. We need to examine carefully what relationship exists between the virtual representation of the learner and the learner herself, and in my empirical study I will point towards some promising research avenues. Whether this has any influence on the process of identity-creation that some researchers consider vital in a new language and culture (e.g. Schwienhorst, 2003), and whether there is a wash-back effect on the real persona largely remains a question for future research. However, it is important to at least recognise the online character as a tool to work towards a new identity in the target language and its community.

Another feature of the MOO is that every communication can be automatically recorded and sent to the learner and teacher. These transcripts can serve a variety of purposes. First, they allow the learner to re-read and analyse previous conversations, e.g. look up unknown words and phrases, or analyse instances of miscommunication. The availability of transcripts also frees up time and processing effort during the actual MOO sessions; unknown words that are not essential for comprehension can be looked up after the event. As such, the availability of transcripts can have an immediate effect on learner behaviour during sessions. Other tools can be imagined, arising out of recent research (Schwienhorst & Borgia, 2006) that give learners more control about their discourse both during and after the event. As I will demonstrate in the next chapter, the Bilingual Tandem Analyser (BTA) analyses automatically the proportions of L1 and L2 used in learners' communication, and provides accurate feedback in the form of detailed statistics.

For now, I can say that the essentially written nature of the MOO can support processes of awareness and reflection in the following ways: first, the online character may provide a scaffold for identity creation in the sense of creating a new persona in the target language, and also (through its written representation) allow for processes of detachment that are a first step towards reflection; second, the availability of transcripts and automatic forwarding to e-mail accounts of learners almost forces them to confront their own output in the target language and enables them to monitor and use live communication with a native speaker (as in tandem projects) for later analytic tasks, such as new vocabulary items, instances of miscommunication, etc. Online diaries and the creation and use of virtual objects contribute to this process as well. Research in these areas is very much in its infancy, though I will try to point towards some promising research avenues in my next chapter.

2.2.2 Interaction in the MOO

How can the user structure and maintain communication on the MOO? Communication tools are quite diverse in MOOs. There are synchronous and asynchronous communication tools available to users, and in many ways one could say that the MOO tries to emulate the variety of real life communication tools in a virtual setting. It is important to note that many commands, in particular communication commands, lead to different output on screen, depending on the speaker and the audience or addressee. Thus the <say> command, used by the user <Peter>, would appear to him as <You say, "Hello"> whereas other users would see it as <Peter says "Hello">. There are some more obvious advantages of a written communication medium for language learning. Thus, having to type obviously slows down communication and thus simplifies decoding at the moment of reception/display of the message. In addition, the written medium also entails that decoding is simplified after reception of the message, either short-term (learners can scroll back to read previous messages and connect them to current messages) or medium- to long-term (learners can re-read transcripts of previous sessions.

Let us look at asynchronous tools first. MOOmail works like an internal mailing system within the MOO. Messages are not sent to e-mail accounts but to character names. However, it is possible to forward MOOmail to e-mail accounts. Interfaces for this system used to be text-only, so all messages had to be compiled in a crude text editor (via <@mail>, <@send>, <@reply>, and similar commands). enCore, in version 2.0, added a form-based WWW interface that allows users to organise, send and receive their e-mails in a form-based interface without having to type in commands (Holmevik & Haynes, 2000:56-60). MOOs also have internal mailing lists at their disposal. Usually they range from administrative, building, or programming issues to general announcements, or the announcement of special events. New mailing lists can be created quite easily from generic objects, and access to them can be restricted to certain user groups if desired. Another asynchronous tool is the use of virtual notice boards. They could be installed in a classroom to give information to users who regularly inhabit this space. Again, access to these objects can be restricted. The <@gripe> command can be used to send complaints to the wizards, and various commands such as <@bug>, <@typo>, and <@suggest> can be used to send suggestions to the owners of rooms. Finally, there is the <news> feature which is usually controlled by the wizards or managers. On connection, users will be told if there are new news items available, and how to read them. Typical announcements in the <news> section are general events regarding all users of that MOO, for instance if the server has been upgraded, or has been disconnected, or the promotion of managers. There are also the <letter> and <note> objects available that can be written on and read by some and restricted to other players.

While this list of asynchronous tools is quite comprehensive, MOOs are really known for their synchronous communication tools. We can distinguish many-to-many, one-to-many and one-to-one conversations, restricted and open, verbal and "non-verbal" (of course, strictly speaking, all communication in the MOO is textual and thus verbal, but we are referring here to representations of non-verbal communication in the MOO). As many-to-many communication tools we would label commands that are potentially available and visible to all users, as one-to-many all commands that are only available and visible to one or a very select group of users and going out to many users, and as one-to-one we would label all commands that are restricted to two participants. We should again emphasise at this stage that MOO characters are located in various (textual) locations in the same MOO. Usually, in terms of communication these locations function like locations in real life, i.e. only conversations that take place in the same location will be "heard" (in MOO terms: seen as text output on the screen). Let us first look at the most common settings:

- many-to-many
  - (location-dependent, verbal): The <say> (shortcut: < " >) command will send a message to all players in the same location, but not to other locations.
  - (location-dependent, but directed): The <to> command will go out to all players in the same location, but everybody will see that it is directed towards a specific user. This is also referred to as "stage-talk" (Cherny, 1995:212): "Use of the directed speech option functions like naming an addressee to help to pin down the intended respondent in an adjacency pair...It also functions like eye contact" (ibid.:218)
  - (location-dependent, hyperpersonal): the <think> command will show a message in an ASCII speech bubble and is used for non-intrusive comments or questions (ibid.:154). There is no equivalent to this in real life, thus we can call this hyperpersonal, in Walther's terminology (Walther, 1996:5). An application of this command: during a lecture on a MOO, the speaker used some lesser known acronyms. A member of the audience used the think command, and everybody in the room saw it as: <Peter . o O

(NSF???)>. Three other users reacted and whispered the solution. The lecture was not interrupted.
  - (location-dependent, emphasis): the <bigsign> command will be shown to all users in the same location and comes with a large ASCII box drawn around the message. This is useful for adding emphasis to an important message, such as the impending shutdown of the MOO, and its real-life equivalent would probably be supported by non-verbal communication.
  - (location-dependent, "non-verbal"): the <emote> (shortcut: < : >) command is used to transmit actions, such as gestures or facial expressions of the sender, to all users in the same location. According to Cherny (1995:187) it is also "used to mix action or narrated material with material that would otherwise be 'said,' including intentional dysfluencies and addressee labels". enCore has additional verbs in the Social Verbs Feature. Verbs (some of which can be used with direct objects) can trigger whole pre-programmed sentences. These verbs, also know as atmospheric commands (Carlstrom, 1992), are sometimes useful for immediate feedback. Example: <vnod> used by <Peter> triggers <Peter nods vigorously.>
  - (location-independent, verbal): the <Channel Feature Object> allows users to communicate with each other in different locations. It has been compared to walkie-talkie channels.
  - (location-independent, inter-MOO): the <LinkNet> system allows users to set up channels across several MOOs.
- one-to-many
  - (location-independent, all users): The <@shout> command will send a message to all connected users in the MOO. As it is perceived as impolite, it is hardly ever used and only available to administrators.
  - (location-independent, group-specific): The <@gpage> command allows teachers to contact specific groups of users, wherever they are located.
- one-to-one
  - (location-dependent, verbal): The <whisper> or <murmur> command will send a message to the player mentioned in the command.
  - (location-independent, verbal): The <page> command (shortcut: < – >) goes to a specified user in another location. If used in the same location, it works in the same way as <whisper>.
  - (location-independent, "non-verbal"): The remote emote command < + > shows "non-verbal" actions to a recipient in another location. This also could be called hyperpersonal, as it has no equivalent in real life.

- (interrupting individual users): The <@gag> command screens out any output from individual players and can also be used for bots. Again, this is used carefully. The command falls into the hyperpersonal category.

It should be noted that certain MOOs offer special features to organise communication in large groups. Ken Schweller describes the <$classroom> tool, and there are lecture tools in most MOOs that allow for the moderation of formats such as panel discussions (see Schweller, 1998:94–95). There is also the <$intercom> tool in enCore that allows teachers "to monitor and record activity in up to five rooms connected by a central control room" (ibid.:94).

There has been some research on MOOs and interaction, some of which has focused on task-oriented scenarios examining computer-supported cooperative work (CSCW) and some of which has examined the development of interpersonal relationships. The fact that all communication can be recorded greatly supports collaborative work (see O'Day et al., 1998; Haynes, 1998; Evard, 1993). Bruckman (1997), in her thesis on MOOSE Crossing, a MOO for children, explored the interplay of collaboration and construction within a text-based VR. Based on theories of constructionism and peer collaboration (see section 1), her case studies demonstrate that

Table 2.1 Overview of basic synchronous MOO communication commands

m/m	*o/m*	*o/o*	*LD*	*LI*	*V*	*NV*	*EX*	*HP*	*Direct*	*I-MOO*	*Commands*
+			+		+						<say>
+			+		+				+		<to>
+			+		+			+			<think>+
+			+		+						<bigsign>
+			+			+					<emote>
+				+	+			+			<Ch. FO>
+				+	+			+		+	<LinkNet>
	+			+	+						<@shout>
	+			+	+				(+)		<@gpage>
		+	+		+				+		<whisper>
		+		+	+			+	+		<page>
		+		+		+		+	+		r. emote <+>
	+				(+)		+	+	+		<@gag>

Key: m/m = many-to-many; NV = non-verbal; o/m = one-to-many; EX = exclusion of users; o/o = one-to-one; HP = hyperpersonal; LD = location-dependent; Direct = directed chat; LI = location-independent; I-MOO = Inter-MOO; V = verbal; + = feature is present.

both creating new artefacts through MOO building and programming, and collaborating and communicating with peers becomes an inseparable context for learning: "community and construction activities are mutually reinforcing. Working within a community helps people to become better [...] learners" (ibid.:16). She also considers the value of help networks in collaborative networks: "Asking for help, receiving help, and giving help are all social acts which help to build networks of relationships. Help is not merely information" (Bruckman, 1997:128).

Parks and Roberts (1997; also see Parks & Floyd, 1996) compared interpersonal relationships on newsgroups and in the MOO. They found that the formation of relationships in MOOs is very common and usually transfers to other contexts. MOO relationships showed several similarities to face-to-face relationships (Parks & Roberts, 1997; also cf. Jacobson, 1996) and they conclude that "MOOs provide an inherently social and powerful context for the creation of personal relationships" (Parks & Roberts, 1997). Roberts et al. (1997) also reported that users felt less inhibited and less conservative in MOOs, and that some noted carry-over effects into their off-line lives, such as an increased confidence in their social interaction skills and their ability to relate to others.

Communication in MOOs goes far beyond simple chat facilities. It tries to replicate the multitude of communicative situations we encounter in real life and thus also the classroom, and adds to it several hyperpersonal tools that are unavailable to users in real life. When I discussed the variety of classroom communication scenarios and the concept of teacher autonomy in section 1, I emphasised that this variety also needs to be present in a CALL environment. The "availability of different modalities of communication in network communities adds richness and depth to online interactions" (Mynatt, O'Day, Adler, & Ito, 1998:138) and can therefore be considered a desirable element in any CALL environment. Although MOOs may not provide many social context cues, it has been reported that they enhance collaboration and can create social relations between users and the feeling of a shared culture and community not found in point-to-point conferencing.

2.2.3 Experimentation in the MOO

In this sub-section I will look at those features of the MOO that relate to experimentation and participation. I will begin by looking at the resources/tools; functionality; and access that the MOO offers. Then, I will look at the customisation of online characters, before I look at MOO building and programming to demonstrate the openness of the MOO. Following that, I will briefly look at the issue of interface metaphors and immersion versus detachment, and finally look at some research on MOOs that has focused on experimentation and participation.

As I mentioned in section 2.1.3, learners' experimentation with language and learning depends on the type and variety of resources available, their functionality, and access to them. As an Internet program, the MOO allows users to integrate their own resources and in principle, there is no limit to the amount or type of Internet source they want to integrate. The functionality is sheer limitless in its scope. Some learners may just want to integrate a web dictionary; others may want to program a new object with new functionality. I will return to the range of object creations in my next chapter. In terms of access, the MOO requires Internet access and, ideally, networked computer rooms. However, we have also experienced quite regularly that learners, while being out (of the physical classroom), logged on to the MOO during our class sessions, for example from their home computer. As the MOO interface is programmed in Java™, it shares the same interface across all computer platforms. Nevertheless, it seems that many learners prefer to modify their screen workspace to a certain extent. That includes customising the layout; their onscreen character; their onscreen learning environments. In the MOO, there are hardly any limits to customisation, and learners in our projects have always made use of customisation. One problem that the MOO has is in some ways unavoidable. Operating all this functionality, these resources and tools, in an environment that is mainly textual sometime impedes access to more complex functionality. This is where pedagogy needs to come in and help connect the learning opportunities with the learner's level of autonomy. The freedom and control of this experimentation and participation translates into one central goal of learner autonomy: the learner takes responsibility for and control of her learning. Without fundamental access to all levels of the learning environment, learners cannot develop a feeling of ownership of the learning process.

I will briefly give some examples for how learners navigate on the MOO, and how they manipulate and create objects. Two examples for navigation are the <@go> verb plus a location number, or the location's name. If learners want to join a particular other user, they use the <@join> verb. They can also use hyperlinks to click on the room name to be moved to that room.

When MOO users register, they receive a unique name, password, and object number. The user name and password can be changed at any time. They can set a description of themselves, give additional information about their research interests and activities, attach pictures to their name, etc. Each user can also set certain text messages that are triggered by commands or user movements and which are displayed to other users. Thus, when a user enters a room, the other users in that location will see a message in which the entry is described.

MOO users can participate in the extension of the virtual environment, provided they have moved up to the status of builder (usually after an introduction by the administrators of a MOO). Builders are allowed to either build a certain number of objects or occupy a certain part (in bytes) of the MOO database. When building, users select from a number of templates, or so-called generic objects with certain features/affordances. Generic objects function here as a scaffold, not as a restriction. Thus, a generic container object can be used to store other objects. Many simple building processes are now done through a menu-driven and form-based interface. All new objects can then be modified and their use can be restricted. One example is the <Generic Classroom> (<#99>) which allows owners to add furniture, including a blackboard. Virtual furniture is here used to regulate communication: users can stand up if they want to speak. All objects are located in relation to other objects. Nearly all rooms are connected to other rooms, so that after a while a network of locations emerges. One of the more interesting objects is the <Generic Bot> which can imitate real conversation partners and be programmed using pattern-matching and random responses and questions. For language learning purposes, bots could be useful as vocabulary trainers or grammar checkers, or simply as a tool to experiment with discourse patterns (I will look at one example in my next chapter).

In some situations, however, it may become desirable for a builder to add new features such as verbs and properties to an existing object. In order to do this they need to become MOO programmers and they need permission by administrators. I do not want to go into the details of programming, as MOO programming has been treated in detail elsewhere (Holmevik & Haynes, 2000:97-124; Busey, 1995; Curtis, 1997). Nevertheless, MOO programming is much more straightforward than many other forms of programming, due to several features:

- Generic objects can be used as templates, and with very little programming expertise, sections of code can be modified. As the MOO programming language can be considered a high-level programming language, it is easy to identify relevant sections of code and replace them.
- All code is visible to programmers. Even on other MOOs, administrators are very willing to share code and allow objects to be ported from MOO to MOO. We know from the rapid spread of html, Java™, and JavaScript, what effect freely available programming and scripting code has on the development of software.
- There is an active and very helpful community of MOO programmers/ administrators on the Internet, who has formed a useful network of support. Very often, MOO programmers might log on to your MOO "live" to look at code and make it work while I was able to "look over their shoulder". I have encountered dozens of in some cases anonymous programmers who have invested hours of their time to solve programming problems.

Recently the discussion around free or open-source software projects has become increasingly prominent in the discussion of software development. Major advantages of this form of software development are: a much wider base of developers, much more reliable applications, much more software components, and easier access to software development in general for newcomers. Given the proper pedagogical framework, experimentation and participation can definitely be better realised in open, collaborative programming environments.

In section 2.1.3, I also discussed three interface metapors. The MOO combines elements of all three. The enCore MOO system allows input via hyperlinks and command-lines; however, it has also direct manipulation elements as the learning environment operates along a spatial metaphor. As I mentioned, this is not without problems. A large variety of functions and resources is difficult to access via text. The implementation of bots allows for easy and highly beneficial experimentation with artificial intelligence in conversation, an area we have only started to explore. When objects have real-life counterparts (i.e. "blackboard"), learners will bring certain expectations to the object in terms of resource/tool and functionality, and then find out how to access it. We have also noticed that more and more hyperlinks have greatly simplified much of the functionality.

What the MOO manages is to create a learning environment where every learner (and teacher) can bring in her own personality. Each can experiment and participate in its creation, up to the highest level. Learners can become absorbed in this environment, but we do not know whether they become completely immersed as someone operating, for example, in an "Immersive Rooms" environment (Fakespace Systems Inc., 2005), where you are transported to a 3D world with gloves to input information. We do not even know yet whether, for language learning, it is desirable to aim for full immersion, where the learner does not perceive a notable difference between her physical identity and the representational character, or some form of detachment, which as I noticed previously, may be more likely to support processes of awareness. Maybe for our purposes it is better to emphasise the gap between the experimentational representation and the physical self.

I would like to conclude this section with a glance at research conducted in the field of MOOs and experimentation. How do users of MOOs perceive the virtual environment? Does something like immersion or presence occur at all in a text-based virtual environment? Very little research is available that provides empirical evidence of social presence in text-based VR. Towell and Towell (1997) surveyed 207 users of text-based virtual environments. They found that 69% of them experienced presence in this communication medium. While they were unable to determine whether social presence referred to being with others or being within an environment, they confirmed some findings of previous CMC research: "Some subjects indicated that the sense of presence was dependent on whom they were with in the virtual environment and, for the scientists [taking part in the study], their interests and involvement in the topic of the discussion" (ibid.). In their research on MOOs as virtual communities, Roberts et al. (1996b) found that most MOO users see MOOs as real communities, but that the extent of this sense of community may vary within and across MOOs: "Smaller MOOs were generally seen as friendlier, with a closer sense of community than larger MOOs".

Research by Roberts et al. (1996a) and Ryan (1995) has shown that MOO characters develop towards real-life descriptions and real-life behaviour (also see Turkle, 1995:205 and 312). In their study, Schiano and White (1998) found that less than 25% of users ever changed their MOO character. The development of telepresence may be more difficult in IRC: "For some IRCers, achieving telepresence is hard work and may not be considered worth the effort involved. The degree of telepresence experienced on IRC may fluctuate for each individual" (Roberts, Smith, & Pollock, 1996a).

A study by Tromp and Dieberger (1995) found that "users can make cognitive maps of the spaces they travel through as long as the different rooms have local Euclidean relationships, and the rooms contain obvious and distinctive landmarks" and that communication between participants is an essential element for navigation (also see Dieberger & Tromp, 1995; Tennison & Shadbolt, 1998). Bruckman and Resnick have also examined social relations and the creation of a "third place" through communication in text-based MOOs (Bruckman & Resnick, 1995; Bruckman, 1992). This idea brings us back to the social aspect of virtual environments: online communication, maybe more than photo-realistic representations of space, can create a shared virtual environment.

In this sub-section I have looked at features in the MOO that support experimentation and participation. I made the point that the MOO allows, in principle, unlimited access to every part of its programming. It also provides various forms of scaffolding for learners to take on more and more control over their experimentation. It is as yet unclear what the issues regarding online representation and learner identity are, but it is important to recognise this area. Deservedly, recent years have seen an intensive debate on learner identity in language learning and learner autonomy (see Palfreyman & Smith, 2003; also cf. Debski, 2003; Kramsch, 1998).

2.2.4 Teaching in and researching MOOs

For the teacher and researcher working with MOOs, I consider the following aspects to be important, relating to section 2.1.4. First, I will look at how the roles of the teacher as facilitator, counsellor, and resource can be facilitated or supported in the MOO. Second, I will consider the MOO as a research tool. Third, I will consider the MOO as a program for teacher education and collaboration.

In all the MOO projects I have conducted over the years, one prominent factor has always been how much the role of the teacher changed, in terms of workload, as a figure of authority in class, as a helper on the side. As a facilitator, the teacher in Germany and I simply organised a pedagogical framework and modified the technology beforehand. During the project itself, the teacher almost becomes invisible. Even more so, it has been our experience that it is almost impossible to modify the environment or pedagogical framework substantially while a project is running, as learners take control of their learning partnership.

The function of counsellor has rarely surfaced in our MOO projects, probably due to the reciprocal nature of tandem exchanges and the dual role of native speaker expert and non-native learner. However, future plans include the inclusion of an electronic version of the European Language Portfolio which could easily form the basis for teacher-learner counselling. It would be easy to use the online learner diaries for counselling sessions, although due to lack of time this was not part of our tandem projects.

Possibly the biggest change in the teacher's role in MOO projects involves the teacher as a resource. This function was now adopted by the tandem partners and peers in the offline classroom, who would ask each other for missing words, or point out words and phrases on their screens. In that respect, the MOO environment together with the pedagogical framework based on learner autonomy makes this function superfluous. This behaviour, of course, attests to the fact that learners were simply taking charge of their learning.

A second area deals with the teacher as researcher. One great strength of the MOO is its ability to be used for data collection. I have personally used the MOO to collect data of the following form:

- MOO transcripts: They can be sent to the learner, and the administrator (automatically). They give an almost complete account of all communication channels and all interaction with virtual objects, with the sole exception (currently) that transcripts are not time-stamped (except for beginning and end of a session). Automatic collection of transcripts has greatly simplified the work by MOO researchers (see, for example, Schwienhorst, 2000b; O'Rourke, 2002; Kötter, 2002), who were then able to tag the data and analyse it with the help of concordancers and other tools.
- Learner diaries: These can be collected and viewed at any stage, and provide valuable qualitative data on language, linguistic, and metacognitive awareness and mechanisms of planning, monitoring, and evaluation.
- Learner interviews: My colleague O'Rourke and I have used the MOO to conduct interviews with learners, initially because interviewees were at the opposite side of the campus and because they provided us with finished transcripts of data rather than tapes that

> had to be transcribed. We quickly realised that conducting interviews had a number of other advantages, such as that learners were communicating in and reflecting on the very medium that we interviewed them about, which aided their memory and made it easier for them to visualise different scenarios. In this way, when asked retrospectively about the MOO project sessions, learners were able to comment on the medium while communicating within the medium at the time of the interview (almost introspectively). A second advantage was that learners seemed to be less inhibited in their answers: they were physically removed from the interviewer and in a comfortable environment (mostly among peers in the computer labs or at home).

Researchers can also at any point look at how users have customised their online character and what objects they have experimented with. Additional tools that we devised for the MOO already have built-in mechanisms for data collection, e.g. the Bilingual Tandem Analyser (see next section). As MOO software is open-source software, more research mechanisms can easily be built in, whereas commercial software developers are often simply disinterested, unwilling, too slow, or even hostile. The MOO fulfils several of Chapelle's criteria of functionality in CALL software (Chapelle, 2001:170–175) as cited in sub-section 2.1.4: It lets teachers, researchers, and learners analyse linguistic output; organise and create learning objects; analyse process-oriented data for the analysis of learner processes; author learning conditions; and delivers everything via a familiar interface. More research tools are currently being evaluated and planned, especially in the area of learner models; feedback; and the assessment of task difficulty.

A third important area is teacher education. I personally have very little experience in using the MOO for this purpose, except for occasional sessions with Higher Diploma students here at Trinity College. However, there are two Norwegian projects that are of particular interest in this context[1]. PROFFT (Program for fransk og tysk i skolen, Program for French and German in schools, *http://profft.no/*) is an Internet- and MOO-based study program for German and French language teachers who want to improve either their grammatical or communicative competence. PROFFT is a common program of all four Norwegian universities and several "høyskoler" (university colleges) and is co-ordinated from Oslo. The technical support function and language teaching components are provided by the University of Bergen. There are tendencies in Norway, as in many other countries today, to use standardised e-learning platforms across universities. It is encouraging to see that the MOO platform was chosen as a major mode of delivery, in spite of its age and some weaknesses in administrative tools. However, positive pedagogical experiences with the enCore database were apparently more important.

1 I am grateful to Carsten Jopp for providing me with information on these projects.

In Norway, there is a two-semester add-on which provides a formal qualification as a teacher. In French and German teacher education, MOOs were extensively used within the INVITIS project (Innovasjon med IKT i språklærerutdanningen, Innovation with ICT in language teacher education, http://www.uib.no/invitis/). Not surprisingly, the project was organised by Turid Trebbi, who has been promoting the concept of learner autonomy for many years. In this project, MOOs were used, for example, to simulate real classroom situations, prepared and acted out by students. Afterwards, transcripts were analysed and discussed, for instance as regards conflict situations or alternative actions (see Trebbi, Jopp, & Coco, 2003). This implementation of technology is exemplary, as it fulfils the demands I emphasised earlier about teacher autonomy. We can only expect teachers to encourage learner autonomy and have an open attitude towards the use of technology if they have experienced both first hand.

In this sub-section, I looked at the features of the MOO that concern the role of the teacher/researcher. I made the point that the roles of facilitator, counsellor, and resource are well supported, but that in practice the teacher becomes more often a connecting element between the technology/pedagogy combination and the level of autonomy that the learner has already achieved. In this process, the MOO is particularly effective. In terms of research, the MOO already fulfils many demands of modern CALL software, not least because of its structure as open-source software. Finally, the MOO has also been shown to be a very useful and central tool in teacher education, as demonstrated by the variety of projects currently underway in Norway.

2.3 THE MOO AND SECOND LANGUAGE ACQUISITION

My discussion of learner autonomy in section 1, and previous research on MOOs indicate that language learners can very well benefit from text-based CALL environments, for task-based collaboration as well as the development of interpersonal relationships, and for the development of a learning culture that unites the demands of learner autonomy. But what research is already available on linguistic features, and in particular language learning in MOOs, and how can we put this research into context?

I have previously made the point that I would like to avoid making rash and generalised judgements about CMC. We should thus be careful whether it is useful and justified to transfer conclusions, for example, from an open chat channel on a music network site with a carefully monitored, dedicated, language learning environment. If these two settings "produce" different kinds of language, then this is hardly because of "the nature of CMC", but maybe because of specific features such as: lack of thematic focus; anonymity; lack of ownership; or lack of access restrictions; to name a few. I have emphasised that every chat technology has particular features that set it apart from others, and we also have different pedagogical frameworks that have been employed. I will therefore try to focus on MOOs and on tandem learning, as the technology and the pedagogical frameworks used in my research.

The definition of MOO language has been as difficult as defining other types of CMC discourse. Cherny (1995; later published as Cherny, 1999) probably provides the most comprehensive overview of linguistic MUD/MOO discourse features to date. She suggests the Rational Actor Hypothesis to account for MOO communication, and sees the language found on MOOs as a new emerging register. Her Rational Actor Hypothesis suggests that "[u]sers operate within the system constraints and affordances as rational actors modifying their behavior to achieve maximal communicative benefit" (Cherny, 1995:19). Her view confirms previous communication research models (Hiltz & Turoff, 1981; Walther, 1992).

The issue of turn taking is important in MOO discourse. As all messages only become visible after they are completed and sent off via the enter button, the potential for multi-threaded topics is high and can thus seriously impede task-oriented exchange. Cherny reports that MOO users adapt by sending smaller grained messages (i.e. a smaller length of single messages, and/or utterances that conclude in dots to indicate ongoing messages, see Roberts, Smith, & Pollock, 1996b) and frequent back channels (Cherny, 1995:207). In the MOO, rather than establishing turns as intentional units, it becomes more relevant to establish who holds the floor (ibid.:209, Edelsky, 1993; Shultz, Florio, & Erickson, 1982; Hayashi, 1991). Where conversations become disorderly, "repair mechanisms come into play, which are specific to the medium, like signals of premature preemption, explicit explanations of disorderly lines, or pasting into focus in the conversation at a later point" (Cherny, 1995:222). Back channels are of vital importance in a CMC medium. These may include non-verbal cues such as nods or body movements or verbal interjections like "oh", "aha", "right" (for back channels as confirmation feedback, see Oviatt & Cohen, 1988) and are seen as "one common way in which conversational cooperation is communicated and monitored" (Gumperz, 1982). The existence and variety of back channel emotes in MOO discourse is a strong argument against reduced cue perspectives or theories suggesting a lack of feedback in CMC (Daft & Lengel, 1984).

Cherny shows how a speech community has developed its own "routines, conventional vocabulary and abbreviations, syntactic and semantic phenomena, and turn-taking and repair strategies in the register" (Cherny, 1995:ii). Her analysis of back channels and other emoted utterances illustrates how attention and understanding can be signalled to the conversation partner in a cue-restricted medium, and her thesis thus provides vital insights into linguistic phenomena on the MOO.

Warschauer (1995) was probably the first to collect a number of papers on language learning and multi-user VR, particularly MOOs. Again, most of these are experience reports and suggestions for teachers who want to use this technology, rather than empirical research. Sanchez (1995) mentions the possibility of logging conversations and then using them for out-of-class work. Falsetti and Schweitzer (1995:231–232) and Turbee (1995) note that students find MOO exchanges motivating. Turner (1995) points out the importance of the three-dimensional aspect of MOOs which raises learners' awareness of the facilities around them.

A year later, Warschauer (1996d) published a further collection of papers that included some on MOOs. Sanchez (1996) emphasises that students have more time and meaningful opportunities to engage in TL communication and that the new identity as a telepresence lowers the affective filter and enhances role-playing. David Pinto's study of MOO discourse (1996) can be considered to be one of the first empirical studies on MOOs. Pinto points to some serious conversation management problems, but the study suffers from flaws in the categorisation of conversational moves and overly simplistic conclusions. He maintains that the technical demands and multi-threaded topics can impede interaction, but still considers MOOs to be useful for developing conversation management skills.

The CALLMOO project (Aarseth & Jopp, 1998) has largely been behind the development of the enCore database, the creation of several multilingual MOOs, and extensive applications of the MOO for language learning within a tandem learning context. Aarseth and Jopp's evaluation of the first project phase contains some valuable empirical data. Within their research, they evaluated data from a Norwegian-German tandem project between Bergen Norway, and Kiel, Germany, and a distance education course in German. They report the beginnings of a self-motivated and self-directed approach towards language and intercultural learning. Many students perceived the communication situations as authentic and realistic. The threshold at which students overcome inhibitions was clearly lower in the MOO than in otherwise similar face-to-face settings. Students reported having been transported to a "third place" (see Bruckman & Resnick, 1995; Schwienhorst, 1998), of being absorbed in the environment. Students demonstrated in their use of emotes that they became not only more comfortable with the command functions over time, but were also able to provide more appropriate back channels. The interplay of pressure/challenge and freedom/control of involvement was perceived as positive and stimulating in terms of language production. The traditional roles of the teachers also began to change from central instructor to almost intruder in a communication (similar to Donaldson & Kötter, 1999).

Shield & Weininger (1999; also see Shield, Davies, & Weininger, 2000:47), in their discussion of a monolingual MOO project, look at group work within the MOO. In the learners' work with shared applications and the extension of the synchronous MOO communication to incorporate other tools such as dictionaries, external web links, and asynchronous communication tools, students were reported to become more effective in task-oriented work. However, they also reported organisational and technical problems, as well as difficulties in collaborating within diverging pedagogical frameworks.

Donaldson and Kötter (1999) provide an empirical account of a successful bilateral project that used the MOO between adult evening class participants and American college students within a framework of tandem learning. In many ways, they confirm previously mentioned research, such as that on repair strategies (Cherny, 1995). One of their most surprising findings was the degree to which teacher intervention was suddenly seen as teacher intrusion as students took responsibility for the agenda of their MOO meetings. Most of the tandem pairs had made use of the ability to paraphrase, repeat, or translate difficult phrases in conversation. Students spent a large part of their communication engaged in negotiation of meaning (also see Pellettieri, 2000; Toyoda & Harrison, 2002; Tudini, 2003) which forces them into cycles of interaction and reflection. They reported a marked increase in interest in the TL culture and hence more motivation.

Kötter's (2002) PhD thesis was probably the first published monograph that dealt in detail with MOOs in language learning, more specifically in the tandem learning context. I will only summarise some of the more important results from his very detailed study here. In terms of attitude, he reports that learners needed time to adapt to the new language environment, and to establish a working partnership with their tandem partners. Several learners contributed to the learning environment by creating their own spaces, modifying their online character, or experimenting with online objects. Repair work and aspects of online interactions increased learners' metalinguistic awareness, and they became more and more aware of the importance of nonverbal communication, different forms of writing, and the simple fact that all information they wanted to convey had to be put into words. In this context, emotes played an important role and were used extensively, as were non-standard punctuation, spelling and icons. Kötter also notes the changed role of the teacher, as learners assume more responsibility for their exchanges (also see Darhower, 2002). Because learners' output was quite high during the exchanges, it forced them to improve their reading skills dramatically to keep up with the conversation. Although learners' proficiency was not measured at the beginning and end of the project, Kötter claims that they not only improved their language proficiency, but also their linguistic and metalinguistic awareness during the project. In this context, corrective feedback became less important, as it was felt to restrict the flow of communication. Errors, however, can be a useful source of exercises offline (also see Yuan, 2003). The study also points out the importance of a strong pedagogical and organisational framework (also see Lee, 2004).

In a tandem exchange between American and German students, Kötter (2003) reports in MOO exchanges a much higher proportion of clarification requests and less indirect repair strategies such as confirmation checks, repetitions, and recasts. He concludes that in tandem exchanges even learners with different L2 proficiencies can benefit from their encounters, and that the study confirms "the importance of the provision of explicit 'positive feedback' in written real-time CMC" (Kötter, 2003:163) as reported by Pellettieri (2000).

In the last few years, MOOs have moved more and more into the foreground of CMC discussions, and fortunately we can see more and more hard evidence supporting claims that were made on the basis of mostly anecdotal reports in the mid- to late 90s. Kötter's (2002) study was probably the first published full-scale analysis of MOO discourse within the pedagogical framework of tandem learning, preceded by my own doctoral thesis (Schwienhorst, 2000b) and followed by my colleague's (O'Rourke, 2002). More research needs to follow, and these studies provide promising starting points.

In this chapter, I have begun by looking at the features of CALL environments that are theorised to be particularly beneficial for supporting reflection, interaction, and experimentation/ participation. Repeatedly, I emphasised that CALL technology needs to go hand in hand with a sound pedagogical framework. In the second part of the chapter, I looked in detail at how these theoretical features are realised in the MOO environment, and how the MOO supports teacher autonomy. I concluded this sub-section with a selective but hopefully representative overview of published research in MOOs and language learning. I now turn my attention towards the bilateral projects carried out between ICT students from the Fachhochschule Bonn-Rhein-Sieg in St. Augustin, Germany, and ICT students at Trinity College Dublin, Ireland.

3 The Dublin/ Bonn-Rhein-Sieg MOO Project

In Chapter 1, I set out a definition of learner autonomy that was built around the three cornerstones of reflection, interaction, and experimentation, on the basis of what we know about language learning and learning processes in general. I also introduced a pedagogical implementation of these principles, tandem learning. I followed this in Chapter 2 with a look at CALL environments and the MOO in particular, focusing on those features that are most likely to support the three areas of learner autonomy. In this chapter, I will provide empirical data to show whether CALL environments, in practice, actually support the development of learner autonomy in the three areas of reflection, interaction, and experimentation. My research neither seeks to prove the effectiveness of CALL versus traditional classroom instruction, nor attempts to address all the issues that are involved with my definition of learner autonomy in Chapter 1. In the analysis of my data, I will provide examples for reflection, interaction, and experimentation in learners. In each of these three areas I will describe and analyse various forms of data, and provide a number of starting points for further research. My research topics within these sections are not randomly chosen; they are merely some of the more prominent ones that lend themselves particularly well to analysis in this context. I will conclude each sub-section with a short analysis of my findings.

3.1 THE MOO-PROJECT– RESEARCH METHODOLOGY

I argued in Chapter 2 that CALL environments in general and MOO technology in particular, can support learner autonomy in several ways. First, learners are supported in becoming more reflective learners. The written medium supports language and linguistic awareness; the virtual representation can encourage processes of detachment that I consider a vital step towards awareness; and the interactivity between the virtual representation, the learner, and the virtual environment can lead to greater awareness of cognitive tools. Second, the MOO allows learners to interact with peers and native speakers in a stress-reduced environment. The written medium gives them more time for processing; they have a variety of interaction modes at their disposal; and learners are more likely to give appropriate feedback in a situation where they fluctuate between learner and expert; while discourse may be challenging, it rarely goes beyond the ZPD, as both learners try to maintain a situation of optimal flow. Third, the MOO environment is a medium that learners can really participate in and make their own; learners can use virtual objects as cognitive tools to experiment with and monitor language output, while at the same time they are able to edit and modify their own input.

In the following sub-sections, I will first look at the organisational context of the project; second, I will look at the participants; and third, the data collection method. When referring to my own research, I will use the first person, but will use "we" when referring to issues that were organised in cooperation with other teachers or researchers, which will be clarified by the respective contexts.

3.1.1 Context

The undergraduate degree in Information and Communications Technology (ICT) at Trinity College contains a language course as a required component, which means that courses have a very low attrition rate. Students have a two hour classroom session plus a one hour individual tutorial per week. Native speaker assistants (mostly Socrates exchange students) assist the teachers during the second half of the classroom session by moderating group work and providing TL input for learners' project work.

Each class has to complete four group projects during the course of the year. For first year students, these include a web site creation, a debate, a focus-on-language project (the creation of exercises in the TL), and a newsletter presentation. For second year students, the projects are focus on language (as in first year), a software review, a web site review, and a more general debate around a topic that deals with computers and society. During the two-hour class sessions, learners begin by working in groups on authentic texts relevant to their project, while in the second half each project group is supported by a native speaker, mainly to improve pronunciation by encouraging learners to communicate more in the TL. The weekly one-hour tutorials normally focus on the students' individual progress in class. Most of the data in this section is drawn from a project in 1999-2000, for two main reasons: first, I would like to present some of the early mistakes we made, to show that even minor changes to the technological or pedagogical set-up can solve seemingly major problems; second, the data collected during that academic year forms the most extensive data collection I have conducted of any MOO project. The project was prepared well in advance, and we as teachers agreed on 10 weeks between October and December 1999, which was within the term structure of both institutions. Curricular and institutional obstacles need to be resolved, such as the booking of labs and technical support. We produced booklets and leaflets containing tandem principles and technical information (in addition to online resources), and planned induction workshops at which these would be introduced and discussed (also see Schwienhorst, 2000a).

For the project, we used the enCore database with its web-based interface. We set up our own private MOO for the project, with 22 virtual rooms or study areas to channel communication. In each room, learners found hyperlinks to four different ICT topics (see Appendix B), each with bilingual support in English and German. These were related to topics that were treated in some form in class. However, we also made it clear from the beginning that the topics were only an incentive; students were free to discuss other topics if they considered them to be more relevant. We also included a link to a picture gallery with photos of all students, though anonymous as to make them a topic for conversation. Successful follow-up tasks in an asynchronous mode were included in the following years, such as reformulation tasks and the collaborative writing of stories and fairy tales (see O'Rourke, 2002). Teacher intervention and pressure to provide results was thus very limited. Instances of adolescent behaviour such as obscene language were extremely rare, and were met with strong opposition from classroom peers.

The administrative side of the set-up was facilitated by the intuitive interface in enCore. Setting up our students with MOO characters was a matter of minutes, and building the virtual locations was equally simple. The only change we made (with the help of Jan Rune Holmevik and Sindre Sorensen, the programmers behind enCore) was an automatic means of collecting all learner logs or transcripts. This meant that after each MOO session, I would automatically receive individual learner logs by e-mail. The complete transcripts contain all communication, all emote commands, and all programming commands in the text interface, from the view of each learner, which means that the complete corpus contains at least two similar (though not identical) records of each tandem pair. Altogether the 1999–2000 transcripts form a corpus of 745,605 words.

Students also received a transcript of their own session after each session, which they were able to access through their MOOmail program (for two complete sample transcripts, see Appendix A). In addition, we used the notebook-function of the MOO, a crude word-processor, as a learner diary. Similar to Dam's classroom (Dam, 1995: 40–41), we asked students to write down what they worked on, what went well, where they experienced problems, and how they intended to proceed in the following session. Throughout the project, the MOO proved very stable. There were few technical problems with the MOO itself, except for some time-out settings. Unfortunately, these initial problems severely reduced the number of diary entries, as learners were not all able to open the online diary at the same time.

3.1.2 Participants

As the regular German teacher, Jackie McPartland, had to go on maternity leave, another teacher, Peter Kapec, took over her classes. During the summer of 1999, the three of us regularly met online in the MOO and discussed MOO technology, pedagogy (learner autonomy and tandem learning), and practical considerations (topics, tasks, scheduling, etc.). We also agreed on similar booklets (see Appendix B), containing a detailed technical and pedagogical introduction, and printed versions of the MOO topics we prepared. These booklets were discussed during initial introductory workshops in class. By using the MOO as a location for teacher collaboration, we became much more aware of the advantages and disadvantages of the system.

Both our courses consisted of two weekly class hours plus one hour in the computer lab. In this single hour, our plan was to use half of it to talk German and half to talk English. We both managed to organise sufficient lab space, but noticed that several students on both sides connected from their private machines at home or other computer labs on campus (there is evidence from diaries and transcripts that some students even connected when they were out sick).

We chose to involve the second (which is also the final) year ICT students from Ireland (with L1 English), and first year German ICT students (with L1 German), although the German students represented the higher proficiency group in their year (probably around B2 level according to the *Common European Framework of Reference for Languages*). This compares to a rather low language proficiency in the Irish ICT students (around A2/B1). On the German side, we had 22 students, on the Irish side 29 students. As in our e-mail project, we decided to double-date remaining students, i.e. creating 2+1 groups. This was also our strategy in case students did not turn up for class and needed a temporary new partner. During the course of the project, some students also occasionally decided to form bigger groups, such as 2+2 or 2+3.

Students, to the extent that, of course, all students needed to be involved, were able to select their partners (this process had been suggested by the students themselves) from e-mails the other class sent to me. Students repeatedly mentioned during the project that the actual shared interests are less important than the fact that they are given control and responsibility for their partner. We assigned tandem pairs to virtual MOO rooms, so that the initial process of finding the partner would take less time. All students were asked to agree to the data collection, and with two exceptions, all students signed this agreement; this concluded the institutional preparations for the project. All learners were given builder status by default, as we wanted them to be able to participate in the environment.

Once a MOO project starts, there is a noticeable change of role for us teachers, compared to the classroom. While students are working in the

MOO or even on e-mails, the teacher's role as a dispenser of knowledge disappears almost completely. Students are so involved with their partner that they may not even request offline assistance from their peers. Our work is and was basically limited to the following activities:

- Starting the session, making sure that every student was connected; helping with password problems.
- Monitoring that all students are active. The Who-list in the MOO not only gives information about who is connected, but also about how long students have been inactive (idle). Inactivity was due either to the fact that students had technical problems or that they were multi-tasking, i.e. accessing other programs, for example, because their partner had not turned up. In that case, we would suggest to students that they should join other groups.
- Announcing the switch to the other language. In sub-section 1.4, I emphasise the bilingual format of tandem learning. This was also a major principle of our exchange, so after about half an hour I made a system-wide announcement to switch languages. Since 2002-03, this became unnecessary, due to the Bilingual Tandem Analyser tool.
- Announcing the end of the session and suggesting a learner diary entry. In some cases, students continued their exchange in the MOO long after the teachers had left the class.
- Near the end of the project, we distributed a questionnaire to our students (see Appendix C), and some time after the project, in early 2000, I conducted online semi-structured interviews (see Appendix D) in the MOO with nine Irish and one German student. Throughout the project and the data collection afterwards, students showed strong support and encouragement for the project.

3.1.3 Data collection

I decided on a mixed-mode approach to data collection, combining and, where possible, triangulating data from various sources: learner transcripts, learner diaries, questionnaires, semi-structured interviews, and learners' object creations, their own participation in the learning environment. The evaluation of projects in electronic media has obvious advantages. An e-mail environment such as that developed by Appel and Mullen (2000) or the enCore MOO database, modified by the automatic logging of transcripts, will automatically collect all linguistic data, and even format it. This facilitates the easy quantitative and qualitative analysis of data.

Learner diaries, questionnaires and semi-structured interviews can help us understand affective factors in language learning. Not only can we see what motivational aspects are important for students, but we can explore the attitudes and beliefs that may not necessarily surface in the actual linguistic data. Part of this evaluation process can and should take place on an ongoing basis in class. A crucial principle of learner autonomy is that students need to be confronted with their own learning in such a way that they reflect on it, become aware of the underlying processes of planning and monitoring, and define new goals for themselves. We encouraged learners to use the diary throughout the project, at the end of each MOO session. The questionnaire was handed out in week five of our project. It was in some respects based on the questionnaire we had used in our e-mail tandem project (Little et al., 1999: 16). As there was no time to deal with it at length in class (as in our e-mail project, where it was used as an awareness-raising instrument), some students did not return the questionnaire until the end of the project. All German students (22) and all but three Irish students (26) returned the questionnaire. The interviews were conducted online in the MOO early in 2000, as students had problems fitting it into their class schedule. I was therefore only able to conduct nine interviews with Irish students and one with a German student.

An additional tool of data collection was the students' contribution to the learning environment, i.e. what changes, if any, they made to their virtual character, and what objects, if any, they created in the course of the project. While we encouraged students to create objects, we largely left it to them whether they wanted to create or experiment with any objects themselves; we never formally introduced them to object creation.

Altogether, the project provided me therefore with a wide range of data, only some of which I can analyse here. In order to protect the anonymity of our students, I have replaced their names with GER+ a number (for German students) and IRL+ a number (for Irish students). All the learner data has remained unchanged; any misspellings are their own. My analyses will, where possible, triangulate quantitative and qualitative data to assess how learners express their autonomy and how we can further support learners to become more autonomous language learners and users; in other words, how they can become more reflective, communicative, and experimental learners. The following sub-sections will present relevant data for each of the three approaches to learner autonomy, followed by a summary analysis.

3.2 MULTIPLE SOURCES OF EVIDENCE FOR REFLECTION

In this section, there are two important aspects to reflection that I would like to focus on. First, there is the question of whether learners view MOO language more like spoken or written communication, which indicates their ability to use the interaction for reflective purposes. Second, there are indications of reflection in the transcripts themselves: self-correction and re-use of vocabulary are two examples.

The following structure of sub-sections is in my opinion a useful progression. I will first look at learners' perceptions of MOO discourse as spoken or written discourse, before exploring in more detail how learners perceived their ability to monitor and evaluate MOO discourse. Two important indications of monitoring and evaluating, self-correction and re-use of new vocabulary, are then explored in the third and fourth sub-section, respectively. I then examine the specific use of online diaries for the development of metalinguistic awareness. I will conclude section 3.2 with a summary analysis of my findings.

3.2.1 MOO discourse as spoken or written communication

Let us first look at learners' perceptions of MOO discourse as spoken or written language, and how this perception affects learners' views of MOO communication for language learning (for a more detailed account of this section, see Schwienhorst, 2004a). In the relevant interview question, I asked: "Would you describe MOO language more like writing or speaking, or both? Why?" Learners' responses are in Transcript 3.1 (all utterances preceded by "You" are by the interviewer).

Transcript 3.1 Learners' perceptions of MOO discourse as spoken or written language (interview data)

IRL1 says, "Definately both, you have to spell out all the words but I guess it's really like a slowed down conversation"

IRL5 says, "More speaking I suppose,as it is a conversation"

IRL9 says, "Well you basically write what u would say if you was speaking to the person face to face"

IRL11 says, "well, a mixture. It's just a different type of communication. It comes in the form of writng, mainly but has many of the advantages of speaking."
You say, "like?"
IRL11 says, "but, obviously not all of them"
IRL11 says, "well, as I say, facial expressions and gestures. (virtaul) In the real world these make communicating more efficent and faster."

IRL12 says, " more like writing i suppose but it was a little different when you can see a picture of the person you are talking to"
You say, "how?"
You say, "how is it different then?"
IRL12 says, " it feels different when you are writing to a person that you don't know and you don't know what they look like but it's different when you can get a physical appearance in your mind of who you are writing to like we could see the German people we were talking to"
You say, "ok"
You say, "did it become more like speaking then?"
IRL12 says, " yes a little bit"

IRL15 says, "i suppose a bit of both"
You say, "how so?"
IRL15 says, "cos you have to write in what your saying (obviously) but the replys are just like that person is speaking to you - more informal than normal texts"
IRL15 says, "its more relaxed"

IRL16 says, "I think it is both."
You say, "in what way?"
IRL16 says, "If you are trying to talk about something you say anything(type anything related to the topic"
You nod.
IRL16 says, "But then you look at the screen to see if you have made any error"
You say, "ok"
IRL16 says, "Well I did anyway"
IRL16 says, "That's why I thought it hewpled, because it is writing and speaking!"

IRL23 says, "I would say both. Because, it is like a conversation but a written one and you have to think as you write while at the same time keeping an eye on grammar. "

IRL26 says, "well, i'd say it differs from person to person. for myself, moo language is more like speaking"
You say, "How?"
IRL26 says, "i think of it like i'm speaking to the other person..."
You nod.
IRL26 says, "its the way i envision it in my head"
IRL26 says, "and to me, grammar matters less"
IRL26 says, "(as in speaking)"

GER1 says, "ah, back to your question, of course it's a mixture."
GER1 says, "[...] just because it IS written, you spend a little more time thinking before typing."

Most students perceived it as a mixture (IRL1, IRL11, IRL15, IRL16, IRL23, GER1), some see it as speaking (IRL5, IRL9, IRL26), and one student as writing (IRL12). For IRL12, it depends whether a picture of the partner is available. Reasons why it is more like speaking are: conversational style, inclusion of virtual gestures or mimics (see sub-section 2.2.2 and the emote command), and the focus on informal language, whereas an element of writing is a focus on spelling. IRL16 and IRL23's comments are interesting, as they indicate the psychological processes that are behind learners' perceptions. The example of error correction shown in Transcript 3.2, illustrates the point.

Transcript 3.2 Example of error correction

GER18 says, "But she's studying farer away"
IRL26 says, ""further away""
GER18 says, "Yes... when I pressed return I noticed the mistake"

For these learners, MOO discourse is spoken language in the process of formulating and sending off an utterance, at which point it is transformed into writing, a resource or record for evaluation. As such, composition appears to be quite a different process in the MOO than in the medium of e-mail, where revisions are usually made before the message is communicated to the partner.

In my next interview question, I asked how this relates to language learning: "What are the weaknesses/strengths of communicating like that for language learning?" The responses are collected in Transcript 3.3.

Transcript 3.3 What are the strengths and weaknesses of communicating in the MOO for language learning? (interview data)

IRL1 says, "an advantage of this type of communication is that when you don't know or understand something in German it can be explained to you on the spot and you see how words are spelled. You can see german in a more natural enviornment"

IRL5 says, "Strengths were that it was learning with fun,learning not just German but also about German culture and how things work over in Germany,and a motivation for learning German..." [...]
IRL5 says, "Weaknesses,I couldn` t say much only perhaps you wouldn`t really be gathering more information more so using information you have." [...]
IRL5 says, "Well what I mean is,that you don` learn many new things ,its more about practising things you already know"

IRL9 says, "it can be hard to explain certain phrases"
You say, "why is that?"
IRL9 says, "well if it is a irish phrase the german students might not have a german equivalnet i.e. slang"
You nod.
You say, "is it just difficult because of the typing?"
IRL9 says, "no probably just the language barrier"

IRL11 says, "well i found it a strength that i wasn't under too much pressure to answer straight away in a different language. I had time to think and compile my scentence."
You nod.
IRL11 says, "if I had been face to face with him i couldn't have just stood there not saying anything"
IRL11 says, "so I would have made lots of mistakes in my haste"

You say, "I see"
You say, "any weaknesses?"
IRL11 says, "A weakness is that you arent actaully talking to each other, so sometimes the conversation can get confused from time to time. for example....."
IRL11 says, "when I was talking to [GER8] and he would say something in german that I wouldn't understand and I would ask him to rephrase it. but he might have already typed another scentance. and then I would reply to the new scentance and he would reply to my request. thus we have both trailed off on different tangents. if you know what i mean"

IRL12 says, " A strength is that you don't feel that they are total strangers once you have a picture of who you are talking to"
You nod.
IRL12 says, " I suppose that you can talk to them on a friendler basis"
You say, "any weakness?"
IRL12 says, " no weaknesses really come to mind"

IRL15 says, "well i suppose that its good to see how people actually talk - the format i mean and general slang etc"
IRL15 says, "people type in stuff that theyd actually say"
IRL15 says, "so i think thats good for general knowledge"
IRL15 says, "but not so good for formal writing"
You say, "why?"
IRL15 says, "well that is if the person you speak to is speaking generally in slang - which some people in the moo did."
IRL15 says, "but then again i did as well"

IRL16 says, "Obvously you don't actually get to speak with the person.
Your oral won't improve"
IRL16 says, "Your accent"

IRL23 says, "well the strengths are that if you are just talking then grammar is not as obvious and so you do not have to be as precise, and so the Moo makes you aware of grammar. The weakness, is that because you have to be careful with grammar, it is not always easy to say exactly what you want to."

IRL26 says, "well the weakness is that it's far to easy to just speak english the whole time"
You nod.
IRL26 says, "the germans are happy to practice their english and the irish students are kind of lazy and like speaking english"
IRL26 says, "well *i* do, at any rate :)"
IRL26 says, "the strength is that you get to hear more qulo..damn i cant spell that word....."
IRL26 says, "what i mean is 'local phrasing' etc"

IRL26 says, "that you mightnt see in books or texts from class"

GER1 says, "The strength of course is that I can read the words (listen to) a native speaker of my age who just wants to communicate and not wants to perfect my grammar."

You nod.

You say, "weaknesses?"

GER1 says, "plus after some minutes you just write quicker and more fluently and this for sure helps to speak "free""

You say, "oh, why do you write quicker? do you mean type quicker?"

GER1 says, "You see, it's just like talking. If you want your partner to get your point, you will have to find a quick way to express yourself by utilising your limited vocabulary."

GER1 says, "that's why moo-conv. is more like talking. you can't use a dictionary to look up every word."

As perceived by the learners, strengths of this communication mode are: immediate feedback on spelling, the focus on authentic language use, more motivation, more time, less pressure, supportive partners, more awareness and focus on grammar issues, whereas the perceived weaknesses are: focus on using existing knowledge rather than expanding it; the problem of translation; the problem of turn-taking and multithreaded topics; no appropriate support for formal writing; no support for pronunciation practice; the difficulty of being precise; and unbalanced bilingualism. While I expected some of these comments, I was surprised by the fact that several students obviously attended more to accuracy in grammar and spelling than I thought. Some CMC studies had reported that for many users of text-based communication, spelling is not important (for instance, see Day, Crump, & Ricky, 1996: 300).

3.2.2 Ability to monitor and evaluate MOO discourse

I explored the issue of monitoring and evaluating input further in the interviews to find out how learners compared MOO discourse to face-to-face native/non-native speaker discourse either in class (with language assistants) or in some other situation. I first asked them: "How much were you able to monitor your own and your partner's output when you compare it to face to face communication in German/English (for instance with the assistants)?" The answers are in Transcript 3.4.

Transcript 3.4 Perceived ability to monitor input (interview data)

IRL1 says, "Because you can look back at the session the output on both parts is clearer than normal conversation in the MOO and I think that with the assistants you can speak in stutters and a lotof english and bad german and they still know what your saying also because it is said so fast its hard to see exactly how bad my output is"

IRL5 says, "Yeah,well by the end i was using words in German that my partner used often and vice-versa"
IRL5 says, "german was more cooloquial"
You say, "was that because of being able to see everything on screen?"
IRL5 says, "Yeah,i could recognise the words easier then"

IRL9 says, "well you always had a log of the session and the screen enables you to look back at the conversation"
You say, "did you make use of that?"
IRL9 says, "yep if i wanted to see how the german student had previously said something you can just scroll through and find it"

IRL11 says, "well I mean the fact that you have the whole converstaion logged on the screen in front of you means that you can look back to find words he used or whatever"
You say, "ok"
You say, "did you make use of that?"
IRL11 says, "yes, like I said. If i didn't know the word for 'guitar' and he starts talking about them, well then I will obviously start replying using the new word. Or if I noticed a phrase he used and then ,later, I might come across a place where I would like to use it, i would look back up the converstaion to find it. I din these kind of things often, and I noticed he would often use some of my 'dublin' phrases back to me also."

IRL12 says, " When things are in more conversational style you tend to remember things more than when their on a teaching form and wea had a notebook to keep track of everything"

IRL16 says, "Obviously if you typed somewthing wrong you could correct it ,but"
You hmm.
IRL16 says, "in with the assistants it was tougher because it was face to face"
You say, "where was it easier to keep track of what you and the other person said?"
IRL16 says, "But it wasa better as you could improve your oral because you could speajk!!"
You say, "I see"
IRL16 says, "On the copmuter as you can read above what you and they just said!"

IRL23 says, "I don't know about that one! I think I was better able to monitor it with the assistants"
IRL23 says, "Oh no sorry,It was easier to kleep track of waht was said with the moo partner"

IRL26 says, "well, when speaking to assistants, i dont remember what i said two seconds later or how i said it..."
IRL26 says, "with the moo it records what you say and you can go back and look over it, if you wanted"
IRL26 says, "which is definitely a good thing"
IRL26 says, "so, it was much better for monitoring myself and my progress"

GER1 says, "hmm, im the moo because of the logging. but I don't think I would need this feature often in a face2face conversation."

Learners show a preference for the MOO to monitor their own progress and keep track of their partner's output, as the text remains on screen or is easily available to them by scrolling back. IRL11 illustrates how the learner and his partner used this monitoring to re-use new words. In addition, the log provides a permanent record of all sessions (IRL9, GER1) and the notebook/diary provided an additional record of learner activities (IRL12). In the follow-up question, I asked: "How much were you able to evaluate your own output when you compare it to face to face communication in German (for instance with the assistants)?" The responses are in Transcript 3.5.

Transcript 3.5 Perceived ability to evaluate input (interview data)

IRL1 says, "I mean that if I say a sentence with very bad german to the assistant its faults are not as clear than if it was in the MOO because you can read back over it and it takes longer"
You nod.
You say, "what do you mean by it takes longer"
IRL1 says, "to type the sentences out as opposed to saying them-you have to think harder"
You say, "is that good or bad?"
IRL1 says, "good"

IRL5 says, "well I wasn` really corrected in the MOO,so I` have to say the assisstants there"
You say, "how could we improve that"
IRL5 says, "maybe encourage partners to correct or improve on things said?"

IRL9 says, "well the assistants can easily point out your errors and correct them but in the moo you have to rely on yourself and who ever else is there "
IRL11 says, "well the assistans and my moo partner would reguarly correct me. But when I was in Germany it was natural just to try to understand each other rather than to correct each other."
You say, "so both situations were equally good in knowing whether you were correct and understandable?"
IRL11 says, "yes, I think so"

IRL12 says, " not as well as the assistants could show you to your face what you are constantly doing wrong"
You say, "I see, do you mean by frowning etc.?"
IRL12 says, " sorry say for instance grammer when you are translating a text in front of them"
You say, "yes?"
IRL12 says, " or when you are translating something you had already written in german being always corrected from translating literally helps you more I think"

IRL16 says, "You could see what you had typed wrong...w"
You nod.
IRL16 says, "whereas in speaking ,you find it hard to see if you said anything wrong"
You say, "Yeah, that can be so"
IRL16 says, "It just comes out of you ,yolu don';t have to think" [...]
IRL16 says, "With the MOO ,you think what you type"
IRL16 says, "With the MOO ,you think what you type"
You hmm.
IRL16 says, "You can see where you need to improve"
IRL16 says, "Look back and point out your mistaqkes"

IRL23 says, "Well I think it was easier with the germans assisants because they were there to correct me and my Moo partner did not correct me as much."

IRL26 says, "um....well i'm not sure exactly what you mean, but in terms of seeing if i'm understood, the speaking to assistants is better because you can tell from their body language or frowns if they know what i'm saying"
You nod.
IRL26 says, "on the moo...if they dont understand you, the sometimes just do a smiley and change the subject"

GER1 says, "even if you made a mistake, you barely have the time to read it all through after you sent it."

There is a marked difference to the previous question about monitoring. Some students interpreted this question in terms of self-evaluation, and others in terms of other-evaluation, such as corrective feedback. Thus some students prefer the MOO for self-evaluation (IRL1, IRL16), whereas a larger number of students prefer the face-to-face feedback by language assistants in class (IRL5, IRL9, IRL12, IRL23, IRL26). For IRL9 and IRL11, both environments are equally productive for evaluation, with an emphasis on the MOO for self-evaluation, and the classroom for other-evaluation. Clearly, some learners perceived language assistants to be better for evaluation because of the MOO's lack of non-verbal cues (IRL12,

IRL26), i.e. the perceived restraints of the medium, and because corrective feedback was perceived as part of the assistants' role (IRL5, IRL9, IRL23). This reflects a definition of assistants as fulfilling a classroom or teacher-related role whereas the tandem partner was regarded more as a fellow student.

The majority of learners reported that monitoring was perceived as far more convenient and effective than in the face-to-face contact with language assistants in class. As regards evaluation, we need to distinguish between self-evaluation and other-evaluation. Here, other-evaluation by assistants was perceived as more effective in the classroom, partly because of perceived technical limitations of the medium (see sub-section 3.3.2), and partly because of role definitions of assistants and tandem partners. Self-evaluation, however, appears to be more effective in the MOO medium. The ability to monitor and evaluate own interlanguage output and the partners' L1 input is crucial for the development of linguistic awareness. It affects a number of areas, of which I will mention two: spontaneous self-correction and the re-use of new vocabulary items.

Table 3.1 Evidence for self correction (transcript data)

Self-correction by Irish students:	*Self-correction by German students:*
14/10/99: IRL25 says, "my name is [own name misspelled] goddammit!!"" IRL25 says, "that's [own name]""	14/10/99: GER11 says, "Have a close at our English, its not nuch better" GER11 says, "Oh, have a close look I meant"
IRL25 says, "I'm not sure Iknow how to make a new room, I think we're mweant to stay in the scarlet room" GER15 laughs IRL21 chuckles maniacally IRL25 says, "that's 'meant' not 'mweant'"	21/10/99: GER14 says, " You mean wo wars du am WE ? [...] GER14 says, " Sorry wo warst du am WE!" {GER14 says, "You mean where wer you at the weekend? [...} You mean where were you at the weekend}
21/10799: IRL4 says, "Ich abe schmerzen"" IRL4 says, "habe"" GER16 says, " ahh you got hurt"	GER19 says, "ich bin 23, morgen were ich 24 ;)" GER19 says, "s/were/werde/" IRL17 says, "Herzlichen Glueck Wuencshe" GER19 says, "danke, und wie alt bist du?" IRL17 says, "I bin 19" IRL17 says, "s/I/Ich" *GER19 says, "I am 23, tomorrow I'm going to be [misspelt] 24 ;)* *{GER19 says, "s/going to be [misspelt]/ going to be/"* *IRL17 says, "Congratulations"* *GER19 says, "thank you, and what age are you?"* *IRL17 says, "I [English] am 19"* *IRL17 says, "s/I[English]/I [German]"}*

3.2.3 Self-correction and awareness

Learners' perceptions of monitoring and evaluation are closely related to the issue of corrective feedback on the one hand, and self-correction on the other hand. I will discuss corrective feedback in sub-section 3.3.2, as it is more connected with processes of negotiation and collaboration. Here I will look at self-correction as a form of intrapersonal dialogue which is not prompted by the partner. Spontaneous self-correction is an expression of linguistic awareness as defined in Chapter 1 (Masny, 1997: 106).

Here are some examples for self-correction from the transcripts:

When we sort the instances of self-correction into a table, we get the following:

Table 3.2 Number of self-corrections in transcripts

Self-correction	*in L1*	*in L2*	*no. of students*
Irish students	16	10	15
German students	18	20	14

In the examples (see Table 3.1), self-corrections were not prompted by partners, thus not an instance of miscommunication (see sub-section 3.3.3). Although there are some examples for self-correction, mainly spelling, it is not a wide-spread phenomenon. It is interesting to note that instances of self-correction occur not only when learners are communicating in the L1, but also in the L2. This is even more evident in the case of the German students, when we take into account that ten of the German L1 self-corrections are related to the fact that they were unaware that umlauts were missing from the program during the first four weeks. The low number of self-corrections indicates that the urge to "talk", to compose a message and send it off, is for many students a priority in the process of composition. Here, the fact that learners are "technically" writing is not sufficient for writing to trigger processes of awareness; the impression that they seem to be "psychologically" speaking, i.e. wanting to continue with the conversation, is stronger.

Table 3.3 Questionnaire question 12

	Responses for each of the 5 options					*Average*	*Total*
	never	rarely	sometimes	often	whenever possible		
Irish students	3	9	10	3	1	2.46	26
German students	2	8	8	–	–	2.33	18

Table 3.4: Comments on questionnaire no. 12

Comments by Irish students:	*Comments by German students:*
"usually kept to my own basic vocab" (IRL2) "not off hand" (IRL4) "at the start of some sentences I would use the word 'Also'" (IRL6) "'es tut mir leid' 'genau'" (IRL13) "I cannot think of any at the moment, but I would sometimes use verbs they have said maybe a couple of minutes ago" (ÍRL16) "Just taking words they used in the question and recycling them in the answer" (IRL18) "verbs especially" (IRL20) "I cannot think of any off hand" (IRL21) "I can't think of any at the moment but I know I" (IRL22) "sometimes if he asks me a question I will answer using the same words he used in asking the question" (IRL24) "although I really should be doing so. eg: once he told me how to say a particular sentence and I used the structure a few times after" (IRL26) "I generally replied in own words espicially when I was guessing a translation" (IRL29)	"I never paid attention whether I did so or not" (GER5) "Isn't it better for the vocabulary to try choosing other words/phrases?" (GER6) "don't know" (GER7) "'I'd love to...' is one" (GER8) "Ich denke, das ist vielleicht unbewußt passiert, aber ein genaues Beispiel fällt mir da auch nicht ein." (GER11) {"I think that this maybe happened subconsciously, but I cannot remember a specific example" (GER11)} "I think that rarely but I cannot remember" (GER13) "I don't know any, sorry" (GER15) "I can't give an example, but when I saw a new or nice expression, I used it later by myself" (GER18) "I don't know" (GER20) "fällt mir spontan keins ein!" (GER22) {"Can't remember anything off-hand!" GER22}'

3.2.4 Attention to correction and feedback

Another area apart from self-correction where learners show the ability to monitor and evaluate their own output and their partners' input is in their use of new vocabulary items that their partners have introduced. In question 12 of the questionnaire, I asked students: "Have you ever consciously reused words or phrases that your partner used?" I wanted to find out whether students were able to transform input into intake by focusing on their partner's input and using it in their own production.

Both groups have an average score between rarely and sometimes, although slightly lower for German students. I also asked them: "If so, can you give examples?" to determine whether students were able to recall any particular items from long-term memory. These are collected in Table 3.4.

Two Irish students were able to recall phrases, and two mention "verbs"; four Irish students note that they used words immediately after their partner introduced them. Some answers by both Irish and German students indicate that re-using vocabulary is seen as negative. Just one of the German students recalls an example, and another makes a more general statement of having used "new or nice expressions". Clearly, more work needs to be done to encourage students to use their partners' input to extend their own vocabulary range. However, it is encouraging to note that some students reported having used vocabulary immediately after being introduced to new phrases. This is an important difference between my results and tandem e-mail exchanges, where we reported that almost no students actively re-used their partners' vocabulary or were able to give examples (Little et al., 1999: 48–49). Here the immediacy of the medium, at least to some extent, appears to have a greater potential than the e-mail medium to encourage re-use.

As I reported in our analysis of tandem e-mail exchanges (ibid.), it is difficult to assess students' attention to input and their re-use by looking at transcripts of exchanges. In addition, re-use is naturally more difficult to assess when learners' proficiency levels are very high, as in the example of the German students. First, their vocabulary range would be wider and thus be less likely to be enhanced by their partners, and secondly, it would not be as easy to detect the re-use of new items in the transcripts, as they may already be part of their active or passive vocabulary.

However, as learners taking part in the MOO project reported having re-used new words or expressions immediately after their partner introduced them, it is slightly easier to assess the issue of re-use in the MOO context. We can therefore ask: what evidence of re-use is there in the transcripts? Was this re-use prompted by a preceding translation or correction, or was re-use merely effected by the introduction of new lexical items? Table 3.5 shows some instances of re-use in the transcripts.

When we count the examples according to group, we get results as shown in Table 3.6.

There are only very few instances of re-use of vocabulary in the transcripts. We clearly need to include awareness-raising exercises and online vocabulary lists, for example produced after each session, to widen learners' active vocabulary range and support a transfer into long-term memory.

3.2.5 Metalinguistic/metacognitive awareness and the use of diaries

In this sub-section, I would like to look at additional evidence of metalinguistic/ metacognitive awareness, both in transcripts and in diaries. I will first look at some examples from the transcripts, and second, explore the learners' diaries. With Dam (1995) I would agree that a learner diary can be a particularly valuable tool to support the development of metalinguistic awareness in learners. This can be demonstrated through reflection on and manipulation of language. While many examples of metalinguistic awareness in the transcript corpus refer to perceived differences in proficiency, in the diaries many learners also concentrate on their own difficulties, plan future sessions, and evaluate past sessions.

Table 3.5 Re-use of vocabulary items (transcript data)

Irish students:	*German students:*
18/11/99: GER15 says, "besonders die Szene mit dem Apfelkuchen"[...] IRL17 says, "Es hat clips von American Pie mit den Szene mit dem Apfelkuchen" {GER15 says, "especially the scene with the apple pie" [...] IRL17 says, "It has clips from American Pie with the scene with the apple pie"}	21/10/99: GER6 says, "How do you do?? (I leant this from [IRL5]...)"
GER4 says, "du würdest es nie verstehen" [...] IRL5 say, "du verdest es nie verstehen" GER4 says, "würdest nicht verdest" IRL5 say, "whoops" {GER4 says, "you wouldn't understand it" [...] IRL5 say, "you wouldn't [misspelt] understnad it" GER4 says, "wouldn't not wouldn't [misspelt]" IRL5 say, "whoops"}	GER2 says, "Then in February all people wear a (Kostüm) and the make parades through the big cities and they drink a lot of alkohol" IRL29 says, "does everybody wear costumes?"[...] GER2 says, "I don't like to wear a costum. I don't know why" IRL29 says, "do you feel stupid when you wear a costume"

Table 3.6 Re-use of vocabulary items (number)

	prompted	*not prompted*	*Total*
Irish students	2	9	11
German students	1	5	6

Let us first look at two examples of metalinguistic awareness in the transcripts as shown in Transcript 3.6.

Transcript 3.6 Examples of metalinguistic awareness (transcript data)

14/10/99

IRL21 says, "[GER11], Ich habe schon mit vielen Deutscher gespricht. Ihre
Englisch ist viel besser als unser Deutsch" [...]

GER11 says, "I think German is a more difficult language to learn" [...]

IRL21 says, "Genau, aber es gibt weniger unterschiede zwischen Englisch und
Deutsch als Englisch und Franzozisch"

{IRL21 says, "[GER11]. I have spoken with many Germans over the years. Your English is much better than our German" [...]

GER11 says, "I think German is a more difficult language to learn" [...]
IRL21 says, "Exactly, but there are fewer differences between English and German than English and French"}

9/12/99
GER21 says, "You are lucky. I still have to do something. Apropos, is your PC Y2K-compliant?"
IRL28 says, "I dont know I think so What is Apropas"
GER21 says, "Oh sorry, I thougt that is an international word. It means "By the way" or "What we were just talking about""

Many examples for metalinguistic awareness deal with the perceived differences in proficiency levels between Irish and German learners, and I will discuss these below in sub-section 3.3.5. In the first example, IRL21 and GER11 briefly discuss the differences between learning English, German, and French. In the second example, we can see an instance of L1 transfer. GER21 perceives "apropros" to be "an international word", but is then able to paraphrase it in the L2. Transcript 3.7 shows an example of metacognitive awareness.

Transcript 3.7 Example of metacognitive awareness (transcript data)

11/11/99
IRL21 says, "Have you ever done any online courses?"
IRL22 arrives from CLCS Foyer
GER15 says, "no, i've never done any....i don't think that this kind of course is good"
IRL22 leaves for North Corridor
IRL21 says, "why not?"
GER15 says, "I need some direct communication, if i don't learn autodidactically"
GER15 says, "yu know...someone you can ask, if you haven't understood something"
IRL21 says, "Yeah I understand what you mean. "
IRL21 says, "Do you think you could learn with the level of communication in the MOO?"
GER15 says, "maybe...perhaps you get a little more used to writing a language practically...other than just reading text-books and so on"
GER15 says, "you don't learn a language, if you don't like to...and communication on the MOO is more interesting than speaking a foreign language in front of a class"
IRL21 says, "In my opinion language must be spoken to be learned but I think other things could be learned online"

IRL21 says, "It is less embarassing when you make a mistake online:)"
IRL22 arrives from The Pink Room
IRL22 leaves for North Corridor
GER15 says, "maybe...perhaps this has to do with learn-habits"

IRL21 and GER15 discuss at some length online learning (based on the given topic 4). They emphasise especially the use of spoken language; the existence of authentic partners; immediate feedback; motivation and face-saving ("speaking a foreign language in front of a class"); and speculate about learning habits.

We encouraged learners to keep an online diary of their activities, asking themselves what they had done in the session, what went well, what did not go well, and how they wanted to improve. These diaries show more evidence of metalinguistic/metacognitive awareness.

Transcript 3.8 Evidence for metalinguistic awareness (diary data)

GER4	"My partner speeks a better German now than at the beginning."
GER15	"Within the conversation, there were no problems of understanding. "
GER17	"today was a productive conversation which means there was not much "talking crap". The conversation had a good flow, even the german part went well"
GER18	"Next time I want to meet my own partner again or just work on the next tasks, because its fun talking to the irish people and improve the vocabulary while having fun."
GER18	" I would like him to get more exercise, but the biggest problem is that they don't know the vocabulary to express what they want to say."
IRL3	"hard to keep up the speed of typing hard to be precise in german"
IRL4	"Its much harder to talk about the course as we dont understand the others "jargain". It was much better when we talked about our interests"
IRL14	"I also asked a few times what certain words were in German etc.... and how certain things are said."
IRL16	".I learned a few German phrases"
IRL25	"My german has fallen lower than I thought it had."
IRL26	"damn, his english is good. mental note: must learn some german sometime soon."

There is also some evidence for metacognitive awareness (see Transcript 3.9).

Transcript 3.9 Evidence for metacognitive awareness (diary data)

GER1	"Next time I'm going to talk about hobbies and about topic 2"
GER5	"philosophic discussions with a bit comedy. Next time be more specific."
GER6	"What I plan to do next week - to ask my partners some more questions about IT - than working on next theme....."
GER13	"I fear that it can be hard working with them, because they do not seem willing on working. We will see...just the first impression!"
GER14	"I noticed i am no good at explaining, i totally failed to explain where i live. i will write an e-mail about this, i believe!"
GER18	"Last week we worked very fast so I'm sure I didn't waste too much time today. Its really fun working with the moo system, and the knowledge about the functions will help working with it. Next week I hope my partner is there again [...] I think its more intensive working with your own partner."
GER18	"This moo session was very concentrated and task focussed... [IRL25] and me talked about learning on-line and our web sites, if we did on-line courses yet and so on... I think we reached the point we get used to our partners and climb up to the next level of communication :-) This may sound a bit weird, but I noticed that its not the "how are you today" thing at the beginning any more, we just started off with the fourth task and discussed the topics."
GER22	"Next time, I´ll make more corrections so that we can learn form each other."
IRL1	"Ich lerne ein paar worten und sehe den Text(Comprehension) Ich mochte es nicht zu tun nachste zeit- es ist so lang, ein kurtzer Text ist besser." {"I learn a few words and see the text (Comprehension) I wouldn't like it to do next time- it is so long, a short text is better."} "I got a bit lost sometimes today as they spoke more German but I felt it was more beneficial." "Ich mochte nachste woche mehr Duutsch sprachen. Heute wir sprachen zu viel Englisch." {"I would like to speak more German next week. Today we spoke too much English."}
IRL25	"Maybe some preparatory work should be done in future."
IRL29	"Never gor to ask him about the project I have to do. Make sure to do it next week." "Didn't ask him about my project yet but will do it next week. Promise"

Several students consciously define short-term goals for the MOO sessions. Some students use the diary to evaluate whether these goals have been met. They define their learning agenda, and feel responsible to adhere to the principles they themselves have defined, by using commands directed at themselves (IRL26, GER5) or addressing the diary as a character (IRL29). A number of students report on their strengths and weaknesses in the TL, and some discuss strategies on improving (e.g. GER14).

The results from the diaries are encouraging. Many learners enter into a real dialogue with themselves, planning, monitoring, and evaluating learning. Diaries were not part of course work, as we did not have time to integrate them properly into a bilateral framework. This also meant that not all learners made diary entries, and not all sets of diaries were completed for each session. However, learners' initial diary comments were surprisingly reflective, and in following projects we integrated online diaries more within the assessment and task specifications. Other promising approaches could be in the form of a critical incident questionnaire, where students would focus on particular moments when they learnt a new word, when they felt uninvolved, etc., as an awareness-raising exercise (see Brookfield, 1995).

3.2.6 Summary analysis of data on reflection

In this section, I have looked at various aspects of language and linguistic awareness. A discussion of MOO discourse as spoken or written language showed that many learners perceived MOO language as a mixture of both. This is largely due to the fact that MOO discourse was on the one hand perceived as direct, immediate, "natural" discourse with a native speaker, and on the other hand sometimes used for monitoring, and self-evaluating learners' own input and their partners' output; in short, activities that show linguistic awareness. In describing monitoring, some learners' comments indicated that MOO discourse, especially in tandem, involves other psychological processes than e-mail. In the act of composing a message, MOO discourse appears more like speaking, whereas it becomes writing — as some learners' comments indicate — as soon as it appears in the output window in the MOO. This influences self-correction, which occurs in L1 as well as L2 discourse. There is very little indication for re-use in the transcripts compared to our previous e-mail project. I noted that the primacy of communication flow may be responsible for this.

Examples of metalinguistic awareness are very prominent in the diary data, where learners frequently plan short-term goals, evaluate them, and enter into an intrapersonal dialogue about their learning process. The use of online diaries confirms the positive results that Dam (1995) has achieved with her learners. I would even go as far as saying that the MOO diary can achieve higher levels of linguistic awareness than a diary in the real-life classroom, as it is embedded in an equally immediate, but in addition solely text-based communication medium. I can summarise by saying that one of the central concerns of learner autonomy, raising awareness of the learning process and language itself, can be realised very effectively in the MOO, most likely due to its combination of immediate communication with the written medium, although more pedagogical work is clearly necessary.

3.3 MULTIPLE SOURCES OF EVIDENCE FOR INTERACTION

In this sub-section, I will look at some of the factors that support collaboration and interaction in a tandem partnership. First, I will focus on topic negotiation. Here I will look at the topics our learners discussed, but also examine who initiated the topics and how they were initiated. Second, I will look at error correction, which had been a prominent form of reciprocal support in our e-mail data (Little et al., 1999). Third, I will deal with repair strategies by learners. When communication breaks down or some other form of miscommunication occurs, learners will employ various strategies to repair deficient discourse so that communication can resume. Fourth, I will look at input modifications, and fifth, I will look at a central principle of tandem learning, the principle of bilingualism. Throughout the exchange I noted that much more communication took place in English. Although this was not desirable, it was to be expected, given the huge differences in proficiency between the two groups of learners. I will therefore also report on more recent developments that deal with the problem of imbalanced bilingualism in tandem exchanges.

3.3.1 Topic negotiation

In this sub-section I look at the topics that the learners discussed. As mentioned in sub-section 3.1.1, we had prepared four topics for our students, but made it clear that these were only optional topics for discussion. I will therefore first focus briefly on what topics our learners discussed with their partners. Secondly I want to explore whether native speakers or non-native speakers initiated the topics, and how topics were initiated.

In question 1 on the questionnaire, I asked learners: "1. What kinds of topics have you discussed with your tandem partner?" Learners discussed the following topic areas: (i) aspects of personal life; (ii) aspects of intercultural comparisons between Germany and Ireland; (iii) aspects of information technology; (iv) aspects of course work. These topic areas are largely supported by the transcripts. It is not surprising that private discussions were often triggered by current events: two such examples were the MTV Music awards ceremony that took place in Dublin and the falling of snow in Bonn, an unusual event for Irish learners. There is little evidence in the questionnaire that language learning was discussed as a topic, although I noted at various points in section 3.2 that there is ample evidence for this in the transcripts. Topics often have a strong personal dimension; in the transcripts we can even find examples for highly sensitive topics such as drug habits. Here the MOO obviously provides enough anonymity and encourages interpersonal relationships. In terms of tandem learning, learners discuss matters that they can relate to personally meaningful experience. This personal dimension is one of the great strengths of tandem learning, and is confirmed by the results of our previous tandem e-mail study (Little et al., 1999: 19).

In a recent paper (Schwienhorst, 2004b), I analyse in detail the issue of topic initiation. I will just summarise some of the major points here. Topic initiation in foreigner talk discourse (FTD), as reported by Long (1981), is usually initiated by native speakers, and in many cases they use questions to do so. I wanted to find out whether this also holds true for FTD in tandem in the MOO.

When analysing the transcript corpus, I arrived at the following results. First, in spite of the proficiency differences between the Irish and German learners, topic initiation was far more balanced between the groups than could be expected from previous research for face-to-face FTD (see Long, 1983: 133). In English, 49.19% of topics were initiated by Irish students and 50.81% by German students. In German, the number of topic initiations was exactly split 50/50 between the two groups when pooled across all sessions. Second, the more proficient group, the German learners, used far fewer questions than the Irish group to initiate topics in the L2, a result that was to be expected. Third, wh-questions formed the majority of questions in topic initiations. Fourth, when communicating in the higher proficiency language, the two groups displayed much more NS-NS like features (lower number of questions, higher number of wh-questions, etc.). There were no significant changes of topic initiation behaviour over the course of the project.

In summary, I can say that learners discussed a variety of topics during the MOO sessions. They did not discuss course-work related topics exclusively nor did they "chit-chat" for any extended amount of time. Here we can see one of the strengths of tandem learning: it encourages content-driven discourse that is of interest and concern to both parties. My discussion of topic initiation in MOO discourse indicates that topic initiation within a reciprocal tandem learning framework has different implications than (one-sided) FTD. I noted that, in general, learners did not use questions as often as Long's (1981) subjects, and that topic initiations in both languages are far more balanced than reported from face-to-face FTD.

3.3.2 Error correction and encouragement

I have noted in the sub-section on self-correction that some students used the output window in the MOO for post-editing their input. In my analysis

Table 3.7 Sample comments on questionnaire nos. 2 and 3 (sorted by tandem partnerships)

	What did you correct?	*What did your partner correct?*
IRL1	"Small bits of grammer; natural phrases" (IRL1)	"vocabulary, typical german mistakes (sensitive => sensible etc....)" (GER1)*
IRL2	"Colloquilisms ??" (IRL2)	"vocabulary, typical german mistakes (sensitive => sensible etc....)" (GER1)
GER1	"Grammar: personal pronouns, conjugation, declination" (GER1)	"Vocabulary" (IRL1) "Grammar (sentence structure)" (IRL2)
IRL4	"Not much...it is excellent, but occasionally his tenses. " (IRL4)	"No corrections made by my partner" (GER3)
GER3	"sequence of words in sentences; no need to correct them, quite a good speaker" (GER3)	"Most of it!!! No – only joking. Although he should correct most of it, he picks out big mistakes" (IRL4)
IRL6	"Grammar and expression" (IRL6)	"he doesn't correct me" (GER5)
GER5	"I correct wrong words (wrong meaning a context)" (GER5)	"Verbs, grammar, expression but generally we try to kept the conversation going" (IRL6)

*This was a 2+1 tandem partnership. As the partner's response refers to both partners, I have repeated it for both learners.

of error correction, I wanted to find out how much support learners gave and received in the form of error correction.

In the questionnaire question 2, I asked: "What aspects of your tandem partner's English/German do you correct in the MOO, or help him/her with most?" I also asked the reverse question: "3. What aspects of your German/English does your partner correct in the MOO, or help you with most?" In Table 3.7, I compile the responses to both questions, as they can show differences and similarities between learners' perceptions of error correction and their partners'. Some examples of students' comments are shown in Table 3.7.

The responses by learners may suggest a high degree of error correction. However, I found very little evidence for error correction in the actual transcripts. Some learners marked corrections similarly as in the previous e-mail project, while other corrections were unmarked (see Transcript 3.10).

Transcript 3.10 Examples for correction styles (transcript data)

IRL18 says, "Haben sie the BLAIR WITCH PROJECT GESEHEN""
GER13 says, "Nein! Aber du kannst mit "dutzen"...: Hast du..."
{IRL18 says, "Have you [formal] seen the BLAIR WITCH PROJECT"
GER13 says, "No! But you can say "Du"...Have you [informal]..."}

GER18 says, "But she's studying farer away"
IRL26 says, ""further away""

IRL11 says, “ Ich habe eine andere bild gesenden”
GER8 says, “x Ich habe ein anderes Bild gesendet. “
GER8 says, “oder x: Ich habe noch mehr Bilder gesendet.”
{IRL11 says, “I have sent another [wrong gender] picture”
GER8 says, “x I have sent another [right gender] picture”
GER8 says, “or x I have sent more pictures”}

IRL16 says, “Es ist nicht schlecht,du hast gut Ehglish!” [...]
GER11 says, “man sagt : Du “kannst” gut Englisch”
{IRL16 says, “It is not bad, you have good English” [...]
GER11 says, “we say: You “can” [speak] good English”}

IRL3 says, “Ich interessiert mich fur Computers...” [...]
GER2 says, “Ich interessierE mich fr Computer”
{IRL3 says, “I is interested in computers...” [...]
GER2 says, “I AM interested in computers”}

In the Table 3.8, we can see the actual number of corrections in the transcript data. Those corrections that were made for learners other than the selected partner are in brackets.

Table 3.8 Actual number of corrections in transcripts

Corrections by	*spelling*	*idioms/styles*	*morphology*	*syntax*
Irish students	2 (2)	7 (1)	2 (2)	–
German students	6 (3)	10 (3)	15 (4)	2

There is very little evidence of error correction in the narrower sense in the transcripts. My analysis of error correction and learners’ comments confirms, nevertheless, some observations I made earlier in sub-section 3.2.2 on evaluation. On the one hand, several learners obviously do not see it as part of their role in a MOO tandem partnership to correct each other, but emphasise instead the communicative function of the exchange. In this context, students often perceive error corrections as a disturbance of communication flow. There was also very little evidence of learners making general comments regarding their partners’ errors, or explicitly co-ordinating correction strategies.

Transcript 3.11 Instances of learners discussing error correction (transcript data)

21/10/99:

IRL1 says, “[IRL4 + IRL1]-I would appreciate it if you might correct some of the mistakes that I make -not all though I’m sure there are lots

GER18 says, “Its the other way round: We are here to correct you and to help you to talk German”

GER18 says, "You help us to increase our skills and we help you"
GER18 says, "Thats the deal"

28/10/99
GER11 says, "you can also correct me, I wont be insulted"

4/11/99
You sense that GER6 is looking for you in The Lime Room.
It pages, "You may correct me.... I sometimes write shit..."

This should not be interpreted as a complete lack of error correction nor lack of reciprocal support. Reciprocal support can be and has been provided in a number of other ways. Some students were asking for and giving direct translations of unknown words, an issue we will not explore in greater detail here. An important element of reciprocal support in the MOO is the encouragement they give each other. In Transcript 3.12, there are two typical examples from the first two sessions.

Transcript 3.12 Examples of encouragement (transcript data, first three sessions)

14/10/99:
IRL21 says, "ACHTUNG. Mein Deutschverkenntnisse ist nicht sehr gut. Ich muss sehr
langsam sprechen. ENTSULDIGEN sIE BITTE"
GER15 says, "ok, we'll type slooooowwwllyyy" [...]
IRL21 says, "Vielen Dank" [...]
GER11 says, "Have a close at our English, its not nuch better"
GER11 says, "Oh, have a close look I meant"
{IRL21 says, "ATTENTION. My knowledge of German is not vey good. I have to speak very slowly. I am sorry"
GER15 says, "ok, we'll type slooooowwwllyyy" [...]
IRL21 says, "Thank you very much" [...]}

IRL26 says, "wir konnen kein Deutsch" [...]
GER19 says, "wir koennen auch kein Englisch ;)"
IRL26 says, "heh" [...]
GER7 says, "Wie lange habt Ihr denn Deutsch"
IRL26 says, "seit 6 Jahren"
IRL9 says, "Ich studiere deutsch sechs jahr aber my Deutsch ist nicht so gut"" [...]
GER2 says, "[IRL9]: keine Sorge, meins ist nicht besser :)"
GER19 says, "[IRL26], Du kannst doch Deutsch. Sehe ich doch..."
{IRL26 says, "we don't know any German" [...]
GER19, says, "we don't know any English either ;)"
IRL26 says, "heh" [...]
GER7 says, "How long have you had German"
IRL26 says, "for 6 years"

IRL9, "I have been studying German six year but my German is not so good" [...]
GER2 says, "[IRL9]: no worries, mine isn't any better:)"
GER19 says, "[IRL26]. But you can speak German. I can see that..."}

The mutual encouragement of learners is noticeable throughout the project. In many cases, learners became more confident as the exchange progressed, and Irish students apologised for their lower proficiency level much less than at the beginning. This certainly contributed to increased levels of confidence, an important factor for motivation.

In summary, there is very little evidence of direct error correction in the transcript corpus. Some partnerships used this form of reciprocal support more than others. In commenting on error correction in the relevant questions on the questionnaire, very few partnerships show similarities in the areas where they corrected each other. Not the least of which because we included other areas that the partner "helped with" in the question, some students may have included support mechanisms apart from error correction here. There is some indication that error corrections were perceived as interruptions to the communicative flow of conversation, and some lack of corrections may be due to the perceived role of the tandem partner as discussed in sub-section 3.2.2. I also argued that other forms of support such as encouragement were more important. We should not forget that language learners are often very embarrassed to speak in the TL, so maybe it is considered more important to get them to "speak". Other forms of reciprocal support, such as repair strategies and input modifications are explored in the next two sub-sections below.

3.3.3 Repair strategies

On the basis of my observations on error correction, I would expect repair strategies to occur more often in the exchanges than error corrections, as repair strategies are a direct consequence of a breakdown in communication, as opposed to the mere occurrence of a deficient form. I will therefore look at repair strategies in some more detail. Again, as I have focussed on repair strategies in a separate publication (Schwienhorst, 2002a), I will only summarise the major findings here. In this case, however, I will also include statistical analyses (missing from the original publication) to underline my points. It is important to distinguish between what learners say in questionnaires (their **intentions**) and the actual **realisations** of repair strategies in transcripts.

In questions 4 and 5 in the questionnaire, I focused on repair strategies that were used by learners to resolve instances of miscommunication (for a detailed categorisation of miscommunication, see Gass & Varonis, 1991; Milroy, 1984). Similar to Donaldson and Kötter's (1999) study I expected evasive strategies (such as ignoring utterances) to be less frequent, while active strategies (such as translation) were to be more widely used. It is important to note that, as in previous tables, not all of the subjects answered all the questions. Therefore I will give the total number of responses for each option, as well as an average mark, calculated by multiplying each result with the frequency value, adding each multiplication and dividing it by the total number of responses for each section. Students were also able to include comments with both question 4 and 5. I asked in question 4: "What did you do when you did not understand what your partner was saying in your **target** language, German/English?"

For both groups, an Anova (Analysis of Variance) test was carried out. For the data in Table 3.9, there was a significant difference between the various strategies employed ($p < 0.05$; F ratio: 10.31) as follows: between, on the one hand, asking partner for translation, and on the other hand, changing the subject/ignore what s/he said; on the one hand, asking partner to repeat, and on the other hand, changing the subject/ignore what s/he said; on the one hand, asking partner to say it in other words, and on the other hand, changing the subject/ignore what s/he said; on the one hand, guess the meaning, and on the other hand, changing the subject/ignore what s/he said.

In Table 3.10, the statistically significant differences were as follows ($p < 0.05$; F ratio: 24.03): between, on the one hand, asking partner for translation, and on the other hand, changing the subject/ignore what s/he said/; on the one hand, asking partner to repeat, and on the other hand, changing the subject/ignore what s/he said; on the one hand, asking partner to say

Table 3.9 Question 4 Results for the Irish group (26 subjects)

	Frequency (1 = very low, 5 = very high) Responses for each of the 5 scale points					*Average (1–5)*	*Total Responses*	*Std Dev*
	1	*2*	*3*	*4*	*5*			
change the subject	16	1	3	1	0	1.48	21	0.93
ignore what s/he said	7	8	3	2	0	2	20	0.97
guess the meaning	1	5	7	7	3	3.26	23	1.10
ask partner to repeat	6	1	4	6	4	3.05	21	1.53
ask partner to say it in other words	4	3	4	5	7	3.35	23	1.50
ask partner for a translation	3	1	6	6	9	3.68	25	1.35

Table 3.10 Question 4 Results for the German group (22 subjects)

	Frequency (1 = very low, 5 = very high) Responses for each of the 5 scale points					*Average (1–5)*	*Total Responses*	*Std Dev*
	1	*2*	*3*	*4*	*5*			
change the subject	18	1	0	0	0	1.05	19	0.23
ignore what s/he said	16	3	0	0	0	1.16	19	0.37
guess the meaning	3	2	11	3	1	2.85	20	1.04
ask partner to repeat	4	3	6	5	2	2.9	20	1.29
ask partner to say it in other words	2	1	1	5	12	4.14	21	1.31
ask partner for a translation	5	4	4	3	3	2.74	19	1.45

it in other words, and on the other hand, all other categories; on the one hand, guess the meaning, and on the other hand, changing the subject/ignore what s/he said.

The data suggests that the students rarely used evasive strategies. Topic changes because of non-communication were avoided, as was ignoring the partner's utterance (although both were more acceptable to Irish students). Guessing the meaning was far more acceptable than suggested in Donaldson and Kötter's study, and it is by far the most unobtrusive strategy of the three: communication flow would not immediately be affected, and the guess might, at least at some point, result in partial understanding.

For those repair strategies that clearly involve negotiation of meaning, the results are less pronounced, although overall they are valued higher than the first two. It is important to note that the option "ask partner to repeat" is technically redundant in a MOO, where the previous text messages are at all times accessible to the learner. However, the transcripts reveal that students used exact repetition only in very few instances. It may therefore well be the case that the question was understood to refer to paraphrasing rather than exact repetition.

It is interesting to note that for Irish students, asking for a translation into English was slightly more important than paraphrasing the unknown word or phrase, whereas for German students the preferences were the opposite; paraphrasing was far more important than translation. This may point towards a combination of higher levels of proficiency and more advanced stages of learner autonomy in the German students. It is, of course, easier for less proficient learners to paraphrase in their native language, while more proficient learners have fewer problems translating into the TL.

In question 5, I also asked the reverse question: "What did you do when you did not understand what your partner was saying in your **native** language, English/German?"

Again, for both groups, an Anova (Analysis of Variance) test was carried out. For the data in Table 3.11, there was a significant difference between the various strategies employed ($p < 0.05$; F ratio: 5.12) as follows: between, on the one hand, asking partner for translation, and on the other hand, ignore what s/he said; on the one hand, asking partner to repeat, and on the other hand, changing the subject/ignore what s/he said; on the one hand, asking partner to say it in other words, and on the other hand, changing the subject/ignore what s/he said; on the one hand, guess the meaning, and on the other hand, changing the subject/ignore what s/he said.

In Table 3.12, the statistically significant differences were as follows ($p < 0.05$; F ratio: 24.53): between, on the one hand, asking partner for translation, and on the other hand, changing the subject/ignore what s/he said; on the one hand, asking partner to repeat, and on the other hand, all other categories; on the one hand, asking partner to say it in other words, and on the other hand, changing the subject/ignore what s/he said; on the one hand, guess the meaning, and on the other hand, changing the subject/ignore what s/he said.

The low number of total responses in the Irish group, together with their comments, shows that this question had little relevance for them. They repeatedly pointed out in their comments the high level of their partner's

Table 3.11 Question 5 Results for the Irish group (26 subjects)

	Frequency (1 = very low, 5 = very high) Responses for each of the 5 scale points					*Average (1–5)*	*Total Responses*	*Std Dev*
	1	*2*	*3*	*4*	*5*			
change the subject	11	2	0	1	1	1.6	15	1.24
ignore what s/he said	11	2	2	0	0	1.6	15	1.24
guess the meaning	2	4	4	3	5	3.28	18	1.41
ask partner to repeat	5	1	2	4	4	3.06	16	1.65
ask partner to say it in other words	3	2	6	2	6	3.32	19	1.45
ask partner for a translation	7	2	3	2	2	2.38	16	1.50

Table 3.12 Question 5 Results for the German group (22 subjects)

	Frequency (1 = very low, 5 = very high) Responses for each of the 5 scale points					*Average (1–5)*	*Total Responses*	*Std Dev*
	1	*2*	*3*	*4*	*5*			
change the subject	18	1	0	0	0	1.05	19	0.23
ignore what s/ he said	17	1	1	0	0	1.16	19	0.50
guess the meaning	2	1	5	8	4	3.55	20	1.19
ask partner to repeat	7	3	3	5	2	2.6	20	1.47
ask partner to say it in other words	1	4	3	6	5	3.53	19	1.26
ask partner for a translation	2	1	4	11	3	3.57	21	1.12

English. Again, the first two evasive strategies are not considered to be important by both groups. Guessing the partner's meaning was far more important than the first two options, and in both groups, guessing took second place among the given alternatives, though only by an insignificant margin.

In relation to negotiated meaning, Irish students said they requested exact repetition more often than the German students, although, as mentioned before, the learners' interpretation of repetition is unclear, as the transcripts show very little evidence of it. Nevertheless, for the Irish students, asking for an exact repetition and guessing the meaning clearly rate higher than asking for a translation of the unknown word. Asking the German students to paraphrase (in English) is rated higher than translation. For the German students, on the other hand, asking their partners to translate into English is now slightly more important than asking for a paraphrase (in German). In their comments, both Irish and German students show that they were very aware of the different proficiency levels.

I should make clear that in the preceding paragraphs I am referring to learners' perceptions of repair strategies, not their realisations in the actual transcripts. If judging only from the questionnaires, the answers and comments by learners show a marked difference in repair strategies between native language and TL conversations. When talking to their German partners in English, Irish students clearly preferred to ask for paraphrasing (in English) rather than translation into German (Table 3.11), which was also, by far, the preferred strategy for German students (Table 3.10).

When talking German, these strategies would change, although the differences were now less pronounced (Tables 3.9 and 3.12). Irish students would prefer to ask for translation rather than paraphrase, as would German students, though only by a narrow margin. Some comments for questions 4 and 5 had indicated that some learners perceived the questions as "what if" scenarios. Thus, many Irish students reported that they had hardly ever had to correct their German partner's English. It is therefore useful to look at the transcripts.

One noticeable difference between the questionnaire and the transcript data is the form of clarification requests. In the transcripts, learners very rarely, if ever, indicate a clear preference for either translation or paraphrase (or indeed any other specific type of repair), and most requests for clarification take the form of "I don't understand", "What does <unknown word or phrase> mean?" or "<unknown word or phrase>?". We therefore need to look at what type of clarification they **received**, rather than what type they **asked for** (in the actual request), or specified in the questionnaire responses. In the order of Tables 3.9–3.12 these are as follows:

When Irish students requested clarification while communicating in the TL (German), Germans replied in 17 instances with paraphrase, in 70 instances with translation. This difference is far more pronounced than in the questionnaire, where there is only a slight preference for translation.

When German students requested clarification while communicating in the TL (English), Irish students replied in 14 instances with paraphrase, and in 27 with translation. Although the ratio between translation and paraphrase is lower than in the previous scenario, this stands in contrast to the information shown in Table 3.10, where Germans expressed a clear preference for paraphrase.

There were significantly fewer requests for clarification by native speakers when communicating in their L1. When Irish students requested clarification while talking in their native language (English), Germans replied in 6 instances with paraphrase, and in 5 with translation. In Table 3.11, Irish students had indeed expressed a preference for paraphrase in this context.

When German students requested clarification while communicating in their L1 (German), Irish students replied in four instances with paraphrase, and in nine cases with translation. Again, the data in Table 3.12 confirms this: German students had expressed a (very slight) preference for translation.

In this sub-section, I evaluated parts of a learner questionnaire and learner transcripts. I found some evidence for Donaldson and Kötter's (1999; also see Pellettieri, 2000) findings that active strategies, or to be more exact, processes of negotiated meaning are far more prominent than instances of non-engagement or misunderstanding in native speaker/non-native speaker MOO discourse. I noticed that the function of guessing and repetition for discourse management is difficult to assess, and additional data from diaries and interviews was needed to explore the issue further. A study of transcripts provides us with some valuable insights into the **realised** use of translation and paraphrase in bilingual MOO discourse in relation to learners' **beliefs** expressed in the questionnaire data. The questionnaire data suggests that German students, when helping their Irish partners with German, would adapt to or move towards the Irish students' preferred/intended strategy, translation, whereas the Irish students, when helping their German partners with English, mostly would adapt to the German students' preferred/intended strategy, paraphrasing.

A closer look at the preferences for paraphrase and translation, however, reveals that the intentions expressed in the questionnaire were only to an extent realised in the transcripts. Native speakers preferred to translate when conversing in their L1, although the ratio between translation and paraphrase was much higher in the case of German students (in the German language context). While the preferred/intended strategy for Irish learners in TL discourse, translation, was realised by the German students, the preferred/intended strategy for German learners in TL discourse, paraphrase, was not realised to the same extent by the Irish students. Native speakers, on the whole, made very few clarification requests when conversing in their L1. When assuming the role of expert, native speakers do not request clarification from their partner as often as in the TL context or "learner" role.

The data shows how both learner groups worked towards finding the most effective strategies for their very different levels of proficiency, adapting to each other's needs and capabilities. The fact that in so many cases learners used native speaker partners as informants suggests that in terms of repair strategies, reciprocity in MOO tandem partnerships involves processes of adaptation and scaffolding (as discussed in sub-section 1.1.2), even when there are marked differences in proficiency levels.

3.3.4 Input modifications

In non-native/native speaker interactions, the phenomenon of foreigner talk emerges, whereby the native speaker will adapt to the proficiency level of the non-native speaker by modifying her output, such as adopting a smaller range of vocabulary or a simplified grammar to facilitate communication. These input modifications can give us an important insight into the adaptive processes used and realised by native speaker experts in a tandem partnership.

I dealt with the issue of input modification in two questions on the questionnaire. I first asked: "10. Would you say that you have adapted the use of your native language (English/German) to your partner's level? If so, in what way(s)?" The responses are shown in Table 3.13.

Table 3.13 Input Modification by Irish students

	Frequency (1 = very low, 5 = very high) Responses for each of the 5 scale points					*Average (1–5)*	*Total Responses*
	1	*2*	*3*	*4*	*5*		
avoided certain words	6	4	5,5	4,5	4	2,85	24
avoided idioms and colloquial phrases	6	3	6,5	2,5	6	2,98	24
made sentences less complex	4	5	7,5	3,5	5	3,02	25

An Analysis of Variance (Anova) test on the data indicated that there was not a significant difference in the mean scores between the categories ($p > 0.05$; F ratio: 0.09).

Transcript 3.13 Comments on Questionnaire no. 10 (Irish students)

"The germans are so good at English I don't really have to" (IRL1)
"kept sentences very basic" (IRL2)
"I didn't really have to adapt. He seemed to know what I was saying most of the time" (IRL3)
"His English is excellent" (IRL4)
"I don't really need to do this because his German is so good." (IRL12)
"I try to explain colloquial phrases." (IRL14)
"My partners German is very good. There is not much that I need to avoid, but sometimes we speak alot simpler just to make it simpler!" (IRL16)
"His english is near perfect." (IRL18)
"Only sometimes" (IRL20)
"I sometimes teach him some slang and idioms" (IRL24)
"His english is so good, that the only thing he can really learn from me is colloquial phrases...and maybe some big words." (IRL26)
"I avoided slang words and little phrases cause I knew he couldn't understand but for the most part he understood my english perfectly" (IRL29)

From the Irish learners' comments in Transcript 3.13 we can see that they were very much aware of the high L2 proficiency of their German partners. Four students mention that colloquial/slang language had been avoided.

An Analysis of Variance (Anova) test on the data indicated that there was not a significant difference in the mean scores between the categories ($p > 0.05$; F ratio: 0.19).

Table 3.14 Input Modification by German Students

	Frequency (1 = very low, 5 = very high) Responses for each of the 5 scale points					*Average (1–5)*	*Total Responses*
	1	*2*	*3*	*4*	*5*		
avoided certain words	1	2	9	4	5	3,48	21
avoided idioms and colloquial phrases	1	1	8	5	6	3,67	21
made sentences less complex	2	-	7	6	6	3,67	21

Transcript 3.14 Comments on Questionnaire no. 10 (German students)

"You always think, to help someone, when adjusting to his/her level" (GER6)

"I tried to use 'plain' German- not too much 'slang' or special/technical words that would have been too hard to understand" (GER15)

"There is no doubt that their level is not as high as our level, so I tried to use simple phrases and common expressions so that they understand what I say.""(GER18)

"I do make sentences less complex, after I find out, my partner dosn't understand the original phrase" (GER19)

The number of input modifications, as can be expected with the differences in proficiency levels between the groups, is markedly higher for German learners than for Irish learners. In both groups, the most frequent modifications were perceived to lie in the area of sentence complexity, although the differences between the given categories are not significant. Again, the comments in Transcript 3.14 indicate that many learners of both groups are concerned with the input being comprehensible. This emphasises my earlier argument that communicative flow is highly prioritised in MOO tandem discourse.

I also wanted to find out how students perceived their partner's adaptations, and whether there were similarities to my previous question: "11. Would you say that your partner had adapted his/her native language (German/English) to your level? If so, in what way(s) do you think he/she did?" The results are shown in Table 3.15.

An Analysis of Variance (Anova) test on the data indicated that there was not a significant difference in the mean scores between the categories ($p > 0.05$; F ratio: 0.78).

Table 3.15 Perceived Input Modifications: How Irish Students See Their German Partners

	Frequency (1 = very low, 5 = very high) Responses for each of the 5 scale points					*Average (1–5)*	*Total Responses*
	1	*2*	*3*	*4*	*5*		
avoided certain words	--	3	7	6	3	3,47	21
avoided idioms and colloquial phrases	1	3	4	6	6	3,65	20
made sentences less complex	1	2	3	8	8	3,91	22

Transcript 3.15 Comments on Questionnaire No. 11 (Irish students)

"I'm not sure, they probably do but they always explain things I don't understand" (IRL1)

"He didn't make sentences very simple but I think he made them less complex than he usually would" (IRL3)

"He helped me a lot" (IRL4)

"We haven't 'spoken' in German enough to answer this question" (IRL8)

"My tandem partner seemed to use idioms which were quite difficult to translate during the course of our conversations." (IRL13)

"My German is not as good as my partners, but still it is a challenge to use complex sentences and colloquial phrases. If you stay on the same language level, you won't improved, therefore we would push complexity of sentences" (IRL16)

"Hard to say if he is or isn't as I don't know how he would normally speak" (IRL18)

"It's hard to say. I think he does because I usually ask him to repeat most of his sentences so the second time around, I can see that it is a less complex sentence but I can't tell why." (IRL19)

"I really have no idea" (IRL22)

"He was quite amazed at how long I had been learning german for- considering how bad I am at it!" (IRL26)

"I guess he made his german a little bit easier so I could understand it" (IRL29)

It is remarkable how similar the results in Table 3.15 are to the ones in Table 3.14. Irish students seem well able to assess how much their German partners have modified their input. Some of the comments in Transcript 3.15 indicate that input modification was signalled by some form of miscommunication, i.e. it was not perceived as a pre-conceived strategy, but a necessity to guarantee communicative flow.

Table 3.16 Perceived Input Modifications: How German Students See Their Irish Partners

	Frequency (1= very low, 5 = very high) Responses for each of the 5 scale points					*Average (1–5)*	*Total Responses*
	1	*2*	*3*	*4*	*5*		
avoided certain words	5	4	4	4	–	2,41	17
avoided idioms and colloquial phrases	4	3	2	5	2	2,88	16
made sentences less complex	5	3	4	5	–	2,53	17

The German group also perceived input modification in much the same way as their Irish counterparts in the previous question (see Table 3.16).

An Analysis of Variance (Anova) test on the data indicated that there was not a significant difference in the mean scores between the categories ($p > 0.05$; F ratio: 0.57).

Transcript 3.16 Comments on Questionnaire No. 11 (German students)

"Can not testify that he used a easier style, do not know his normal speaking" (GER3)

"I can't say whether my partner used 'easy' English. Probably he did it. I felt that could understand all and that the language wasn't too hard." (GER5)

"It seems like this, because I was able to understand my partner(s) very well" (GER6)

"Ich glaube schon, daß meine Partnerin vieles aus ihrer Umgangssprache außen vor gelassen hat, was aber auch verständlich ist, da ich denke, daß sie fast nichts verstanden hätte, wenn ich in meinem lokalen Dialekt gesprochen hätte." (GER10)

{*"I do think that my partner leaves out some of the colloquial language, but this is understandable, because I think that she wouldn't have understood a thing if I had spoken my local dialect." (GER10)*}

"Man kann schlecht beurteilen, ob der Partner das geändert hat. Allerdings fände ich es auch nicht gut, wenn der Partner seine Sprache zu simpel gestaltet, sonst würde sich mein eigenes level auch nicht steigern" (GER11)

{*"It is difficult to say whether the partner has changed this. On the other hand, I wouldn't think it's such a good idea if the partner simplifies the language too much, because my own level [of proficiency] then would not increase" (GER11)*}

"It seemed to them that I understand everything" (GER13)
"Actually, I think our english was a lot better than our german conversation- it was more fluent and much more complex" (GER15)
"I think they really used the words and phrases they use when talking to their friends. I enjoyed the level of their speech and extended my vocabulary" (GER18)
"same as q10" ["It's hard to say. I think he does because I usually ask him to repeat most of his sentences so the second time around, I can see that it is a less complex sentence but I can't tell why."] (IRL19)
"I guess he figured that I understood him very well" (GER20)

The results in Table 3.16 are similar to those in Table 3.13, with the exception of the second option, adaptations in idioms and colloquial language. Here German learners seem much less certain of their partners' adaptations. In Transcript 3.16, GER11's comment reflects a central idea of the Vygotskian ZPD that I presented in section 1, sub-section 1.1.2. Some learners do not want input modification to go too far: for them, TL input still needs to be beyond their current proficiency level for learning to take place. A two-sample t-test with an alpha level of 0.05 was carried out to show whether there was any significant correlation between received modifications and given modifications, between Tables 3.13 and Table 3.16 on the one hand, and Table 3.14 and Table 3.15 on the other hand. For both pairs, the differences suggest that there is a correlation between the various categories.

In summary, the German group, as could be expected, had to modify input much more than the Irish group. It is remarkable how well both groups seem able to assess each other's perceptions regarding the amount of input modifications. There are no clear preferences for particular areas of input modification over others, although some Irish students mention slang and colloquialisms. Although it is difficult to assess the actual input modification in transcript data, these results for one of the core principles of tandem learning are encouraging. They show that learners, even with widely diverging levels of proficiency, seem well able to adapt to each other. Input modification in foreigner talk is one of the central preconditions for learning in the ZPD.

3.3.5 Bilingualism

As I noted in sub-section 1.2.3, one of the core principles of tandem learning is bilingualism. In our evaluation of an e-mail tandem project (Little et al., 1999) we mentioned that bilingualism in e-mail tandem is important to make sure that both partners receive an equal amount of TL input and are required to produce TL output.

I have repeatedly referred to the imbalance in MOO transcripts between English and German content. This has several obvious reasons. First, we noted that there was a large imbalance in L2 proficiency levels between the two groups, to the extent that both learner groups perceived communication in English as non-problematic and simple (cf. sub-section 3.3.4). Second, although we had created bilingual support for four topics, the rest of the MOO interface, such as its command language and object names, is displayed exclusively in English. There is evidence in the transcripts that a number of German learners communicated with one another, sometimes outside scheduled class sessions, in the TL (English) without any prompting from their teacher. Third, it is difficult to say what we mean by equal amounts of both languages when we are talking about a synchronous medium; do we mean equal amounts of time spent on composition; equal amount of utterances; or equal amounts of text length in the TL? Several transcripts show that students switched from English to German immediately after it was announced by one of the teachers and continued to communicate in that language until the end of the session. Nevertheless, the length of the German transcript part would be substantially shorter than the English text, because of the proficiency differences we mentioned above. We found that on the one hand, learners simply had no tool for monitoring their bilingualism; on the other hand, learners did not have to focus on projects that had a particular bilingual outcome, a specific goal.

In a separate but similar MOO project one year later with Irish and German learners, my colleague O'Rourke (2002) looked at bilingualism in the transcripts and came to the conclusion that it was indeed very imbalanced. Pooled across all sessions, learners used 84% English and only 16% German (see Transcript 3.15). This gave us both the first real indication how imbalanced the exchanges were. I wondered whether a technological tool would help, and how much pedagogical support would be necessary. In Appel and Mullen's e-mail tandem web site, they had built in tools that gave learners feedback on how much they used both languages, and, if necessary, reminded them to make adjustments. On the basis of my design specifications, Alexandre Borgia then programmed the Bilingual Tandem Analyser (BTA), which was used for the first time in a MOO project in 2002-03. Detailed results from this project were published elsewhere (Kapec & Schwienhorst, 2005; Schwienhorst & Borgia, 2006), so I will just summarise the major points here.

When a learner connects to the MOO for the first time, the BTA will ask her to select the native language and the L2 from drop-down lists. The BTA then automatically analyses data as soon as learners produce an utterance and press the ENTER key. Utterances are analysed using n-gram analysis (Cavnar & Trenkle, 1994). At any point during a MOO session can the learner call up statistics on language proportions, as well as average word and sentence length. When a learner re-connects, she is automatically

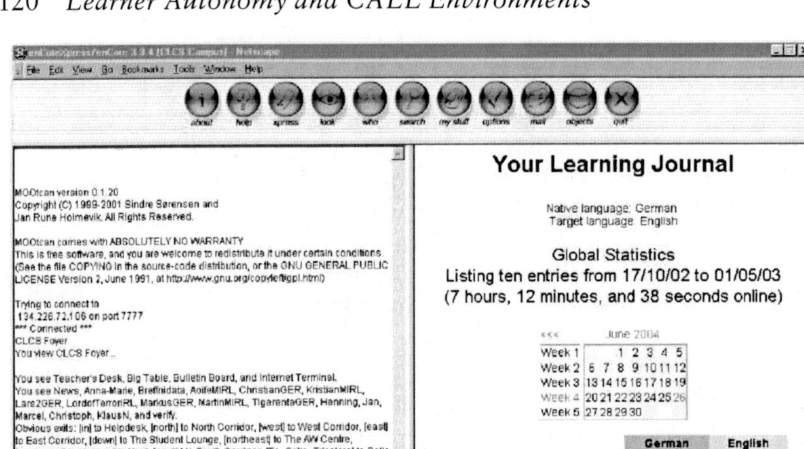

Figure 3.1 A sample screenshot of the MOO with the BTA.

presented with the statistics, and she can call up overall statistics, or statistics calculated by day, week, month, etc. (see Figure 3.1)

We did not yet provide reminders of imbalance, but these could be implemented quite easily. My first major concern was whether this tool would be exact in analysing utterances. I was fortunate in that I had

Table 3.17 Comparison between machine & manually parsed results (based on 97 transcripts, O'Rourke, 2002)

	No. of English utterances	*English (%)*		*No. of German utterances*	*German (%)*	
		Manual	*Auto*		*Manual*	*Auto*
Session A	460	76	75	143	24	24
Session B	440	73	73	166	27	26
Session C	331	87	86	48	13	13
Session D	604	97	96	20	3	3
Session E	416	86	84	69	14	15
Session F	292	90	87	33	10	12
Pooled across sessions	2543	84	83	479	16	16

Table 3.18 Bilingual proportions of English (E) and German (G) in global statistics

Student group	*Global statistics average (E:G %)*	*Number of global statistics in 30:70 range*
2000–01	76:23	15 out of 60 (25%); 6 Irish (23%), 9 German (26%)
2002–03	63:36	16 out of 30 (53%);8 Irish (67%), 8 German (44%)

O'Rourke's manual analysis data at my disposal, and I used his data for comparison. Second, I wondered whether the tool would have an effect on bilingualism, i.e. would learners be more balanced in the use of the two languages?

We can see that the tool, both per session and in total, is very close to the manual results O'Rourke arrived at. There are only two major discrepancies in sessions E and F, where the automatic analysis is off by 2 and 3%. The remaining sessions, however, are at most 1% off. This clearly indicates that the BTA analyses at least English and German very accurately.

In my second question, I looked at whether the BTA would by itself lead to substantial changes in bilingualism. I determined a generous proportion of 70:30/30:70 as a range of acceptable language proportions, and looked at the overall (global) statistics for individual students. These were the statistics that were presented to the students automatically when they connected, so each student, whether they called up daily, weekly, or monthly statistics during a session, saw these statistics at the beginning of each session by default. The results of these statistics can therefore be considered more relevant than the results from individual sessions (see Table 3.18). If we consider someone in the 70:30 range as successful, we can rewrite the table as shown in Table 3.19.

Thus, there is a statistically significant improvement in the global score. The biggest contribution is that Irish students do far better. The German students also improve, but the contribution to the elevated Chi-Sq is less.

The average global statistics are much more balanced between the two languages in the 2002–03 group than the 2000–01 group. The number of global statistics by students is probably the most dramatic result: more than double the percentage of participating students (53% compared to

Table 3.19 Successful and unsuccessful sessions in global statistics

Student group	*Successful sessions*	*Unsuccessful sessions*	*Total sessions*
2000–01	15	45	60
2002–03	16	14	30

Chi-Sq = 7.110; DF = 1, P-Value = 0.008

25%) in the 2002-03 project with the BTA was now in the prescribed 70:30 range, a substantial improvement over the 2000–01 group. When I looked at the actual partnerships, I noticed that in three out of the 6 1+2 learner groups in 2002–03 all participants had imbalanced bilingualism, whereas in 1+1 dyads there was at least always one learner within the 70:30 range. It seems, therefore, that tandem dyads are less likely to become imbalanced than 2+1 groups.

In summary, I can say that the imbalance in bilingualism can be improved substantially by using a computerised tool such as the BTA. Although learners are quite aware of a general imbalance, especially when there is a big difference between their L2 proficiencies, they depend on their partner's support and encouragement to use the TL more. While this was done in many exchanges, and in various ways (see sub-section 3.3.2), additional tools such as the BTA are needed and often desired by the learners to give them more support in structuring the session and secure equal amounts of L1 and L2. Other pedagogical tools are possible, such as preparatory work before the sessions, or during and after the sessions with (possibly collaborative) asynchronous tasks that focus learners' attention on the bilingual element of their exchange. In this context, the extended and more systematic use of the diary/notebook can serve to increase learners' awareness and encourage more TL use.

3.3.6 Summary analysis of data on interaction

In this section, I have focused on various aspects of interaction and collaboration in MOO tandem partnerships. I have examined topic negotiation, error correction, repair strategies, input modifications, and bilingualism. In terms of topic negotiation, I noted that learners discussed a wide variety of topics. These included aspects of personal life, aspects of intercultural comparisons between Germany and Ireland, aspects of information technology, and aspects of course work. Clearly, many learners' comments show that they perceived "chit-chat" as least beneficial in terms of learning. MOO discourse was thus content-driven, dealing with topics that were perceived as personally meaningful to the learners.

I then examined briefly the issue of topic initiation. Here, I noted that topics were initiated much more often in English than in German. This is not surprising, given the imbalance in bilingualism. However, it was unusual to see that the difference between native speakers and non-native speakers in topic initiation is not as high as could be expected from previous research, for instance by Long, who reported that in native speaker/non-native speaker discourse, more topics are initiated by the native speaker. While most topic initiations are introduced by a question, this percentage is not as high as in Long's study of native speaker/non-native speaker discourse, but rather tends towards native speaker/native speaker discourse. These results are unusual and could indicate that topic initiation in MOO tandem creates a stress-reduced atmosphere where non-native speakers are encouraged to take more initiative.

Second, I looked at error correction. I noted that there is very little evidence in transcripts of error correction or meta-talk regarding error correction. In commenting on error correction, very few partnerships are able to assess adequately the areas they corrected or that were corrected. However, learners may have misunderstood the question to extend to other forms of reciprocal support. In general, error correction was often perceived as an interruption to the communicative flow, and that many learners did not see error correction as part of their partner's role. Other forms of reciprocal support, such as encouragement to communicate, were used frequently throughout the project and may play a bigger part in MOO tandem.

Third, I looked in more detail at repair strategies. As these directly affected communicative flow, they were far more important to learners than error correction. There was some confirmation of Donaldson and Kötter's (1999) findings that evasive strategies were rarely used. In my questionnaire, the German group expressed a preference for paraphrasing, whereas Irish students preferred translation; this result is probably related to the differences in TL proficiency. However, the transcripts show that translation was the actual repair strategy that was used most frequently. More clarification requests were made by non-native speakers. In general, we can see that the use of repair strategies shows that both groups, in spite of their differences in TL proficiency, worked towards the most effective strategies. In this respect, learners tended to adapt their repair strategies to their partners' preferences. Clearly, the use of repair strategies demonstrates reciprocal processes of adaptation and scaffolding.

Fourth, when looking at input modifications, I found that learners show a remarkable ability for adaptation. As I expected, input modification by the German group was much more pronounced, although Irish learners were still able to identify a number of areas where they also had to modify their input. Finally, I looked at bilingualism, a core principle of tandem learning. I noted that bilingualism is difficult to quantify in MOO discourse. However, while it is safe to say that the majority of transcripts in the 1999–2000 study shows an imbalance in bilingualism, this problem was addressed with the introduction of the Bilingual Tandem Analyser in 2002–03. Not only was this tool very accurate in its analysis of the languages used, but it also provided learners — to my knowledge, for the first time — with a real-time tool to monitor their bilingualism in synchronous text-based communication. From my data, I can say that the introduction of the tool had a noticeable effect on proportions of bilingualism. There is also some evidence that balanced bilingual exchanges were more likely to occur in pair work than in small group work, and more likely in established tandem pairs than in temporary partnerships (e.g. formed because one partner was absent).

3.4 MULTIPLE SOURCES OF EVIDENCE FOR EXPERIMENTATION

In this final section, I want to look at various instances where learners actively experiment with the learning environment. Through experimentation and participation the learner takes control of her learning and determines the learning agenda. There are two obvious areas where they can experiment. First, there is the CALL environment which allows learners to "build" and experiment with objects, although we did not have time to formally introduce them to the way this is done. This includes the learners' virtual character. Second, learner can use a shared mental model of an environment, which should open the door for situated language use. The use of indexical language is linked with authenticity and particularly face-to-face communication, but plays by definition a much more subdued role in telephone or other distance communication modes where no environment is physically or virtually shared.

In the following two sections, I will therefore look first at object creations and virtual identities, before I move on to look at some examples of indexical language in the transcript corpus. I will conclude this sub-section with a look at control in the MOO. Taking control of the learning process is one of the declared goals of learner autonomy, and I will explore how learners feel in control in the MOO as compared to classroom situations or face-to-face contacts with native speakers.

3.4.1 Object creation

Because of organisational difficulties, we did not have the time in the 1999–2000 project to support our learners appropriately in creating new objects, and changing their virtual identity. Only one of the learners changed his online name (GER18), and very few changes were made to personal descriptions beyond setting the gender and similar basics that we encouraged.

We found that 5 Irish students created a total of 9 objects, whereas 13 German students created a total of 51 objects. Four German learners created rooms with descriptions in the TL, but most objects were created from a generic bot which I described in sub-section 2.1.3. One of these object creations deserves a closer look.

GER15 programmed a bot named "Bender Unit 22". The name is taken from a cartoon series called "Futurama", where Bender is the name of a robot. Transcripts show that the learner was personally interested in the programme. In the series, the robot has a number of catch-phrases, which GER15 subsequently transferred into the bot's repertoire. The bot would then be able to react to the appropriate keywords when activated. GER15 also deleted existing keywords, so that only the new keywords would activate responses. Table 3.20 contains the keywords the learner programmed, and their responses.

Table 3.20 Keywords and automatic responses for Bender Unit 22 (Object data)

Keywords	*Responses*
good	You kiddin'? I was a star once...I could bend a gourd the angle of 30 degrees..32 degrees...you name it....31
bye	Well man it was a pleasure meetin' ya...I'm gonna go kill myself.
look	I'm not lookin'...
bend	Seems like one of us has to bend 'dis.
kill	Come on, come on, kill me already.
give	Bring it on, baby.
name	By the way, my name's Bender.
program	I'm a Bender...I bend things...that's what I was programmed for.
hi	Welcome home, pal!
drink	Let's go have a drink...all for me.
sing	A robot would have to be crazy to be wanting to be a folk singer.
do	I'm trying to.
cigar	Cigars just make me look cool.
cool	Cigars just make me look cool.
jerk	Everbody is a jerk...you...me...that guy over there...
grins	Don't grin at me...not even with desperate need.
yes	so?
no	Allright.
help	No one is gonna help you, now...let's get drunk.
never	Never? What time-period is that?
thanks	You're welcome...at least.

Here we can find an illustration of how MOO objects can become a cognitive tool for language learning. In a process of exploration, the learner found out how to program the bot with phrases from a fictional character on a TV show. It indicates that the student not only found a personally meaningful subject for his studies (he also discussed "Futurama" with his tandem partner), but also presupposes that the learner showed initiative to take down the relevant phrases from the TV program. The task the learner got involved in was actually very complex: finding out the appropriate words that would trigger phrases as answers, thus dealing with difficult questions of how discourse is organised. This example shows how powerful MOO objects can be for language learning; the use of bots alone, which can also be re-programmed in more detail, can supply learners with a flexible tool to experiment with language.

It must be said that some of the other bots that were created by learners increasingly caused confusion among learners. As they used the limited selection of pre-programmed keywords and responses, their responses quickly became repetitive and seriously impeded the communication flow between tandem partners in some sessions. There is evidence from the transcripts that some learners collected and deactivated bots when they disturbed communication. In addition, some bots were named after learners or teachers (note that the only difference between these and the representation of the real character was an added full stop). This caused some confusion among students, and some learners whose names had been "hijacked", reported to me during one particular session, so that I had to collect the relevant bots and deactivate them. In subsequent projects, we included the issue of creating bots in our awareness-raising sessions, to alert learners to the fact that creating bots can be a sensitive issue.

Although the other bots were not modified from their default responses, there are some examples in the transcripts where their responses fitted the context and where learners even replied to them (see Transcript 3.17)

Transcript 3.17 Instances of learners replying to bots (transcript data)

11/11/99:
Buffy says, "Who would call himself 'Stefan' anyway?" [...]
IRL16 says, "Why is she being so mean to eveeryone?" [...]
Buffy says, "[IRL16]: I am not mean"
GER11 says, "Buffy is somewhat programmed of the person called [GER18], it is no real person"
IRL16 says, "GER11 where are you?"
Buffy says, "I'm just a poor little bot programmed to answer to anything people say"

18/11/99:
GER16 IRL23 what did u do on the weekend ?
Prof.Neunast says, "That's an interesting question..."
IRL22 says, "Who or what is Prof Neunast""
Prof.Neunast [to [IRL22]]: Don't you know?
IRL2 says, "hey prof"
Prof.Neunast says, "So, you call 'CLCS Foyer' your home?"
IRL22 says, "No""

25/11/99:
Peter Kapec says, "I think The Violet Room is an excellent name for this place, dont you?"
GER15 says, "[IRL21] is ill today"
GER15 hushes Peter Kapec.
Peter Kapec says, "Suppose [IRL21] were not ill today? What then?"

IRL17 says, "OK. It's a great name for this room. I think [IRL21] just finds it difficult to get up in the mornings"

IRL14 says, "What the fuck is going on now? [GER10 misspelt] are you talking to me?"
[GER1.] [to IRL14]: What is so going on now [GER10 misspelt] are you talking to me about fuck?
GER16 arrives from East Corridor
IRL14 says, "Sorry didn't mean to curse, just got a little confused"
GER16 picks up [GER1.].
[GER1.] says, "hmm, is that so.."
GER16 leaves for East Corridor
IRL14 says, "[GER1.], who ever you are, you have a dirty mind"
GER22 says, "what did he say?"
IRL14 says, "It's not what he said, it's what he implied"

Jennifer Lopez says, "I think The Green Room is an excellent name for this place, dont you?"
GER16 leaves for North Corridor
IRL20 says, "yes very original"

Note that student IRL14 even ascribes human-like qualities such as intentionality and deception to a very simple AI implementation, and this in spite of the grave grammatical errors. In one case, it became problematic for the German teacher (Peter) to establish his identity (see Transcript 3.18).

Transcript 3.18 Instance of teacher identitiy and bot (transcript data)

Peter says, "Hello, this is the real Peter Kapec here"
Peter Kapec says, "Suppose this were not the real Peter Kapec here? What then?"
Peter says, "Get off my name!!"
Peter Kapec says, "What about your name?"
Peter says, "There aren't many Peter Kapec's around"
GER1 Peter Hey, Just ANYONE could call himself "the REAL Peter"....

These examples show that although the bots are very crude implementations of AI, they can appear to be quite "lifelike", even with their default settings. We could, of course, interpret them as problematic, as some learners felt they were in some way cheated when they found out. In several MOO sessions with bots and in some interviews and diary entries learners voice their annoyance at bots. However, a more purposeful experimentation with bots as demonstrated by GER15 could open the door to a tool for experimentation that can clearly contribute to language learning in general and support linguistic awareness.

3.4.2 MOO identity

In sub-section 2.1.1 I argued that a certain amount of detachment from the learning process leads to increased levels of linguistic awareness. I also indicated that we need to consider how learners perceive the relationship between their real-life character and their virtual counterpart. I explored this issue further in the interviews where I asked: "Would you say your online character differed from the real-life character? If so, how?" (also see Schwienhorst, 2004a).

Transcript 3.19 Virtual identity versus real-life character (interview data)

IRL1 says, "No I don't think so also when other Irish students were in the same room they seemed the same as always"

IRL5 says, "Ye3ah,i suppose by being online i tried to get as much reaction from the Germans as possible"

IRL9 says, "not really i say what i think and i think i did this for my moo conversations"

IRL11 says, "well, I never thought of it as a different character. but, I suppose for the reasons I already stated, I was alot more confident on the moo, than conversing aloud in german."

IRL12 says, " of course you wouldn't tell a person on line the things you would tell a person that is your friend in real life" [...]
IRL12 says, " being honest I Didn't really talk much german over the MOO but no when I did I didn't behave differently"

IRL15 says, "i suppose maybe a little"
IRL15 says, "because you can make up stuff which can be kindof amusing"
You say, "how?"
You say, "make up stuff?"
IRL15 says, "i didnt really do it that much"
IRL15 says, "what i mean is that you dont have to be 100% honest about trivial things like your appearance etc."

IRL16 says, "I don't think my character changed,although I wasn't as confident as it is a native German we are speaking with!" [...]
IRL16 says, "Also ,If learning is made fun,you will actually enjoy it!" [...]
IRL16 says, "It isn't as bad as sitting down for hours learning off a Grammar book"

IRL23 says, "Thats a tough one!!"
You say, "for instance, when you compare it to talking in German to the assistants"

IRL23 says, "em, I think so, because I was face to face with my Moo partner I was less worried about saying something stupid, so I said more!" [...]
IRL23 says, "sorry, I mean not face to face"

IRL26 says, "probably not, because i irc quite a lot with my friends in 'real' life who happen to be working instead of in college..."
IRL26 says, "as a result, i'm more myself as i'm very used to this kind of thing"
IRL26 says, "i'm not sure how it would be for other people...i'm just asking [IRL29]" [...]
IRL26 says, "she said she didnt pretend to be someone else, but she found it hard to let her true character come through, due to lack of german" [...]
IRL26 says, "people are less shy online"

GER1 says, "I think it did."
You say, "how so?"
GER1 says, "Maybe I tried to appear more self confident, or more competent hmm, just "cooler".."

This question was understood on several levels. First, some learners interpreted it as being able to express their personality (IRL1, IRL9, IRL26); while IRL29 (as reported by IRL26), found this difficult. Second, some learners emphasised increased levels of self-confidence when compared to face-to-face communication with native speakers (IRL11, IRL23, GER1) or less self-confidence (IRL16; this learner emphasises the fact that communicating with a native speaker was more challenging). IRL15 mentions that appearance does not matter on the MOO, so learners can represent themselves differently. IRL5 comments on her increased initiative on the MOO. Some learners (IRL1, IRL9, IRL12, IRL26) did not report any differences between themselves and their real-life character.

On the one hand, therefore, learners themselves perceive a difference between their online character and their real persona. On the other hand, it is encouraging to note that many learners feel that they can express themselves adequately on the MOO and that virtual character and real personality are seen as a unity. This is also shown in the fact that many learners were irritated when other learners created bots with their names (see section 3.4.1). The fact that the majority of learners perceived their partners as genuine in their representation also contributes to authenticity in this, albeit virtual, environment.

3.4.3 Indexicality

In sub-section 1.1.3, I discussed the notion of indexicality in the context of situated learning. One of the advantages of CALL environments is that

Table 3.21 Instances of "here" and "hier" in the transcript corpus

	Virtual	*Real*	*Ambiguous*	*MOO generated*	*Total*
"here"	795	266	331	569	1961
"hier	191	89	3	-	283

a shared environment enables learners to include indexical language in synchronous communication, thereby creating social presence and shared mental models of space. In order to find out how this is reflected in the transcript corpus, I looked at instances of the words "here" and its German equivalent "hier" (also see Schwienhorst, 2004a). In the following table, I have summarised whether these refer to the virtual environment, the respective real-life classroom, or whether they are used ambiguously. I have also included a section for instances that are generated by the MOO program (which refer to the virtual environment). Table 3.21 includes duplicates, as the transcript corpus contains at least two records of each conversation.

The categories "ambiguous" and "MOO generated" were removed for the purpose of statistical testing. A chi-square test was used, and the differences between the "virtual" and "real" group were significant ($p < 0.05$). For both "here" and "hier", the vast majority of instances in the corpus refers to the virtual environment. It is also noticeable that when "here" and "hier" were used to refer to the real-life context, it was often specified further as in "here in Dublin" or "here in St. Augustin". The results for "here" and "hier" indicate a form of presence as discussed in section 2 (presence as "being there"). Learners form a mental model of the environment that is reflected in their use of indexicality.

I only looked at the distribution of "here" and "hier" in this corpus, but more research clearly could be carried out. A more detailed look at indexicality, possibly combined with a look at the use of tenses, can provide us with important insights into learners' mental models. Again, this confirms what I emphasised at various points in sub-section 2.1.3: learners become more absorbed and more focused in (even text-based) CALL environments than in many other face-to-face or computerised contexts. The here-and now orientation of MOO discourse allows learners to draw on the immediate environment to interpret their partners' utterances.

3.4.4 Control and freedom

Aarseth and Jopp (1998) refer to the various mechanisms of freedom/control and pressure/challenge involved in MOO tandem learning. The reciprocal tandem partnership, where learners constantly need to adapt to their partners' language level and preferred learning strategies to enable communication, allows and in many cases forces learners to take control of their learning process, define goals, work out how to approach them, monitor the learning process, and evaluate whether the goals have been reached.

In this sub-section, I have come full circle to one of the central ideas of learner autonomy — assuming responsibility for and taking control of one's learning. In the interviews, I asked learners: "How much did you feel in control of the learning situation in the MOO, as compared to the classroom or a real face-to-face situation with a German speaker?"

Transcript 3.20 Control and freedom in MOO tandem learning (interview data)

IRL1 says, "I felt very much in control because you can decide what to work on but leaving students to their own devices with no outline could be dangerous-nothing would get done, It was good to have those outlines because it gave us somewhere to start and something to talk about. It might be an idea to broaden that section but not make it compulsary"
You say, "yeah we tried to keep the topics open as much as possible..."
You say, "How would you compare the MOO to other experiences you had with native speakers?"
You say, "In terms of control"
IRL1 says, "I haven't had much expierence with native speakers but in the MOO these people don't know you and it's probably a bit easier- to make mistakes, or say things or suggest topics without feeling stupid"

IRL5 says, "I felt much more in control...as I was not face to face""
IRL5 says, "it didn` matter so much then"
You say, "how does face to face influence things?"
IRL5 says, "O you know,I stumble on words and my accent is bad so.."

IRL9 says, "it was similar you can easily talk to anyone else logged on and if u needed help you just had to ask"
You say, "how would you compare it to the classroom in terms of determining what you wanted to do?"
IRL9 says, "yeah i could see it being hard toactually get some work done if the rest of the people in the room did not want too"

IRL11 says, "well in the classroom the learning is controlled by the lecturer/teacher. If I was speaking to a german face 2 face, I personally would feel more victimised than anything!!!! since it is such a trial for me to converse in German!!! I would not be in control at all. I would just be trying to answer questions rather than asking them. but I suppose the more I converse in German ,the more I get better at it. At least in the moo I could start conversations, or confidently bring up topics, beacuse I knew I could get by with my english vocabulary , so I wouldnt get stuck. "

IRL12 says, " Well I knew I could ask my partner any queries I had so I felt pretty in control"

IRL16 says, "Sadly I felt better using the MOO"
You say, "why?"
IRL16 says, "You are not as concious when you are sending info through a computer" [...]
IRL16 says, "You don;t know if the other person is laughing at you or not... and you don't really care either because you can't see them"
IRL16 says, "You are then more relxed" [...]
IRL16 says, "So you don't mind if you make mistakes" [...]
You say, "where would you say you had more control about what you did, in class or in the MOO?"
IRL16 says, "In the Moo"
You say, "why?"
IRL16 says, "In the MOO ,it was one to one so you didn't have anyone distracting you. "
You say, "I see" [...]
IRL16 says, "Inthe class there are people around and it is hard to concentrate"

IRL23 says, "I think I feel more in contol in the classroom, because it is easier to ask questions and get answers" [...]
IRL23 says, "Well i found it quite easy to talk about what I was interested. I was lucky enough that we were both quite interested in a lot of the same thigs. But it is quite easy to change the topic of conversation and steer it in another direction. "

IRL26 says, "well, i felt a lot more in control than when i'd be in the classroom.... if i wanted to speak german, i'd just speak it, even if i was being talked to in english"
IRL26 says, "in the class, if you try to speak german, most people tell you to stop cos they dont understand" [...]
IRL26 says, "now..in terms of face to face..."
IRL26 says, "i felt more relaxed than face to face, cos i didnt have to worry about my pronounciation"
IRL26 says, "i'm not sure about control, in that situation" [...]
You say, "is that a drawback or an advantage of text?"
IRL26 says, "but i was more forthcoming with german on the moo, than i'd be in a face to face situation"
IRL26 says, "definitely a disadvantage, because myself and indeed a lot of others in the class..."
IRL26 says, "dont have too much confidence speaking german out loud and those presentations are sheer hell :)"

GER1 says, "the pressure to be fast, exact and correct is much bigger in class."

Given the results of the previous sub-sections and the open structure of the MOO sessions, the overwhelming preference for the MOO, in terms of control, is not surprising. However, the issue of control is not only related to the open structure of the project. In Transcript 3.20, learners mention several reasons for their preference of the MOO:

- communication was not face-to-face (the face-saving nature of MOO discourse)
- communication was in text (learners did not have to focus on pronunciation)
- there was less peer pressure when communicating in the TL
- more relaxed atmosphere
- easy to receive immediate support
- encourages learners to take initiative (asking questions instead of just answering)

For IRL9, the MOO is similar, although his comments show that successful project work depends on similarly purposeful partners. IRL23 prefers the classroom as it gives her more evaluative support. IRL11's use of "classroom" as opposed to the MOO sessions is just one of many examples where students contrast MOO sessions and classroom learning like that. It indicates just how deeply rooted learners' beliefs are about classroom learning. If something is perceived as enjoyable as the MOO, it is not seen as classroom learning.

3.4.5 Summary analysis of data on experimentation

I noted in sub-section 3.1.2 that both institutional frameworks left very little time for additional sessions outside class. Because of organisational difficulties, we were unable to adequately support our students in experimenting more with the MOO environment. Under these circumstances, learners created very few objects or experimented with them.

First, I looked at object creations. Very little experimentation went on with objects, apart from creating and renaming them. One notable exception occurred when a German learner created a bot, a virtual version of a cartoon character from a well-known American animation series. This learner meticulously reprogrammed the bot's automatic replies and replaced them with the catch-phrases of the animated character (in the L2). This can be seen as an example where a learner created a cognitive tool as described in sub-section 1.1.1, an artefact that is personally meaningful and allows for open-ended and creative experimentation with language. A variety of other bots were also created.

However, the actual implementation of these bots was sometimes problematic. As some of the examples show, some learners were confused and unable to distinguish between peers or partners and bots, and annoyed or irritated when they found out that their names had been used for some of them. Here, more structure and support by teachers is clearly required, although object creation in itself is certainly not a technical problem any more.

Second, I looked at the issue of virtual identity. Several learners reported that they were well able to express their personality adequately in the MOO medium, and some learners expressed increased self-confidence. Consequently, a virtual identity may encourage learners to take more risks and initiative. In addition, perceiving their partners as genuine contributes to an authentic environment.

Third, I focused on indexicality as an expression of a shared environment. I only looked at two indexical words in the corpus, "here" and "hier", and explored whether these referred to physical reality or the virtual environment. The instances were significantly related to the virtual environment, a strong indication that learners' mental models changed towards a "third place", a shared (albeit virtual) environment. More research on indexicality is needed, but it promises to be a useful and rewarding area to show the differences between virtual environments and two-way conferencing modes.

Fourth, I returned to one of the core issues of learner autonomy: taking control of the learning process. In the majority of cases, learners preferred the MOO over ordinary classroom sessions in terms of control. This may be attributed to the open structure of the project, but learners' comments confirm previous observations in sub-section 3.2.2 that the immediacy of support, the written medium, and a more egalitarian engagement in the learning process were the most important factors for learners when assuming responsibility for and taking control over their learning process.

Experimentation with objects should form an essential part of MOO tandem work, although learners must be enabled to implement them in meaningful contexts. My discussion of indexicality and control points towards two particular strengths of MOO tandem work. First, the use of indexicality shows that learners in a virtual environment share the same reference points and the same mental model for communication. This is a distinct advantage of virtual environments over point-to-point conferencing modes, which by definition exclude the dimension of a shared space. Second, my discussion of control shows that the (synchronous) MOO tandem partnership, even more than (asynchronous) e-mail tandem, forces learners to assume responsibility for and take control over their learning process, a notion which lies at the heart of learner autonomy.

4 Where We Go from Here

In Chapter 1, I defined the concept of learner autonomy and suggested three interrelated principles that should guide any learner-autonomy-based pedagogy: reflection; interaction; and experimentation. I also introduced one of the implementations of learner autonomy principles, tandem learning. In Chapter 2, I argued how CALL environments can help achieve the goals of learner autonomy. Building on the existing research literature, I presented a number of features that make CALL environments, from a theoretical point of view, particularly useful in the process of supporting learner autonomy. I also introduced the MOO system in particular as an example of a CALL environment that supports learner autonomy. Chapter 3 presented research data from my MOO projects, organised according to the three areas of reflection, interaction, and experimentation. My analysis provided some expected and some rather surprising results. In this the final chapter of this book, I will reconsider and review the theory of and the principles behind a learner-autonomy-based pedagogy in the light of my own and my colleagues' empirical research. What are the lessons to be learned from the data? Where do we need to provide more technological and pedagogical support, and what form can this take? How can we usefully connect learner autonomy principles and CALL environments, and how has our research influenced both pedagogical principles and the design of CALL environments? Where are shortcomings in our pedagogy, where do we feel the need for more technological support?

In the second part, I will discuss various CALL tools and pedagogical concepts that we might use (and integrate) to fill the perceived gaps in the four areas of reflection, interaction, experimentation, and teacher autonomy. The third and last part deals with the relationship between CALL technology and a learner-autonomy-based pedagogy. Can software by itself guarantee the support of learner autonomy, or even work against it? Conversely, can learner autonomy be supported without CALL?

4.1 LEARNER AUTONOMY AND REFLECTION

4.1.1 Reflection in the MOO

In the first two chapters, I looked at the importance of reflection and awareness in language learning. In short, the demands of learner autonomy in this area can be summarised as follows: CALL pedagogy and environments need to have mechanisms to support language, metalinguistic, and metacognitive awareness; CALL software needs to support, even force learners to confront their own planning, monitoring, and evaluation in language learning.

First, I think we need to acknowledge that the opportunities for reflection while learners are engaged in synchronous communication (whether text-based or not) are generally less than in non-synchronous communication. My research in general has shown that there is always a primacy of communicative flow; limited time for utterance composition and decoding means that learners can dedicate less time to reflective processes while communicating. Second, written communication, in whatever form, offers opportunities for reflection that we simply do not have in oral speech. More about this later.

As we have seen, there are opportunities for reflection while communicating live (i.e. online) or afterwards (i.e. off-line). I would argue that in these two distinct situations, reflection can be supported by sometimes predominantly technological, and sometimes predominantly pedagogical tools. Let us first focus on opportunities for reflection while learners are engaged in interaction.

First, there is evidence in my research that learners read through their own and their partner's input on screen (after utterance composition). My colleague O'Rourke (2005) has recently demonstrated quite succinctly how learners monitor their own and their partner's output in the MOO during communication. The fact that the MOO makes a limited amount of the interaction still available to both learners makes it easier for learners to monitor, and subsequently maybe "notice" (Schmidt, 1990; Sharwood Smith, 1996) data; a learning process that has been argued to lead to intake. This is a definite advantage of the MOO over oral speech that stems from its nature as written discourse, and the MOO's feature of presenting a certain amount of "speech" in a scrolling window on screen.

But there are also differences between MOO and e-mail writing. While e-mail writing can involve complex processes of editing and re-editing before communicating, MOO discourse happens under some time pressure. Learners want to communicate quickly, and there is neither a pedagogical nor a technological tool yet that hinders them to send off an utterance full of errors. As one student indicated, MOO discourse is like speaking while composing an utterance, but like writing once the utterance appears on screen. This may be a difference I had not considered when starting this research, nor is there enough empirical evidence in my data to claim this is even as much as a tendency. However, it appears to be a useful area to explore further; it may present an explanation for the lack of reflection in composing an utterance, an area that certainly needs more support.

I could think of a whole range of technological tools to support reflection while learners are communicating, and some have already been implemented. These are not vapourware, but are deemed feasible and are currently being planned. The MOO, in principle, allows for formatting options for the output window, including the use of colours. At one extreme, we could have minimal interference with the interaction, by introducing a spell-checking facility while a learner composes a message, or after the utterance has been sent off, then displaying the utterance with the errors marked in a different colour on screen. At the other extreme, we could prevent learners from even sending off or displaying messages with misspelt words, or utterances that are deemed ungrammatical. Clearly, the right balance needs to be found here, not only to support careful editing to eliminate errors, but also to support the re-use of new vocabulary. And after all, these tools should not interfere with or even break the communicative flow that learners establish.

What this discussion leads us to, of course, is the development, implementation, and evaluation of intelligent feedback systems in MOOs and other CALL environments. With the Bilingual Tandem Analyser (BTA), MOO learners now have a tool that gives them accurate feedback on the language proportions used. While this primarily aids interaction (see my next section), initial research also shows that it makes learners more aware of the bilingual principle of tandem learning (Schwienhorst & Borgia, 2006; also see Kapec & Schwienhorst, 2005). Another tool is the shared whiteboard, which we developed in 2004 and which supports learners in processes of noticing when collaborating on texts. The program has various editing features and keeps track of each change that was made in a log file which can be viewed by students and researchers. In this way, the development of a text with all its revisions becomes visible.

There are also pedagogical tools to support reflection while learners are communicating. We can create tasks and activities in which learners have to discuss language and/or language learning explicitly. My colleague O'Rourke (2002) explored this further in his thesis, by introducing a reformulation task. Learners created a text off-line in the target language, sent it to their tandem partner for reformulation; both then discussed the changes/reformulations in the MOO, explicitly focusing on grammar, idiomatic phrases, etc. In later projects, we used a fairytale task, where we gave learners only a starting point ("Once upon a time....") and they alternated in adding sentences. The native speaker then edited and reformulated the story and discussed the changes explicitly with her partner (also see Kapec, 2004). These are all suggested improvements to support reflection in online, synchronous work.

We can, of course, also imagine both more technological and pedagogical support afterwards, in an offline or asynchronous mode. Let us look first at some technology-based tools in off-line work. Since we implemented the BTA, the MOO system "knows" which utterance is produced by which user; whether the utterance is produced by a native speaker or learner; and which native and target language the learner has. The BTA can be used at any time, also offline, to monitor the learner's development of bilingualism. It would be easy to implement a mechanism that automatically tags, archives and assigns each utterance to a database/corpus that is literally expanding with each new user connection. One might expect that this poses far less problems than audio or video corpora. After all, all MOO transcripts contain (if we also add time-stamps for each utterance) the complete communication that took place. This is certainly true, but we also know that learners in chat systems produce many typographical errors, have ways of expressing stress (e.g. "I am SOOOO bored!"), intonation (e.g. "Byyyyyeeeeeee"), pauses (e.g. "hmmm....dunno"), dialect or slang (e.g. "you da man") etc. In other words, learners intentionally and unintentionally produce words and utterances that, if transferred directly into learner or native speaker text corpora, will not be found by researchers or other students if not tagged/coded in some way or at least pose problems for conventional concordancing tasks.

One solution would be that the corpus only accepts words it knows, which would, of course, ignore the great variety of expressive online interaction that learners produce. Another option would be to include a spell-checking device such as that described above that would either check MOO utterances in the process of composition or after they were sent to the MOO via the ENTER-key, before the utterances are added to the corpus. Yet other options would be to get all utterances corrected automatically, or manually, or tag them manually, or just accept all utterances, regardless of individual spelling. This should suffice to indicate that there are many challenges for the design and production of chat corpora; although these are already in a digital format, they contain much information that expresses features of speech, or non-verbal communication. I hope that with the advent of substantial text chat corpora, we will enter a much needed discussion on how to deal with these problematic issues.

Both learners and teachers/researchers could access this database with a concordancer interface to find authentic examples of native language use, or focus on learner language. While concordancing of authentic (native speaker) text corpora has for a good while been an established ingredient of CALL (see, for example, Little, 1996; Aston, 1997; Rézeau, 2001; Beatty, 2003), the use of learner language corpora has only recently become a more widely-discussed topic in CALL (e.g., Granger, 2002; Granger, Hung, & Petch-Tyson, 2002; Granger, 2003; Heift & Schulze, 2003). Learner language, or interlanguage, corpora can form the basis for intelligent tutoring systems that analyse the complexity of learner's interlanguage and provide individualised feedback on that basis. This, in turn, can lead to highly individualised corrective feedback tools (see for example, Trude Heift's E-Tutor at *http://www.e-tutor.org/*). More about this in the subsequent section.

In terms of pedagogical tools supporting reflective work off-line, we need to acknowledge that receiving an instant transcript of a live interaction is something we rarely, if ever, have at our disposal, so much pedagogical work is necessary. Judging from our MOO projects, learners are quite unprepared for the opportunities the material offers. Normal transcripts can, for example, form the basis for vocabulary work, or learners can identify instances of miscommunication. Again, the story-writing task has been shown to be useful in later projects we did, as learners needed to work through their transcripts to fulfil the task of editing a story. In these kinds of tasks, the transcripts become a quarry where learners find the raw materials for text production.

The online diaries were certainly a big success, and I reported that learners really enter into an intrapersonal dialogue about their learning process. However, I also noticed that learners were not consistent in diary entries; they felt they did not have enough time; and some rarely reviewed them or used them to plan ahead. Learners need to be pushed into making diary entries and reviewing them regularly. We have not yet tried to connect the online diaries with the framework of the European Language Portfolio (ELP), which we piloted in our language modules several years ago, but the ELP promises to be more detailed, more structured, and also more standardised than the diary format we have used so far. In addition, the ELP can be easily embedded into the overall evaluation and assessment of the course. I will look at the ELP in more detail later in this chapter.

In summary, I have distinguished between reflection during communication and afterwards, offline. During communication, the MOO's focus on written communication has undoubtedly advantages in supporting reflective processes in learners. These currently lie mainly in increased opportunities for noticing. However, I have also noted that communicative flow seems to supersede corrective feedback mechanisms, and corrections seems to be related to instances of miscommunication, i.e. discourse-related issues, rather than aspects of accuracy or idiomacy. I have suggested various ways in which automated feedback could focus learners' attention on misspelt words, and also pedagogical tools such as tasks and activities that help with this process. The amount of reflective opportunities off-line is vast, but too far removed from the learner's experience so that these remain, for the most part, unexplored. I suggested three different tools that could easily be integrated: intelligent feedback systems; concordancing; and the ELP. These three tools could in my view greatly contribute to more reflective learners. Intelligent feedback systems can be particularly useful in synchronous communication, but– as I will later describe– can also assist learners in work on long term goals. Concordancing and the ELP are both useful tools for learners to access and review transcripts of their interactions.

4.1.2 Reflection beyond the MOO — Filling the gaps

In this sub-section, I will look at some tools that can fill some of the perceived gaps in supporting awareness. I noticed that supporting awareness in learners has quite different implications for synchronous and asynchronous work. On the one hand, a learner who is– maybe for the first time in her life– communicating live with a native speaker, is probably unlikely to reflect on what she is doing while she is communicating without some form of support. On the other hand, a learner who is watching herself on video, is often very quick to point out things she wants to change, things that surprise her, things she was not aware of. This is a distinction that Schön (1987) called reflection-in-action and reflection-on-action.

I mentioned that in the MOO, within a text-based communication medium, reflection-in-action can be easier supported than in spoken, face-to-face or video communication, a fact that is generally acknowledged in the area of Intelligent CALL (ICALL, cf. Cowan, Choi, & Kim, 2003:452-3). First, the MOO obviously pushes learners to read the communication on screen (cf. O'Rourke, 2005). Second, our BTA is already a tool that analyses utterances while they are communicated. In this way, it was also a proof-of-concept, as we found that real-time analysis and feedback was feasible while learners were communicating. We also have tools to support reflection-on-action that are quite successful, and more are under development. The availability of and work with MOO transcripts is already successful, and the diaries are a useful tool in particular for raising metalinguistic and metacognitive awareness. I would therefore briefly describe three areas where I see a huge and realistic potential for supporting reflection: for reflection-in-action, Intelligent CALL (ICALL) systems; for reflection-on-action: ICALL; concordancing; and language portfolios.

One challenge for research is the link between synchronous communication in text (audio and video tools are at this stage vapourware), and intelligent CALL (ICALL) systems that analyse utterances and give feedback to learners while they are communicating and also afterwards, in offline mode. ICALL systems provide automated learner feedback and use the data from learner corpora to create and revise learner models.

I think it is feasible and worthwhile to pursue the following strands in ICALL and apply them to text-based communication media such as the MOO:

- Much of the current work in ICALL, intelligent language tutor systems (ILTS), and automated feedback systems already focuses on learner corpora as the basis for analysis and feedback. Granger (1998; 2002; 2003) and Cowan et al. (2003) make a case for extensive and cumulative learner corpora, and a corpus-based approach to reflection-in-action appears promising.

- Individualised interlanguage corpora provide a more focused basis for error analysis and specific feedback to learners (such as exercises, see L'haire & Vandeventer Faltin, 2003:481).
- ICALL systems need to be able to provide "personalised and meaningful feedback" (Felix, 2003b:150; also see Felix, 2003a:9), which requires separate identification and records for each learner.
- ICALL systems need to focus on a subset of errors produced by the learner, e.g. persistent errors (Cowan, Choi, & Kim, 2003); just one error at a time (cf. Van der Linden, 1993); or errors ranked by importance (Heift, 2003:535).

I think within the MOO and similar text-based systems, much of the potential of the above ICALL approaches has yet to be exploited. I pointed out earlier that I think reflection is difficult to promote in synchronous communication by pedagogical tools; learners might see the benefits of reciprocal error correction, but will rarely engage in it when actually communicating. However, a combination of learner corpora/databases; automated and effective error correction (even just on the level of spelling); and meaningful feedback could provide a technological solution to this problem of reflection-in-action. For reflection-on-action, a comprehensive ICALL implementation in text-based communication media could range from offline work on transcripts with various error analysis tools to the creation of individualised exercise/training programs based on the learners' individual corpora of their MOO output. These options appear feasible for text, but I am unaware of any audio or video system that is even in development that might have these features and that would offer the same flexibility.

A second area I would like to look at is the area of concordancing which is another tool that appears useful to promote reflection-on-action. I have already mentioned that learner corpora seem to be a useful basis for ICALL systems. They provide a wealth of individual learner data that allow analysis of error patterns and aid subsequent planning of learning activities. Concordancing could make use not only of learner corpora, but also native speaker corpora. The language categorization tool in our BTA is already able to analyse what language an utterance is in, and the MOO "knows" from the initial log-on screen of the BTA which is the L1 and L2 of the learner. Thus certain system requirements for the cumulative construction and automatic tagging of corpora are already in place.

A concordancing tool with appropriate corpora can link interaction, reflection, and experimentation processes in several ways, and thus it can be particularly valuable to support learner autonomy. Empirical research that is available points to substantial benefits for learners, whether at intermediate (see Cobb, 1997, 1999) or beginners level (St. John, 2001). However, concordancing is mostly limited to text. To my knowledge, no direct audio or video concordancers have been developed that allow searches by inputting audio or video. There are some examples where text searches lead to audio or video results, but the mixing of media does, of course, pose conceptual problems (e.g., if I search by text, the result will be homographs; but how do I look for homophones?). For audio, there are the very impressive audio corpora at the Institut für Deutsche Sprache (IDS, Institute for German language, http://www.ids-mannheim.de); through their own concordancer interface, COSMAS, they allow access to text, audio, and annotations. Its discourse database (DIDA) uses a special tagging system and much additional information on dialects, speakers, etc. As far as text access to audio corpora goes, I think the IDS corpora and concordancer have gone as far as possible, but the conceptual problems remain.

One of the biggest projects involving video and concordancing has been the Multimedia Adult English Learner Corpus (MAELC) at the Portland State University Department of Applied Linguistics (Reder, Harris, & Setzler, 2003). The MAELC "is a database of video of classroom interaction and associated written materials collected as part of the Lab School Research project since 2001" (no author, n.d.). One major aim of the project is to have examples of learner language integrated with as many other artefacts as possible, such as written work by the student, teacher logs, video, audio, etc. Transcripts contain intonation information, pauses, miscues/repairs, interruptions, paralinguistic information, and non-linguistic information (when used instead of linguistic information). The corpus also includes daily audio recordings of teacher reflections. The MAELC has links between audio/video material and the coded transcripts. The data is used primarily for teacher training purposes and research in second language acquisition.

The IDS and MAELC developments point to some important issues in concordancing. The process of concordancing depends crucially on the corpus that is chosen and prepared. As I mentioned in the previous section, however, learners intentionally and unintentionally produce words and utterances that, if transferred directly into learner or native speaker text corpora, will not be found by researchers or other students if not tagged/coded in some way. One solution would be that the corpus only accepts words it knows, which would, of course, ignore the great variety of expressive speech learners produce. Another option would be to include a spell-checking device that would either check MOO utterances in the process of composition or after they were sent to the MOO via the ENTER-key. Yet other options would be to get all utterances corrected automatically, or manually, or tag them manually, or just accept all utterances, regardless of individual spelling. This should suffice to indicate that there are even many challenges for the design and production of chat corpora; although these are already in a digital format, they contain much information that expresses features of speech, or non-verbal communication. I hope that with the advent of substantial text chat corpora, we will begin a much needed discussion on how to deal with these problematic issues.

In summary, from a teacher's perspective, concordancing requires much pedagogical intervention. Tasks need to be designed; corpora need to be prepared, tagged, or simply chosen; the activities need to be embedded into other classroom work. In my experience, learners find it initially difficult to see the benefits of concordancing, or make use of its affordances, and they are sometimes overwhelmed by too many functions or too large corpora; then, many learners find it almost addictive to work with corpora, finding out more about language by exploring and experimenting. As I mentioned before, our system is already able to tell these utterances apart, for several languages. The same corpora that we intend to exploit for ICALL implementations can be used for concordancing. The particular strength of the MOO transcripts as a corpus is that here we have two types of data that are generated by learners themselves: on the one hand, there is an interlanguage corpus; on the other hand, a native speaker (authentic) corpus. By communicating, learners automatically contribute to future learning resources for themselves and their partners, discussing topics and events that are personally meaningful to them. Thus, both from a motivational perspective as well as the view of reflection-on-action, work on MOO transcripts could move concordancing to a new level. As in ICALL, it is difficult to imagine how similar work could be achieved with audio or video corpora, and there are inherent conceptual problems (e.g., how useful is a search for text strings in an audio corpus?).

Third and last in this section on awareness, I would like to focus on the idea of a language learning portfolio, which has received enormous interest in recent years. This is not least due to the developments around the European Language Portfolio (ELP), based on the Council of Europe's Common European Framework (CEF) of Reference for Languages (Council of Europe, 2001). In some ways, the ELP follows in the tradition of the learner diaries, but also comprises other functions and is much more embedded in the concept of learner autonomy. We had found with our online diaries that they can be a great tool to support metalinguistic and metacognitive awareness, and apart from pedagogical tasks such as reformulation and explicit discussion of text editing, present an excellent tool for learners to reflect on more general concepts in learning. However, the diaries (unless they are discussed at regular intervals with a teacher) do not provide a means to assess whether personal impressions reflect unrealistic expectations, assessments, etc. The ELP is a tool for reflection-on-action, but closer to the "action" than the diaries. With diaries, one danger was always that learners had metalinguistic and metacognitive insights, but often the link to actual partnerwork, to examples from their day-to-day work as a language learner were missing. The ELP, in contrast, comprises a variety of activities from actual essay-writing to detailed self-assessment, goal setting, materials collection, etc. The ELP currently has three components:

- a language passport, which summarizes the owner's linguistic identity by briefly recording L2s learnt, formal language qualifications achieved, significant experiences of L2 use, and the owner's assessment of his/her current proficiency in the L2s he/she knows;
- a language biography, which is used to set language learning targets, monitor progress, plot the development of language learning skills, and record and reflect on specially important language learning and intercultural experiences;
- a dossier, which contains a selection of work that in the owner's judgement best represents his/her L2 achievement. (Little, 2005; also see Little, 2003)

The ELP has both pedagogical and reporting functions (Little & Perclová, 2001:3). As many other types of portfolio, it serves to support the learner in planning, monitoring, and evaluating learning, in short, to make the learning process more transparent. It also serves to report L2 achievement, and allow learners detailed and standardised rating instruments for self-assessment. There are now signs that the ELP will find its way into CALL. Dublin City University is currently in the process of developing a web-based ELP, very much based on the CEF (Veronica Crosbie, personal communication). It is planned that the online ELP will include the following features: learners will be able to create and keep track of their ELP online; learners will be able to save material online (although no specific authoring tool for web pages or multimedia content is provided); learners will be able to share part or their entire portfolio with others. Learners will be able to see the CEF global scales, the "I can do" statements, and these will be linked to their dossier work. It should be noted that Crosbie plans to integrate this online version of the ELP into the Moodle open-source course management system already in use at DCU, conceptually a related environment to the MOO. Recently, the creation of an online ELP has become an EU-funded Socrates project, LOLIPOP - Language On-line Portofolio Project (ISOC/Socrates, 2006).

The opportunity to exchange parts or entire ELPs with other learners has already been implemented in the portfolio by the Amsterdam Faculty of Education (EFA, see Weijdema, 2000). Unlike some electronic versions of portfolios or even ELPs that have been discussed at recent European CALL conferences (e.g. CERCLES, UNTELE, EuroCALL), the EFA has recognised the importance of the ELP and the CEF levels and framework. In addition, it has made first steps towards a similar framework for teacher competencies. As a tool for reflection-on-action, the ELP provides a standardised tool with a wide variety of activities. Additional features such as the sharing of partial or entire ELPs should introduce a more collaborative dimension into online versions.

In this sub-section I have discussed three tools for reflection: Intelligent CALL systems; concordancing; and electronic European Language

Portfolios. It seems feasible that all three tools could be integrated in a MOO-type CALL environment. While ICALL could be useful for both reflection-in-action and reflection-on-action activities and require more technological preparation, concordancing and the ELP are reflection-on-action activities and require more pedagogical input. ICALL (to a growing extent) and concordancing are both relying on learner language and native speaker corpora, almost exclusively in text, exactly the type that is produced in MOO tandem projects. The ELP is one of the most widespread implementations of learner autonomy concepts and is only beginning to be integrated into MOO-type CALL environments. The implementation of these tools can support what is probably the most important goal of learner autonomy: raising language and linguistic awareness or, in other words, supporting reflection.

4.2 LEARNER AUTONOMY AND INTERACTION

4.2.1 Interaction in the MOO

In Chapter 1 I made an argument for the use of the target language at all times in language learning. Strongly connected to this is the emphasis on group work, on collaboration in the language classroom. The communication and collaboration with native speakers is perceived as even more positive for language learning, as it is usually connected with a more authentic context, audience, and purpose than communication with peers or the teacher. The set-up in tandem learning is slightly different, as both partners are fluctuating between the roles of language learner and native speaker expert. I noted that this type of learning partnership should be quite useful, as both partners know what problems can occur from the native speaker's as well as the learner's perspective.

In Chapter 2 I emphasised that CALL environments need to provide a variety of communication modes and collaboration tools. As the MOO as a CALL environment was fairly new and unexplored, I did not know how learners would adapt to this way of communicating. I also mentioned the importance of a learning environment where learners were able to use indexical language, in other words: where they could share a mental framework of a place. One aspect of interaction that I considered in detail was the various forms of scaffolding that are used in this form of interaction.

The first thing we as teachers of the MOO project noticed, even in the first scenario, was that learners interacted; they seemed compelled to do so. A central drawback of many language classrooms is the lack of authentic interaction with native speakers. Even when teachers focus on the use of the target language at all times, learners are rarely pushed into producing comprehensible output. MOO tandem clearly makes it difficult for learners not to communicate.

We also have indications that learners perceive the MOO environment as a shared mental space; indexical language is used frequently and refers in the vast majority of cases to the virtual environment. The fact that they select their own partners at the beginning of the project gave them more responsibility and lead to higher commitment to the exchange. They also appear to be conscious of themselves as a group representing the target language culture, as whenever anybody utters a phrase that can be interpreted as an insult or banter, usually members of the same target language group will clarify the issue or apologise to the receiver, and/ or reproach the speaker. However, we never, even in our first projects, encountered the problem of obscene language that appears to be so much a part of publicly accessible "chat" systems. In that respect, I found that learners, contrary to some common beliefs about CMC, do not engage in "flaming", i.e. using an excessive amount of insults and obscene language, quite the opposite; they overcautiously tried to make sure that every utterance was not misunderstood.

Our pedagogical framework of tasks, and the fact that learners selected their partners, probably assured that learners discussed a wide variety of topics. Learners benefit from initial teacher-produced scaffolding in the tasks themselves, such as questions or additional vocabulary to begin the task. Most effective are those tasks that combine synchronous and asynchronous modes of communication; tasks that have a clear time frame; tasks that are open enough for learners to connect them to personally meaningful events; tasks that have a clear deliverable outcome (such as a textual, visual, or programmed artefact).

Learners appear to be very aware that MOO communication is different and that it has its own rules, so they tend to overemphasise conflict-avoidance signals. The importance of error correction in synchronous tandem learning seems to take second place behind the primacy of communicative flow (as mentioned above). At least as far as it concerns error correction for formal accuracy, this presents a notable, though maybe not utterly surprising, difference from e-mail tandem. In our projects, I noticed that reciprocal encouragement to speak in the target language was very prominent. In other words, learners may decide that it is more important to get the partner to speak; then, and only then, can they think about various forms of careful scaffolding. In the previous section I referred to a possible tool that automatically spell-checks every utterance either during or after composition and colour-codes any errors. This might not only encourage more self-correction but also other-correction. From a pedagogical perspective, I think it is difficult and probably unwise to engage learners in error correction for accuracy's sake, as it would interrupt the interaction too much and be demotivating. Any future changes in error correction need to be careful not to upset the communicative flow. Getting learners to communicate in the target language can be difficult, and several of my students maintained that they had never communicated with a native speaker before (strangely enough, I as the teacher and our native-speaker class assistants did not seem to count as native speakers).

Judging from our MOO projects so far, learners will most likely engage in correction when errors impede the message, which brings us to negotiation of meaning. As I hoped, learners engage in non-evasive repair strategies such as paraphrase or translation. Input modifications are also important, as they contribute to comprehensible input. As can be expected, input modification occurs more often for learners with a lower L2 proficiency. It is difficult, of course, to assess what input modifications a learner really made at any given moment. I did not assess, for example, the complexity of the utterances used with native speaker peers versus language learners, so this is definitely research that still needs to be conducted in future.

A major problem in tandem partnerships, as we found out, was that especially when the L2 proficiencies of the partners differ dramatically, the stronger L2 will dominate interaction, even sometimes becoming the sole language of communication; in other words, the central tandem principle of bilingualism is in danger. This was clearly an imbalance we needed to address, and we have made some significant progress with the Bilingual Tandem Analyser (BTA, Schwienhorst & Borgia, 2006); further fine-tuning of this tool should solve this problem.

On the whole, I am content with the results for interaction that have been achieved so far. Learners interact about a vast array of topics; learners use a variety of communication modes; learners talk like they are in the same space; learners encourage and support each other when miscommunication occurs. We have to reconsider whether reciprocal error correction in this and similar synchronous set-ups is a feasible demand. At this stage, I see more arguments for a technological than a pedagogical solution to this. There seems to be some evidence for input modification, but we need to conduct more detailed research, maybe along the lines of Alcón Soler (2002) and Hegelheimer & Tower (2004). The issue of bilingualism is an area where we have been able to make dramatic progress, through a technological solution learners do not otherwise have in face-to-face communication, in ensuring balanced bilingualism and giving learners a tool to analyse their own discourse in real time.

4.2.2 Interaction beyond the MOO — Filling the gaps

Earlier in this section, I spoke about some of the most obvious gaps in supporting collaboration and communication in the MOO. It is the fact that communication takes place solely by using text. I argued that communicating in text can be a useful mode for language learning, and it should in no way be seen as inferior to audio or video conferencing. Of course, learners need to be exposed to and engage in target language discourse in text as well as via audio and video. Learners would ideally work with a variety of software, both synchronous and asynchronous, and I would even argue that each combination, for example synchronous text-based, can have very different affordances in different programs; compare, for example, the MOO and Instant Messenger. In addition to this variety, I have also argued that learners need to be able to change quickly between various communication groups, such as: 1+1 with a peer (but other learner can see what is said); 1+1 with the teacher (private); 1+3 in small groups; whole class discussion; etc. Although MOO tandem is primarily a 1+1 learning partnership, other communication groups play an important role. We have seen that learners actually make use of this variety in the MOO, and go beyond it. Apart from the communication groups in the MOO, learners also talk to and use their peers in the "real" classroom, and occasionally consult the teacher.

This may all seem very complicated; after all, learners have to use a command-line type input to realise the intricate changes between groups. But what is the alternative? Let us just take a snapshot from our second scenario: learner A is working with partner B; then A consults her peer C in the "real" classroom about a word she does not understand; A and C ask the teacher T who offers alternatives; B is meanwhile sending private messages to another student D who has been working with her the previous week when B was absent, and invites D to join A and B as D's partner is absent. In the MOO, only one extra command would be necessary to realise this, and it would be for the private message, e.g. <-D Hi, is your partner not here?>. One communication is seamlessly linked to the next. How would the same snapshot be achieved using audio or video conferencing, even in an imaginary system? Is there any tool using audio or video that offers similar flexibility? Apart from communication, how else can learners collaborate with each other? In the following, I will look at some communication and collaboration tools and evaluate how useful they are from a learner autonomy perspective: Lyceum, a proprietary system used by the Open University, and various audio and video conferencing systems.

On occasion, I have mentioned that there are alternative virtual environments, using text and/or audio communication, and that there are video conferencing systems that have been used for language learning. To my knowledge, there are not yet any systems for language learning that combine the two technologies of virtual environments and video conferencing. However, systems do exist, for example by Advanced Network & Services Inc. (2004), that synthesise video images of users and computer-generated environments, but these are not a viable option yet, due to technological and cost factors.

In a previous paper (Schwienhorst, 2002c), I discussed 3D environments at length. Since then, few graphical environments have emerged or have been adapted for language learning, with notable exceptions such as the one reported by Svensson (2003). One environment that has received more and more attention over the past few years is Lyceum, "an audio and visual conferencing system for the Internet. Using Lyceum participants can exchange audio messages and share visual applications in real-time."

(Rapanotti & Hall, 2000). Originally, like the enCore MOO, Lyceum was conceived for a variety of courses specifically for Open University, a distance teaching institution; however, it is not an open-source project and not even available commercially. I still think it is useful to present it here, as its researchers have extensively experimented with audio and video conferencing and collaborative tools.

In addition to audio and text chat facilities, the system also includes three collaboration tools: A whiteboard, a concept map editor (later renamed ConceptMapper, see Buckingham Shum, Marshall, Brier, & Evans, 2001), and a screen grabber (or ScreenGrabber, ibid.). The whiteboard, a collaborative drawing and writing tool in real time, has a foreground and background, so that the two layers could remain untouched. The ConceptMapper is similar, but uses matrices, diagrams, and "sticky notes" to organise ideas and is thus somewhat more formal in its structure. Using the ScreenGrabber, users can capture web pages, parts of documents, or other fragments from other applications, and copy them onto the whiteboard as an object or image. Neither whiteboard nor ConceptMapper can cope with files saved in a different format (e.g. Microsoft® Word), but saves files in a proprietary format (Hampel & Barber, 2003:178). Just as the voice conferencing system implements the notion of virtual rooms to structure online communication, each room contains a whiteboard and a ConceptMapper. These three tools are good examples of useful collaborative tools (Buckingham Shum, Marshall, Brier, & Evans, 2001).

Kötter et al. (Kötter, Shield, & Stevens, 1999; Kötter & Shield, 2000; Kötter, 2001) report enthusiasm, but also problems with the voice interaction: on the one hand, learners appreciated the additional communication tools, on the other hand, they were also quite aware of the lack of contextual cues and the differences to other media (including the differences to telephone communication). Kötter (2001:338) reports that, initially, the particular mode of voice conferencing made it easier to hide (cf. Hampel & Barber, 2003:184), but that learners then grew in confidence, took more risks when communicating in the target language, and used Lyceum between sessions (Kötter & Shield, 2000). As in the MOO, the tutor's role changed significantly to that of "administrator, event manager and, occasionally, co-learner" (ibid.). Kötter and Shield also point out the problem of error correction versus communicative flow (ibid.:344).

There are, in my view, two important areas where Lyceum has contributed significantly to CALL from a learner autonomy perspective. In terms of collaboration, it has recognised that various shared workspaces are needed, such as the informal whiteboard and the more formal ConceptMapper. In terms of interaction, it has shown that audio conferencing, properly included with other tools and supported by text chat in a virtual environment, can be beneficial for language learning and, on a broader scale in distance education, building a community of learners. Tracking tools are useful, as are audio recording tools (Hampel & Barber, 2003:175;

also see Hampel, 2003), in spite of their conceptual limitations. Lyceum has become an impressive example of a CALL environment.

However, I would also voice some criticism. Lyceum has not been released as commercial software; it remains a proprietary platform for the Open University. If it would be released, it is questionable whether the source code would be made available, so that others could contribute to its development. We also need more research on how we can use audio records or audio conferencing in general for reflective tasks, not only what audio conferencing can do for the development of fluency (Lamy & Goodfellow, 1999; Lamy, 2003). Learners do not seem to figure as co-creators of this environment, they are presented with a finished product.

Felix (2003b:160) has noted that voice interaction, on the whole, is still poorly supported by web-based tools, yet one of the most pertinent problems in the language classroom is the phenomenon of language anxiety when speaking in the second language. It is interesting to note that video conferencing has not had a major impact on CALL so far; even in Lyceum it was not deemed feasible. I remember a demonstration of video conferencing at the 4th CERCLES conference in Dresden, Germany, in 1996 where, in spite of detailed preparation, dedicated hardware, and a number of experts present, no useful conferencing could take place. I also remember that a year earlier, in 1995, I attended an open day at the Language Centre in Cambridge, England, where the HIPERNET project was presented (Esch, 1996; HIPERNET, 1995), including successful video conferencing.

Cziko and Park (2003) review a number of audio conferencing tools, some of which are combined with video and other channels. Some of the software they review has acceptable audio quality, but video frame rates are described as one to three frames per second, hardly useful for video communication. In spite of the author's optimism regarding viable (multiparty) video conferencing using the Internet, I would agree with Hampel (2003:176) that it has not become a reliable and useful technology yet; Wang (2004) shows that bandwidth, frame rates, resolution, lip synchronisation, are just some of the problems the technology is still faced with.

One audio conferencing tool that has gained some attention is Horizon Wimba's Voice Tools (http://www.horizonwimba.com), originally an asynchronous audio conferencing tool, although now extended to include synchronous audio conferencing. Voice Tools is a suite of communication tools such as live conversation, voice boards, voice e-mail, voice testing types, etc., and integrate with existing course management systems such as WebCT and Blackboard®. Recently, it has presented itself more like a "language lab online"; however, some of its functionality, such as asynchronous voice boards, could be quite useful not only to practice oral skills, but also (through its recording facility) for reflective tasks (cf. Felix, 2003b:163). There are very few research reports available on Horizon Wimba, though there have been some presentations at conferences (Braul, 2003; Chao &

Kabata, 2003; Frei, Dixon, & Van Deusen-Scholl, 2003; Lafford, 2003; McIntosh, Braul, & Chao, 2003).

The findings are, on the whole, positive and suggest that speaking and listening activities are perceived as useful and authentic. It is interesting to see that an asynchronous voice conferencing system can open up a whole range of activities that are useful for the language learner on her way to autonomy. Just as synchronous writing slows down communication and makes it visible on screen, asynchronous speaking allows for preparation, revision, and evaluation of spoken language. From a learner autonomy perspective, Voice Tools can add a reflective dimension to online speaking. It remains to be seen whether the financial implications of this tool will prevent its wider distribution, and there are still some questions about user-friendliness and reliability.

There are severe limitations on audio and video conferencing systems to support reflective processes in language learners; this appears to be the nature of the medium of voice, compared to text-based communication. We need to keep in mind that many audio and video systems will influence communication in different ways: how effective is whispering? Can the learner fluctuate between small group work, pair work, whole class presentation, and teacher advice within a short time? Can the learner control the video signal? Nevertheless, audio and video conferencing, but only when technically feasible, should form part of the CALL environment, just as face-to-face interaction is important in the "real-life" classroom.

4.3 LEARNER AUTONOMY AND EXPERIMENTATION

One of the central misconceptions about learner autonomy is that just by leaving learners alone, they are or become autonomous. However, in my first chapter I made the point that learners need to make useful connection between the level of autonomy they have achieved and the learning environment around them. In other words, they need to connect (or be helped to connect) with the learning opportunities around them; opportunities they may not always perceive as such. I argued that learners can make this connection more easily when they are enabled to actively experiment with the learning environment. The use of our task framework and relevant support material was to provide authenticity; learners had an authentic audience and purpose in the collaboration with a target language speaker. The opportunity to create and share textual artefacts in the MOO served the principles of activity theory, especially because so much on the MOO centers on language and its use. The MOO is also at its core a constructivist medium, more like a framework, an authoring suite, than a finished program. By giving learners easy-to-use tools and templates to create their own, personally meaningful, objects, and by having an online persona, the MOO becomes a constructionist learning environment, where learners can not only experiment with other objects, but also with themselves and their new identity in the target language. The MOO as a situated learning environment together with the framework of tandem learning emphasise the communal activity of learning; in fact, the idea that learning is created through negotiation and sharing, and that this should help in finding one's place in the target language culture, has been crucial to our projects.

4.3.1 Experimentation in the MOO

In the MOO, learners develop virtual spaces and materials rather than exercises. It allows configurability, as authors can progress from simple templates to making complex changes to the heart of the system; this is a crucial point, as many commercial systems do not make source code available and thus prevent more advanced programming changes to the software. The MOO's interface is programmed in Java™ and JavaScript™ and causes very few problems, if any, between platforms. Authoring is done within the environment, so the interface is always consistent and the functionality the same. Installation on a server is not easy for a novice, but there are many forms of help: books (Holmevik & Haynes, 2000), mailing lists, and other MOO administrators. Finally, the MOO has a number of tracking mechanisms and more of these can be built into it quite easily to obtain more user statistics.

The MOO, as an open-source learning environment, can be manipulated by learners, if permissions are granted, to its very core, unlike commercial software. In reality, learners in our projects only very rarely explore the full range and depth of their options, but this is not to be expected when we are looking at exchanges of only 9 sessions, especially when object creation was not a major focus in our first projects. I reported that very few learners engaged in object creations, but given the fact that none of them had any formal introduction to this, the fact that some of them did is encouraging. I have singled out the description of the learner who created a so-called "bot", a crude conversation program, to show how absorbing, challenging, complex, yet playful the work with artefacts can be. Planning in a foreign language what words or phrases one needs to use not only so that a sensible response is triggered but that a reasonable conversation develops is a very complex recursive process that requires and develops higher-level skills on discourse structure. I noted that several learners created rooms and other smaller objects that were not as elaborate. This continued in subsequent MOO projects. It appears that learners will want to take control of creating their own, personally meaningful learning environment if they have the opportunity, even with very little extra encouragement. The weakness or barrier does not lie with the functionality, but with the interface. As a (hyper-)text-based learning environment, it is unavoidable that the MOO requires in many cases textual or conversational input to interact with the vast programming functionality; an interface that many learners are no longer familiar with. EnCore has begun to make many object creations available through hyperlinks and form-field input which is a step in the right direction.

One particular form of object creation is the customisation of the online character. Some comments of our learners indicate that the online persona clearly lowers the affective filter. Some learners, especially in later projects, changed their online name and appearance, but they soon settle on an identity to remain recognisable to their partner (cf. Turkle, 1995:205). While some learners reported crucial differences between their online character and their real self, some maintained they were able to present themselves as they are; some learners reported both forms of behaviour. Perhaps a contradiction, perhaps two sides of the same coin, but nevertheless inconclusive. If we consider identity formation a crucial component of second language acquisition, we need to recognise the differences between various communication media. In the MOO, learners may choose to present themselves differently than in face-to-face communication, and it would be useful to explore this further by using pedagogical tools that encourage learners to experiment with online identity. The fact that all character customisation is in text makes it almost automatically also a linguistic exercise. Learners can, for instance, set messages that appear whenever they enter or exit a room, or when somebody tries to contact them from another room. These messages and descriptions could easily form the basis of further activities.

My research in the use of indexicality was an important indicator of the shared mental space that MOO tandem learners inhabit; indexicality is used in most cases to refer to the virtual location of the MOO, the environment that both characters share as representations. The use of indexicality was not prompted by pedagogy at any stage during the projects, it just happened. Although I only focused on "here" and its German counterpart "hier", my findings were encouraging if we think back to the coffee-and-biscuits problem of collaboration (see p. .). A shared space is vital to establish a common reference framework for interaction and collaboration. More research is needed, but if we consider the use of indexicality a worthwhile goal, we could introduce more shared tools that support this notion. We have already continued this with the creation of a shared whiteboard for collaborative writing.

In my final sub-section on experimentation, I looked at one of the central goals of learner autonomy; the ability of learners to take control of their learning. My research suggests that the framework of MOO tandem encourages learners to experiment more than they would in the normal classroom. The framework of technology and pedagogy allows them to focus more on their task; receive more support; feel less under pressure; and take initiatives. Again, this was a positive result for our MOO sessions (though a sobering one for our classes). It showed that the decision to create separate virtual rooms had paid off, and that tasks were important as scaffolding devices. There are a number of drawbacks relating to the interface which still prevents many learners from experimentation and authoring.

Particularly the last paragraph underlines the fact that learners are not automatically autonomous because they are given absolute freedom. They are seeking, to different extents, a technological and pedagogical framework that challenges their achieved level of learner autonomy. It is then the teacher's responsibility to find a framework that, on the one hand, avoids that learners are disoriented and aimless because it is too abstract or "open", and on the other hand, avoids that learners' autonomy is restricted by specific demands or predetermined pathways. Ideally, an environment should offer ultimate freedom to create (even down to the actual level of programming); on the other hand, it also needs more basic options or authoring tools that are easy to operate for less autonomous learners to participate in. With many commercial authoring systems, learners and teachers will sooner or later reach a point beyond which they cannot make changes to the software; here the principle of open-source software seems to serve the principles of learner autonomy better.

4.3.2 Experimentation beyond the MOO — Filling the gaps

When we use commercially produced language learning material, whether these are textbooks or computer programs, we all make the experience that at a certain point it makes a decision for us that we do not share, or that we are presented with a line that we want to cross or a path we cannot pursue. It is vital that learners feel that the learning environment is not just created by an all-knowing authority for them, but also and foremost, by them, as their learner autonomy grows. Learners need to be enabled to choose, to make decisions, to assemble or develop materials and share them with other learners (cf. Squires, 1999). This choice exists more and more, and increasingly on the Internet, for example in authentic simulation software (see Beatty, 2003; Kern & Warschauer, 2000; Taylor, 1990; Meskill, 1990).

The previous section emphasised the notion of learners as authors of their learning environment; as real participants or agents in the learning process. The MOO as an authoring environment offers in principle unlimited access to the environment, but as I discussed earlier, a major drawback is that this functionality is somewhat hampered by a largely command-line-based input.

Learners creating content for other learners in the target language is a particularly useful activity within the context of learner autonomy. From a motivational perspective, learners create personally meaningful content that is published with a particular purpose for other learners to use. Strangely enough, when talking about authoring programs, researchers often refer to teachers as authors and learners as recipients (see, for example, Wachman, 1999; Beatty, 2003; Godwin-Jones, 2003), a distinction I consider counterproductive for the learner-autonomy-based classroom. First, creating exercises for other learners can be a valuable part of working on deficits; second, creating coherent exercise cycles can help learners in planning and executing future learning targets; third, having to create instructions and relating exercises to skills and levels, such as those of the ELP or CEF, can raise learner's metalinguistic and metacognitive awareness.

In CALL, we now have several authoring tools that help in creating exercises, such as the Wida software (Ebbrell, 1998; Jones, n.d.) or Hot Potatoes (Winke & MacGregor, 2001; also cf. Wachman, 1999). Within the spectrum of authoring software, there are also more general educational programmes, such as Blackboard® (http://www.blackboard.com/), WebCT (http://www.webct.com/), and TopClass™ (http://www.wbtsystems.com/). Often referred to as learning management systems (LMSs), these seem to fall out of favour with many language educators, as they often are too inflexible, too rigid in their programming, and have insufficient tracking mechanisms for more advanced research. An interesting recent project is Moodle (http://www.moodle.org), an open-source course management system that provides a variety of modules for online courses based on social constructionism.

Arneil and Holmes (1999) reiterate some core problems behind the development of authoring tools, taking their software Hot Potatoes as an example. Among the more relevant points are the dichotomy between the sophistication of the software and its "programming feasibility" (ibid.:13); the problem of "configurability versus simplicity" (ibid.:14); the portability across platforms and browser versions; and the availability of user statistics. I mentioned in the previous section that the MOO has tools for object creation, but that it does not yet possess authoring tools for creating content that is specific to language learning.

A recent authoring tool has been in development at Brigham Young University, called WebDVD, which will allow learners to create web-based content around commercially available DVDs. These DVDs can then be played inside the web browser, viewed together with additional content such as exercises, background information, historical references, etc. WebDVD (Hendricks, 2003a, 2003b) did not go beyond being a delivery mechanism, and developed out of combinations of laserdisc and computer software and later CD-ROMs[1]. However, there were plans to extend it into an authoring tool at some stage (see Figure 4.1).

Like concordancing, it is somewhat surprising that learner dictionaries and lexical organisers have not played a bigger role in CALL so far. They allow learners to create and organise their own dictionaries and provide various tools to support the acquisition of vocabulary. In recent years, there has been a shift in focus from syntactic structures towards the lexicon as the "engine of language"(also see Little, 1994). The MOO does not have

1. I am grateful to Harold Hendricks for supplying me with information on WebDVD.

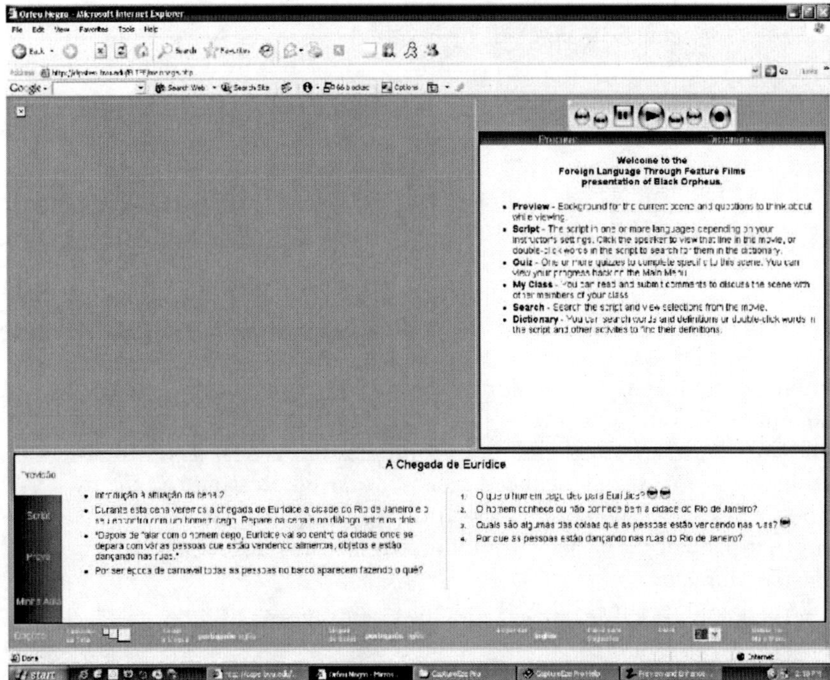

Figure 4.1 Screenshot from Orfeo negro, a WebDVD project at Brigham Young University

any specific support or built-in tools for collecting and studying vocabulary yet, so I will look briefly at three developments that demonstrate new approaches to electronic learner dictionaries: The Visual Thesaurus; KirrKirr; and the Lexical Organiser by my colleague O'Rourke.

The Visual Thesaurus™ (a proprietary software product of Thinkmap, Inc. and available in CD-Rom format and online at http://www.visualthesaurus.com) is probably the least interactive of the three tools, as it offers the user only minimal access to manipulate the underlying dictionary database. It is primarily a tool to visualise relationships between words and meaning within a spatial interface. As such, it is primarily a new interface, a new way of displaying data. Either in 3D or in 2D, learners can visualise semantic and morphological relationships between words, including synonyms and antonyms. On the right of the screen, there is a list of all the words displayed at any moment, including their meanings, organised into parts of speech. Visual Thesaurus™ offers some innovative insights into new dictionary design, and certainly works against the traditional notion of a linear organisation of the lexicon (see Figure 4.2).

Kirrkirr is a research project at Stanford University (Manning, 2004; also see Manning & Parton, 2001), mainly for indigenous languages. From

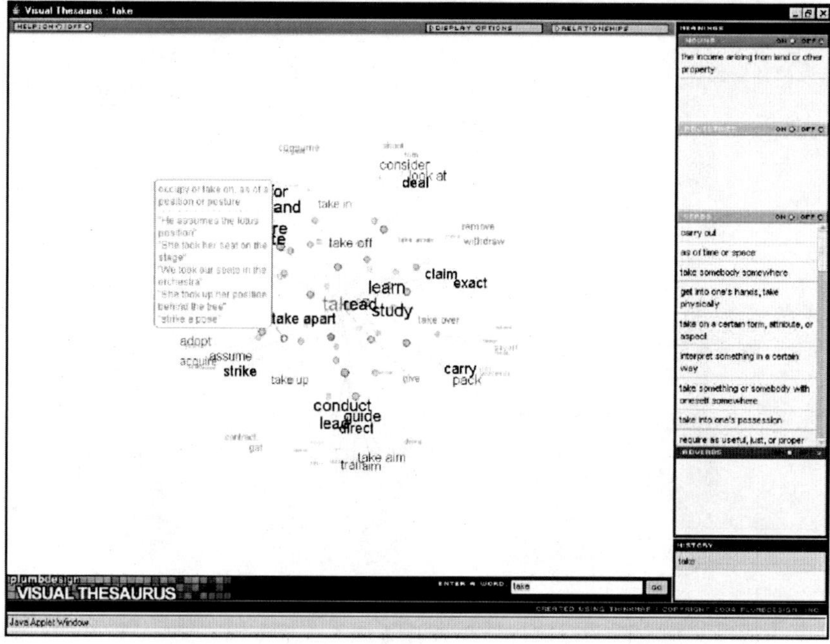

Figure 4.2 One view of the Visual Thesaurus™

dictionary data in XML format, it can generate networks, and the user can then visualise and customise dictionary information. KirrKirr can also integrate audio or visual support for entries, if these are available in the underlying database. In searches, the software allows for fuzzy searches, if the exact spelling of the word is not known. Learners can add notes to dictionary entries, and it is possible to create word games such as crossword puzzles on the basis of the dictionary. One major goal of the KirrKirr project is to provide a reversible dictionary, as many dictionaries for indigenous languages are only available as x-English versions. See Figure 4.3 for a view of KirrKirr with multimedia content.

O'Rourke (1998; O'Rourke & Schwienhorst, 2000) has created the web-based Lexical Organiser which is approaching completion. It is "suitable for shared asynchronous use by learners at a distance from one another" (O'Rourke & Schwienhorst, 2000:129). Created in Java™, it allows learners to gather, organise and annotate lexical items as they work at their computer. As the Visual Thesaurus™ and KirrKirr, it emphasises a spatial organisation of vocabulary and moves away from the linear presentation of many dictionaries. Learners create new tiles with lexical items, which they can then double-click to enter annotations. These annotations can be of three types: "authentic examples of use, the learner's own examples of

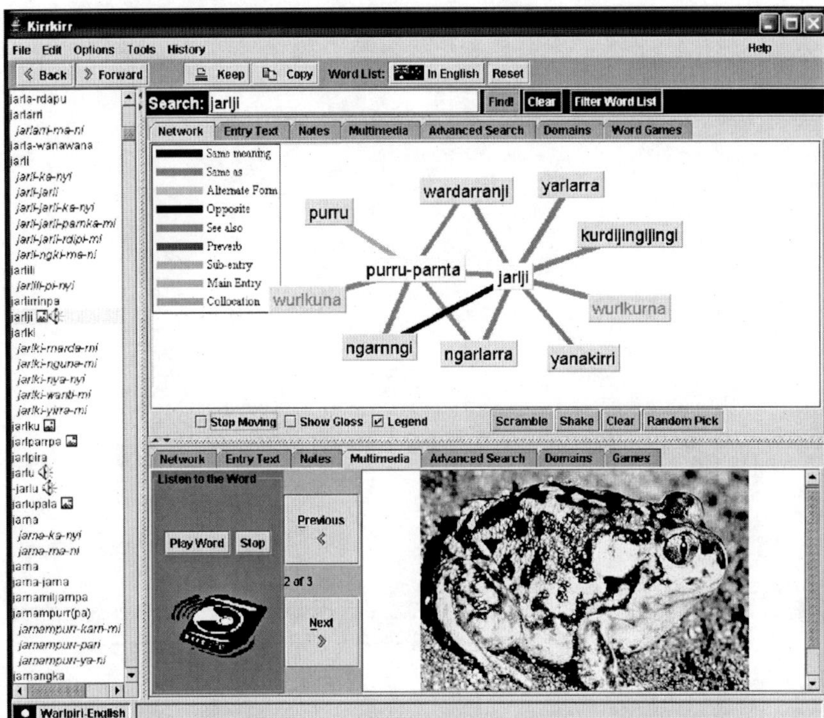

Figure 4.3 A multimedia view of KirrKirr[2]

use, and meaning and usage notes" (ibid.). Lexical items can be arranged in various levels or hierarchies, and the categories can all be defined by the learner "without predefining or implicitly favouring any particular taxonomy, provided that it can be expressed as a hierarchy" (O'Rourke, 1998). Later additions include self-testing facilities and additional drawing tools to aid visualisation in given (sub-)categories (see Figure 4.4).

Building up and structuring a dictionary is only one possible application. Learners can also use the software for written composition, using the boxes to enter paragraphs or longer texts; and learners can share a Lexical Organiser to co-operate and brainstorm on a project (O'Rourke & Schwienhorst, 2000:130). While Thinkmap, Inc.'s *Visual Thesaurus*™ and KirrKirr may have the more impressive interface, the Lexical Organiser has the functionality that is most in line with learner autonomy principles. First, learners are not only encouraged, but almost forced to reflect on language, by making connections between lexical items and the need to organise them; in this respect, it shares the data-driven learning approach of concor-

2. I would like to thank Christopher Manning and Mary Laughlin for permission to use this screenshot.

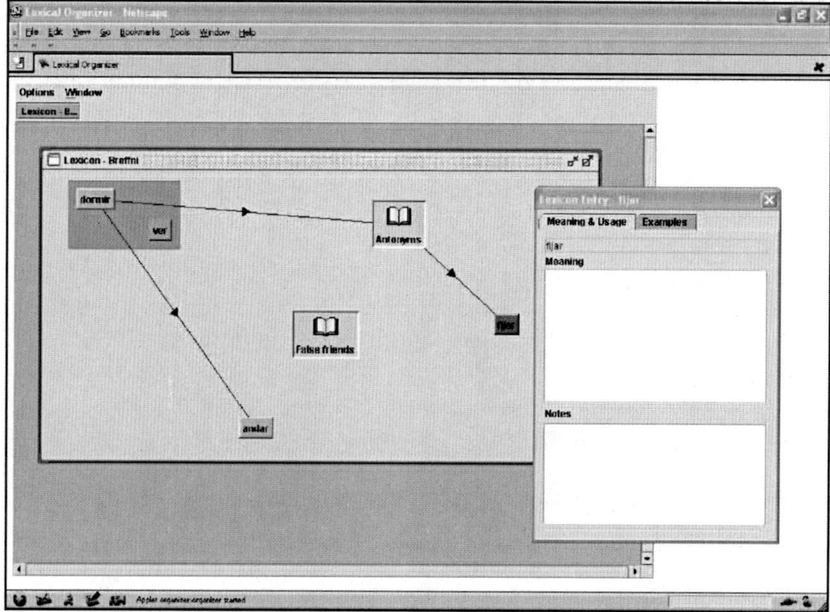

Figure 4.4 Screenshot of the Lexical Organiser

dancing. Second, the Lexical Organiser will allow sharing of dictionaries and can even be used for brainstorming on collaborative texts, both asynchronously and synchronously; by doing that, it encourages meaningful interaction between learners. Third, learners have the flexibility to express themselves; they have tools that are easy to use, yet not restrictive for more sophisticated ideas; they can take full control over their learning. So far, no tracking mechanism has been implemented, except that all the learner dictionaries are stored in a Microsoft® Access database, and thus would be potentially available to researchers.

4.4 LEARNER AUTONOMY AND THE ROLE OF THE TEACHER

In Chapter 2, I cited three functions of the teacher in learner-autonomy-based classrooms: facilitator, counsellor, and resource (see Voller, 1997). For Dam (1995), a dialogue between teacher and learner is essential, and teachers should use similar tools as learners for reflection (diaries, contracts, etc.). Little (1995) has suggested that these principles are essential for teacher education, as teachers will only be able to support learner autonomy if they have experienced it themselves.

4.4.1 The role of the teacher in the MOO

In the MOO tandem context, we as teachers noticed that these principles needed much revision or rather adaptation. First, we noted that the teacher's roles as outlined by Voller are to some extent taken over by the native speaker partner. The partner provides the bulk of session-to-session support and encouragement, and thus fulfils most of the demands as a facilitator. The partner may also be pushed into counselling, although this function is more usefully done by the teacher in small-group introduction and reflection sessions at regular intervals during the project. The function of resource is almost totally relinquished to the native speaker partner, if we ignore the bilingual support in initial task frameworks and activities. One of the most disorienting, even somewhat frustrating, experiences during MOO sessions for teachers is how much they are excluded from the learners' learning process and how little they are consulted. When learners are unclear about something, they ask their partners, or peers, or their peers' partners, but not the teacher (also see Kötter, 2002). Where the teacher is most active is in the planning and organisation of the exchange; the discussion and implementation of tasks and activities; the settting of deliverables and agreement of terms. Monitoring of the exchange can happen during the sessions, or after the sessions, by looking at transcripts and other learner data. Overall evaluation is greatly simplified by the various data collection tools that the MOO offers, and we have found that interviews on the MOO have the particular advantage that learners can reflect on the very medium while they are using it.

As I indicated earlier, I did not use the MOO on a larger scale for teacher education. Using the MOO for our preparation of the exchange was highly beneficial and raised our awareness of the problems and opportunities. I consider the MOO to be fully adequate for the preparation of such an exchange, and even during the sessions, teachers stayed in touch, thus keeping each other up to date about classroom atmosphere.

In terms of teacher autonomy, then, our experience was even more extreme than we imagined. The teacher's role in the classroom is limited to very few but decisive areas. First, the teacher needs to create a pedagogical and technological framework that allows as much flexibility as possible for learners to become more autonomous learners. This framework and its effect is constructed almost completely before the project begins; in other words, when we think back to the two scenarios in Chapter 1, few changes are possible after the initial session. Second, the teacher needs to include introductions and reflection sessions at regular intervals during the project, so that learners become more aware of tandem principles, exchange ideas about tasks and objects; clear up problems with the partner; etc. Third, the teacher needs to keep a diary, in which she can record how sessions are developing. Fourth, it is vital that the teacher stays in contact with the partner teacher at all times; a common framework that is clear and consistent also usually translates into more focused tandem partnerships. Fifth, a thorough evaluation should be an essential part of the MOO tandem project, to see whether technological and pedagogical frameworks need to be modified.

4.4.2 The role of the teacher beyond the MOO — Filling the gaps

When I discussed teacher autonomy in MOO tandem, I discussed the changed role of the teacher. Before the project she becomes more of a designer, during and after the project more of a researcher. Her main role during MOO tandem sessions is to adjust the learning environment and pedagogy to the level of autonomy that the learner has achieved. These roles translate into the following demands: a CALL environment must offer design tools and functionality that can grow with the teacher/learner; it has to include and enable a variety of research tools and user tracking that ideally takes account of all the additional programmes/modules that are built into it; and be above all flexible to cater for the autonomy level of each individual learner if possible.

First, in my experience, many teachers get into CALL by simply using a ready-made programme and expect that this programme will do exactly what they want. At some point they are no longer happy with the functionality of the software, or research facilities built into the program, or the fact that it does not support their pedagogy. My colleague and I certainly had this experience with a learning management system we used. It had neither tools for reflection nor communication facilities beyond a crude forum nor offered students participation or experimentation; nor did it offer any tracking or other research facilities. It was easy to use, though. In the end, we abandoned this, and started using the MOO and dabbled in various programming languages to create our own CALL tools.

Taking control of learning also means taking control of the learning environment, the learning tools. If these remain prescribed or fixed, a teacher or learner who is becoming more autonomous may lose interest in them, or feel restricted. This applies more often to commercial software and less to non-commercial, open-source software. When we approached the company of a learning management system with suggestions for functionality, they thanked us, but refused to implement any changes, or let us or others implement them. With the MOO, suggestions become the focus of discussion and are generally taken on board, and source code is freely available, so that whatever tools we need we can develop ourselves or with comparatively little expenditure. Examples of this are the BTA, the shared whiteboard, and the forthcoming Lexical Organiser we developed at the CLCS. In our experience, therefore, an open-source environment where various modules can be slotted in and out is ideally suited to support learner autonomy. Moodle appears to be such a system, and hopefully we will see more of these.

Second, research tools are much easier accessible in open-source software than commercial learning management systems, although admittedly they are beginning to realise the existing demand. In short, I think that a software like the MOO has been so successful, in spite of its long history, because it offers free re-usable code; open frameworks of programming where new tools can easily be slotted in; support structures that encourage and distribute the development of new ideas and tools rather than suppress them; and finally, is continuously updated and enhanced while maintaining maximum compatibility across platforms and versions. Above all, it allows me as a researcher and teacher to access everything that is produced, every trace of every connection that a language learner makes.

Third, in two papers (O'Rourke & Schwienhorst, 2003; Schwienhorst, 2002b), O'Rourke and I have looked at the relationship between technology and pedagogy and the learner's level of autonomy, and distinguished between pressures, potentials, and affordances. We argue that learning opportunities arise when learning tools are within reach of the level of learner autonomy that the learner has achieved. Sometimes these are pressures, i.e. tools or opportunities that learners will avail of even at a low level of autonomy, almost without pedagogical or technological intervention. For example, in the MOO, almost all learners will "re-read utterances immediately after transmission" (O'Rourke & Schwienhorst, 2003:56). The second group of learning opportunities can be called potentials and is realised by a large group of learners, but the technology or the pedagogy or the combination of both does not intrinsically force them to make use of this. An example of this for reflection is "editing utterances before transmission" (O'Rourke & Schwienhorst, 2003:56). The third group is when learning opportunities merely remain affordances that will almost never be taken up by the learner, unless they have achieved a very high level of autonomy. One challenge in MOO work to support reflection, for example, is that although learners are sent all transcripts of their exchanges, they will not by themselves use them as a learning opportunity or resource. A distinction between pressures, potentials, and affordances provides a more pedagogical view on CALL tools and tells us where more teacher support is needed, either in the form of technology or pedagogy.

I have emphasised in previous sections that the MOO currently falls short not in its functionality nor its flexibility nor its research tools, but in the interface to design the learning environment which is still largely command-line-based. Here, commercial software provides a more intuitive interface, as does Moodle, one of several recent open-source course management systems. This current drawback in the MOO also means that a large number of learning opportunities that the system provides will be lost.

In summary, we can say that the role of the teacher in CALL environments refers to three crucial areas: design, research, and the relationship between technology/pedagogy and the learner's level of autonomy. I noted that the MOO provides the functionality and modularity; research tools; and flexibility, but clearly lacks an intuitive interface to design, which is crucial for teachers and learners to fully exploit their learning opportunities. In this respect, other open-source course management systems such as Moodle have become a serious competition.

4.5 TECHNOLOGY RULES? LEARNING ENVIRONMENTS, PEDAGOGY, AND THE LANGUAGE LEARNER

In the preceding sections in this chapter, I have summarised the major benefits and shortcomings of MOO tandem in the light of my research. I have shown that sometimes we need a modification of the set-up which sometimes requires more technology, sometimes more pedagogy. It is also clear from the two scenarios at the beginning and my research that technology and pedagogy need to and can well support each other, as in MOO tandem, but that technology on its own very rarely compels learners to engage in behaviour that works towards learner autonomy. For instance, I would argue that in principle MOO technology, as open-source and web-based software, allows learners to experiment and participate much more than, let us say, commercial CD-ROM or DVD technology. In the latter two, learners are denied access to the program beyond a certain point, and the medium fundamentally denies change and restructuring. We could call this, by adapting Gibson's phrase (Gibson, 1979, 1966), an affordance the medium has. In many cases, as we have seen, however, the affordances remain unnoticed if not properly supported by a pedagogical framework. Based on my research results from MOO tandem and the gaps I perceived in this combination, I would consider the following features vital for the success of any CALL environment.

- CALL environments need to have mechanisms to support reflection; CALL software needs to support, even force learners to confront their own planning, monitoring, and evaluation in language learning. This is still probably the most difficult but also the most important part of learner autonomy. I have demonstrated that text-based environments and text-based communication can support these processes very well; it is difficult to imagine how an analysis tool like the BTA could be as easily implemented in an audio or video environment. However, I argued that it might be difficult to support processes of reflection **during** communication sessions, as this is perceived to disturb communicative flow. It appears that technological tools might here be more successful than pedagogy. On the other hand, supporting reflective processes **after** communication sessions promises to be easier by using personally meaningful, authentic tasks and activities that fully exploit the material generated in communication and link it to a wider context.

- CALL environments need to have mechanisms to increase and fully exploit interaction with peers and the target language community. My research confirms that the opportunity to switch quickly between pair work; group work; work with a teacher; work with another group; etc. is very important to learners. However, there is a principal dilemma that faces designers, teacher, and learners. If we decide to choose text-only environments, language awareness may be better supported, but communication is slower and possibly somewhat more cumbersome (e.g. due to keyboard commands), and pronunciation is completely excluded. If we choose audio or video communication, pronunciation practice may be useful, communication will be quicker and considered less cumbersome, but its benefits for the support of reflective processes will most likely be largely lost. I also saw that reciprocal support in MOO tandem is very focused on communicative flow. The prime goal for tandem partners is to create an atmosphere where learners feel encouraged to produce output. Communication is, for the most part, only interrupted when miscommunication occurs, i.e. in negotiation of meaning. This is certainly different from e-mail tandem where communication focuses also on error correction without a focus on negotiation of meaning.
- CALL environments need to have mechanisms to facilitate experimentation with CALL environments and the creation and use of cognitive tools. CALL environments need to support learners in assuming responsibility for and taking control of their learning process. Here, I would again like to mention the dilemma of interfaces and functionality. Of course, CALL environments, like any software, will become more complex to operate the more functionality they have, and the MOO offers a huge range of functionality. In our projects, we had some learners who created and manipulated a number of objects, but I would like to see more of this experimentation. The MOO interface needs to offer easier access to the objects that can be created, and more templates, or meta-tools, need to be implemented, a process we have supported through the creation of the whiteboard facility. Experimentation also plays an important role, as I have indicated, for the creation of identity in the target language. I was surprised to see that my students, for example, often did not disclose their real physical appearance to their partner and during the course of the project became very conscious of behaviour that was accepted or not accepted in each other's culture. Learners became more conscious of appearance and experimented with text descriptions and entry messages. Some learners also described that they took more risks in the target language. The issue of how the development of a new learner

identity can be fostered is crucial; yet I see it hardly if ever mentioned in the CALL context.

- CALL environments need to have flexible mechanisms to support the changed role of the teacher. I was astonished at the amount of data the MOO provided to me as a teacher and researcher. As the transcripts arrive via e-mail after each session, they become part of normal e-mail reading, and I knew what needed to be discussed at induction and reflection sessions in later projects. Whereas data collection and retrieval is extremely difficult in audio and video learning environments, the MOO can provide almost all data (so far without time codes, although this could be added) that is actually produced. Online interviews are convenient and allow learners to reflect on the MOO while actually using it. Much of the teacher's work is done before the project begins, when the technological and pedagogical framework is put into place. I was surprised that during the project, only small adjustments are possible; either projects work or they don't. When the atmosphere was chaotic (as in scenario 1), it was difficult to introduce a more rigid structure afterwards; when the atmosphere was focused and structured (as in scenario 2), MOO tandem work was unlikely to revert to chaos. I have slowly, very slowly, become accustomed to the fact that the teacher's participation in MOO tandem classes is hardly required nor requested, and the role changes to close observer, monitoring where learners can make new links between their level of autonomy and CALL environment. Close contact and agreement with the partner teacher is crucial.

We have seen that there are many areas in language learning that MOO tandem alone does not and maybe cannot cover. But I have also pointed towards some promising avenues for research where research has in some cases already shown measurable benefits.

If there is one thing that we have learned from our MOO tandem projects, it is that clearly technology or software tools are not the whole story when we discuss CALL environments. Just as with physical learning tools in the language classroom, the affordances (to use Gibson's term again) of the learning environment remain unexploited if they are out of reach of the learner's autonomy. It is the task of the pedagogical framework, and the teacher's role, to bridge this gap, where the learner is unable to do so, and bring these opportunities within the reach of the learner's autonomy. But that does not mean that the CALL technology or environment is unimportant by itself, something that is somehow value-free until it is used in the name of some pedagogy. Let us consider briefly this relationship between learner, learning environment, and a learner-autonomy-based pedagogy, before returning to pedagogical principles for good learning environments.

Little et al. (1989:2) note that

> there is a fair degree of consensus concerning the kind of context that promotes language learning. Basically, language learning is fostered by contexts which are rich in opportunities for interaction in and with the target language.'Interaction', as the formulation of the last sentence implies, has here a social and a psychological sense.

and elsewhere Little emphasises "that learners are presented with a rich and varied diet of authentic texts in print and other media" and "the role of communication not only as the goal but also as the channel of learning" (Little, 1991:29).

The fact is that any learner is of course surrounded by some form of learning context, or learning environment, which works towards or against the learning domain and the development of learner autonomy. On NBC's *Tonight Show*, one of the headlines quoted was "Beacon students will head to Kentucky to study ocean" (http://www.nbc.com/nbc/The_Tonight_Show_with_Jay_Leno/headlines/H_2955/28.shtml#headline). The humour here comes precisely from the dichotomy between the learning domain "study ocean" and the learning environment "Kentucky" (a US state without connection to any ocean). In this case, without knowing any more details, one might assume that a location near an ocean might perhaps be better suited to study the ocean, independent from the pedagogical approach.

It is reasonable to assume that each learning environment offers different opportunities for learning as regards a particular learning domain. CALL environments such as the MOO have a number of affordances for language learning and the development of learner autonomy that are different from a language lab or a language classroom, and that is before we think about pedagogy. Certain elements in learning environments can be more favourable than others, and in some cases they can by themselves lead to more learner autonomy (Schwienhorst, 2002b).

If we return to our two initial scenarios, for example, we can see that in both cases, learners read scrolling communication on screen (as in the MOO); learners engaged in MOO interaction once other learners were online; and learners used a shared mental model of space when communicating on the MOO. But we would also concede that the second scenario was far more successful than the first. Why? Because the pedagogical framework, and additional technological tools, was adjusted so that more learners made more meaningful connections between the learning environment and the level of learner autonomy they had already achieved.

For the most part the success of MOO tandem relies on an interplay of CALL environment and learner-autonomy-based pedagogy that works towards more learner autonomy. In some cases, this interplay forms such a close unit that it is difficult to tell one from the other. Take the BTA; born out of the perceived imbalance of two languages in MOO tandem (a pedagogical necessity), it runs continuously while learners are connected and learners are regularly confronted with its results (it is part of the learning environment). The BTA only becomes a useful tool if the learner is able to relate the BTA to her own learning and her own level of learner autonomy and this is probably where flexible and creative teacher intervention is most important.

So, why do I think CALL environments like the MOO in combination with tandem learning can support our learners in becoming more autonomous? First, this type of pedagogy/technology mix can support learners to reflect on their learning, by not only allowing them, but even forcing them into planning, monitoring, and evaluating; in short, making decisions about their learning. Second, it can provide learners with and engage them in a variety of communication tools, reflecting various modes. We have to accept that just as we use a multitude of communication tools in "real life", we also need a multitude of tools for online communication, and we also have to accept that we might use these tools and communication channels differently, depending on the affordances they provide. Third, combined pedagogy/technology frameworks such as MOO tandem can support learners in experimenting with and participating in language learning. Learners need to be enabled to co-design the learning environment, and customise all aspects according to their needs and achieved level of autonomy. This can only work in modular and scalable software architectures.

These pedagogy/technology combinations also provide a variety of research and data collection tools to facilitate teacher autonomy. First, CALL environments have the potential to make far more data available to the learner and teacher, and this data can be accessed in far more flexible ways than physical classroom environments or single tools. This means that learners and teachers have a better opportunity to plan, monitor, and evaluate their learning. Second, the CALL environment has many elements that do not have counterparts in the physical classroom, for example instant transcripts of "live" communication. Third, CALL environments allow us as teachers to link up reflection, interaction, and experimentation in ways that are quite impossible in other contexts: Learners in MOO tandem are engaged in personally meaning interaction; the transcripts of this can form the basis of countless reflective activities; both interaction and transcripts also provide a quarry for experimentation with language; these activities, in turn, can form the basis for new interaction. Fourth, CALL environments help us as teachers and researchers understand which parameters are of crucial importance in our pedagogy/technology combination, and thus have repercussions, as we have seen in my research; that the pedagogy may be modified because of the technology used, or the learning environment where language learning takes place. In my view, the question whether a learner-autonomy-based pedagogy can be realised without CALL software misses the point. Of course it can, and very successfully. However, CALL environments like the MOO can offer us more flexibility, more learning opportunities, more focus on individual learners, much more so if they have a learner-autonomy-based pedagogy at heart.

Reflection, interaction, and experimentation are the crucial elements in any learner-autonomy-based CALL environment, and I would argue that it will become most powerful when it combines these three areas: when reflective activities are based on transcripts of communication that learners have produced themselves; when communication is based on objects—cognitive tools—that learners and teachers have created in collaboration; when learners create, modify, and interact with bots to understand how discourse works. The demand that CALL should also offer opportunities for research for teachers and researchers is only an extension of the tools that learners themselves should have at their disposal. Research tools are not just tools to evaluate whether this or that CALL framework is beneficial to learning; they are an essential extension of a philosophy that emphasises learner involvement, learner control, learner responsibility, and learner accountability—the concept of learner autonomy. It is when these areas come together that CALL programs truly become CALL environments.

Appendix A
Sample MOO Transcripts

A.1 [IRL29] AND [GER22] ("YOU")

Log Started: Thursday, November 18, 1999 10:50:16 am GMT
You move to West Corridor
You view West Corridor...
[IRL29] is here.
Obvious exits: (Brown, Cobb, & Eastgate) to CLCS Foyer, [west] to The Olive Room, (North) to The
Silver Room, [south] to The Red Room, [southwest] to The Pink Room, [southeast] to The Lime Room West Corridor
You enter a spacious auditorium with rows of chairs and a small platform stage. Type 'up' to enter the stage.
[IRL29] is here.
Obvious exits: (Brown, Cobb, & Eastgate) to CLCS Foyer, [west] to The Olive Room, (North) to The
Silver Room, [south] to The Red Room, [southwest] to The Pink Room,
[southeast] to The Lime Room
You move to The Red Room
You view The Red Room...
Obvious exits: (North) to West Corridor
[IRL29] arrives from West Corridor
You say, "Hi [IRL29]"
[IRL29] says, "Hey sorry i'm late"
[IRL29] says, "I couldn't get into my computer"
You say, "Doesn't matter ! How are you?"
[IRL29] says, "not too bad"
[IRL29] says, "and youself"
You say, "Nice, thanks. Did you get my E-Mail?"
[IRL11] arrives from West Corridor
[IRL11] leaves for West Corridor
[IRL29] says, "yeah, I got it yesterday, thanks"
[IRL29] says, "sorry I didn't get to write back"
[IRL29] says, "i am really busy at teh moment"

You say, "Want are you doing?"
[IRL29] says, "Everything"
You say, "Oh, that's very much !!!!"
[IRL29] says, "i have loads of projects to do"
[IRL29] says, "and I have to do them, go to work and go to college"
You say, "i understand"
[IRL29] says, "I don't have much time on my hands"
[IRL29] says, "what are you up to"
You say, "next week we have to write our first test, so I'm learning a little bit for it"
[IRL29] says, "you need to study hard then eh"
You say, "no not really "
You say, "what did you do last weekend?"
[IRL29] says, "what is the test on"
[IRL29] says, "last weekend I went to work and I went out on saturday night"
You say, "it's about binary trees, Folgen (i don't know the english word for it)"
[IRL29] says, "I went to see a gig down the road from where I work"
[IRL29] says, "It was pretty good and I got a free record at it"
You say, "what's a gig down ???"
[IRL29] says, "A gig is a small concert and "down" goes with "down the road""
You say, "oh sorry, i'm little bit confused today but i don't know why!"
[IRL29] says, "whats wrong with you?"
You say, "I don't know, I just can't concentrate"
[IRL19] arrives from The Silver Room
[IRL19] leaves for The Pink Room
[IRL29] says, "not to worry"
[IRL29] says, "did you find any music for your girlfriend"
You say, "what's about the weather in Ireland, do you have snow too?"
[IRL19] arrives from The Pink Room
[IRL29] says, "we don't get much snow in Ireland"
[IRL18] arrives from West Corridor
[IRL19] leaves for The Chartreuse Room
[IRL18] leaves for West Corridor
[IRL29] says, "even though its really cold and stuff"
You say, "Yes, I searched for the Corrs in the web and I found some songs, but I didn't have the time to download them"
[IRL29] says, "just download them and go and do something else"
You say, "What's about your journey through Europe? When do start?"
[IRL29] says, "what do you mean "when do strart"?"
You say, "When do you go on holiday (you'll go to Germany, don't you?)"
[IRL29] says, "no, I already went on my trip to Europe"
[IRL29] says, "I went during the summer"

You say, "Ah, when was it?"
You say, "Did you like Germany"
[IRL29] says, "no I have to stay in Dublin until next june which I don't want to do"
[IRL29] says, "I went at the end of the summer before I came back to college"
[IRL29] says, "Germany was really good"
[IRL29] says, "We went to the Oktoberfest in Munchen"
You say, "Ah, did you drink a lot of beer?"
[IRL29] says, "yeah, loads"
[IRL29] says, "it was quite expensive though"
You say, "I was never on the Oktoberfest, but I want to go there"
[IRL29] says, "i think 12DM for one of the pitchers"
You say, "yes, it's really expensive"
[IRL29] says, "have you been to the Oktoberfest"
[IRL29] says, "I met and Italian guy on my travels and he told me the history of the festival"
You say, "Last weekend we were in Cologne and we had to pay 2,5 DM for ,2 l of beer"
You say, "what's the history of it. I even don't know it!?"
[IRL29] says, "is it true that years ago they had the festival because people had to drink all the beer before it went sour?"
You say, "This may be true. But I'm not sure"
[IRL29] says, "2,5DM is really cheap for drink"
You say, "I know that people in Africa make something like beer out of bananas"
[IRL29] says, "out of bananas????"
[IRL29] says, "how do they do that"
You say, "yes, but it's 2,5 DM for one glass of beer and this would be 12,5 for one liter"
[IRL29] says, "thats madness"
[IRL29] says, "i guess the prices work out the same but at the time 12DM for a drink seems very expensive"
You say, "I don't know how you can make beer out of bananas but they do and because you can't store it for a long time they have to drink it in a few days and so they make a big fete"
[IRL29] says, "so i guess it was kinda the same thing years ago in germany"
[IRL29] says, "I wish we had omething like that here"
[IRL29] says, "I seems like such a good Idea"
You say, "Don't you have such big festivals?"
[IRL29] says, "No"
[IRL29] says, "you can't really have big beer festivals in Ireland cause we drink to much anyway"

[IRL29] says, "every night is like a beer festival in dublin espically in Temple Bar"
You say, "Klingt ziemlich gut. Gehst du oft aus?"
[IRL29] says, "We have no beer gardens because it is too cold"
[IRL29] says, "ja, "
[IRL29] says, "Ich gehe aus sehr oft"
You say, "mit mehreren zusammen?"
[IRL29] says, "wenn ich geld habe!!!"
[IRL29] says, "ich gehe aus mit meine freundinnen"
You say, "Du gehst doch so oft arbeiten. verdienst Du dabei nicht genug Geld?"
[IRL29] says, "nein"
You say, "Kann ich verstehen."
You say, "Ich gehen nur noch bis zum 3. Dezember arbeiten, dann läuft mein Vertrag beim WDR aus"
[IRL29] says, "jetzt habe ich kein geld weil ich kein geld von meine Arbeit bekommt"
You say, "wieso bekommst Du kein Geld ????"
[IRL29] says, "donnerstag, habe ich geld, hoffentlich"
You say, "d.h. Donnerstag ist bei Euch Zahltag?"
[IRL29] says, "ich kann das nicht erklaren aus Dectsch"
[IRL29] says, "ja"
[IRL29] says, "12:00 nacht, habe ich geld"
You say, "hast du schon Weihnachtsgeschenke gekauft?"
[IRL29] says, "nein"
You say, "ich habe überhaupt keine Idee was ich kaufen soll!"
[IRL29] says, "ich habe keine Idee was Ich kaufen muss"
[IRL29] says, "und du"
You say, "was wünschst Du Dir denn zu Weihnachten"
[IRL29] says, "ich habe keine Idee"
[IRL29] says, "und du"
You say, "ich lasse mir wahrscheinlich ein paar Bücher für die Uni schenken"
[IRL29] says, "was ist "wahrscheinlich"?"
You say, "das heißt ich weiß es noch nicht genau"
You say, "Mir fällt leider die englische Übersetzung nicht ein"
You say, "Weißt Du schon, was Du am kommenden Wochenende machst?"
[IRL29] says, "Noch, gehe ich in de Arbeit "
[IRL29] says, "es ist nicht so gut"
You say, "Glaube ich Dir !"
You say, "Wir gehen am Freitag zu einem Fest an der alten Schule von meiner Freundin"
[IRL29] says, "was ist der fest"

You say, "Und am Samstag haben wir von der Feuerwehr unseren Martinsabend"
You say, "Fest: eine Fete"
[IRL29] says, "I weiss das aber was willst du machen an der fest"
You say, "ach so, entschuldigung. Da gibt es jede Menge zu essen und zu trinken und man trifft da halt ein paar Freunde"
You say, "Was habt ihr denn für eine 'presentation'?"
[IRL29] says, "haden sie eine Projekt aus English zu machen"
[IRL29] says, "Ich muss uber eine Deutsches Website an Deutsches Musik gruppen spreachen"
You say, "auch ja, und hast Du eine deutsche Seite gefunden?"
[IRL29] says, "ja, Ich weiss"
[IRL29] says, "www.germanrock.de"
You say, "Cool, werde ich mir gleich auch mal anschauen !!!"
[IRL29] says, "kennst du eine Website das ist besser"
You say, "Leider kenne ich keine !!!"
[IRL29] says, "ist die Site gut?"
You say, "weiss nicht, ich kenne die ja auch noch nicht!"
[IRL29] says, "habt du eine Projekt"
You say, "wir müssen noch ein Projekt machen, ich weiss aber noch nicht wann und nicht worüber!"
[IRL29] says, "ok"
[IRL29] says, "cih gehe jetzt"
You say, "ok, ich schreib DIr ne Mail !!"
[IRL29] says, "ich sende eine e-mail, I promise"
You say, "Ok, bis dann und ein schönes Wochenende !!!"
[IRL29] waves.
[GER22] waves
[IRL29] says, "und du"
You say, "bye bye"
[IRL29] says, "bye bye"

Log Stopped: Thursday, November 18, 1999 11:55:24 am GMT
A.2 [IRL16] ("You") and [GER11]
Log Started: Thursday, November 18, 1999 10:51:48 am GMT
ATTENTION: There are new news items to read! Type 'news' for a sum.
[GER11] says, "Hi [IRL16]"
[GER5] has connected.
[GER17] has connected.
[GER11] says, "Good to see you"
[GER11] has connected.
[GER16] have connected.
[GER11] leaves for North Corridor
[GER5] leaves for West Corridor

[GER17] leaves for East Corridor
[GER11] arrives from North Corridor
[GER11] leaves for South Corridor
[GER11] arrives from South Corridor
[GER11] leaves for North Corridor
[GER15] has connected.
[GER19] has connected.
[GER11] says, "[IRL16] ???"
[GER11] arrives from North Corridor
[GER11] leaves for South Corridor
[GER5] arrives from West Corridor
[GER5] leaves for The Student Lounge
[GER5] arrives from The Student Lounge
[GER5] leaves for West Corridor
[IRL14] has connected.
[GER21] has connected.
[GER14] leaves for North Corridor
[IRL14] leaves for East Corridor
You say, "Hi [GER11]"
[GER21] leaves for Peter's Classroom
[GER21] arrives from Peter's Classroom
[GER4] leaves for South Corridor
[GER11] says, "Aha, finally recognized me ?"
[GER21] leaves for The Student Lounge
You say, "Sorry,I was doing something else.How are you?"
[GER4] arrives from South Corridor
[IRL19] has connected.
[GER21] arrives from The Student Lounge
[IRL22] arrives from East Corridor
[GER21] leaves for The AW Centre
[Unknown user] has connected.
[GER21] arrives from The AW Centre
[GER11] says, "Oh thanks, I´m fine, just a little cold and you"
[GER15] drops Bender Unit 22.
[GER8] has connected.
[IRL5] has connected.
[IRL19] leaves for The Sea-Green Room
[IRL29] has connected.
You say, "ok,but feeling a bit under the weather"
[GER21] leaves for The White Room
Bender Unit 22 says, "I'm a Bender...I bend things...that's what I was programmed for."
[IRL27] has connected.
You hear a quiet popping sound; [GER19] has disconnected.
You say, "Have we to go into the Maroon room?"
Bender Unit 22 says, "Sure...that's quite it."

[GER15] picks up Bender Unit 22.
[GER11] says, "Why ? You got bad weather at the moment ?"
[GER4] says, "Hi [IRL5], you had a great week?"
[GER18] arrives from South Corridor
[GER18] says, "Hidiho!"
[IRL27] leaves for North Corridor
[GER18] says, "drop Buffy"
[IRL5] says, "Nah, not really,you?"
[GER18] says, "oh"
[GER18] drops Buffy.
You say, "No, it;s an expresion. It means I'm not feeling the best"
[GER15] drops Bender Unit 22.
[GER18] hushes Buffy.
[IRL25] has connected.
[GER11] arrives from South Corridor
[GER15] hushes Bender Unit 22.
[GER18] says, "Hi Bender"
You move to The Maroon Room
You view The Maroon Room...
Obvious exits: [northwest] to South Corridor
Usage: page <player> <message> Standard page
-<player> <message> Quick page
-<message> Reply to last page
+<player> <message> Remote emote
+<message> Reply to last emote
You say, "[GER11] ,can you go intot he maroon room"
[GER11] arrives from CLCS Foyer
[GER11] says, "We saw the first snow this morning"
You say, "Yippee"
You say, "OOhh,you are so lucky.!"
[GER11] says, "This weekend I go to an GRan Dorado Park with 4 friends of mine"
You say, "Was it very heavy?"
You say, "Where is that?"
[GER11] says, "No, not really, this park is about 500 meters above the ocean"
You say, "What park?"
[GER11] says, "Three hours from here by car"
[GER11] says, "Well, have a look at www.grandorado.de"
You say, "Ok,hold on"
[GER11] says, "Above 300 meteres there is alot of snow and my car has no winter tyres so far :-(("
You say, "You have a car????"
[GER11] says, "Yes"
[GER11] says, "Well, a quite older one, but it drives"
You say, "It's a holiday village?"

[GER11] says, "Yes, that is the word"
You say, "It's a car.I don't have a car"
[GER11] says, "But when I heard of the weather news I don´t look forward to the journey"
You say, "Do you know anything about die fantastischen Vier?WE are doing our group project on it"
[GER11] says, "they reported snow above 300 meters and this holiday village is at about 500 meters"
[GER11] says, "well, it's a German Hip-Hop group, Do you want to know anything special"
[IRL11] arrives from South Corridor
[IRL11] leaves for South Corridor
You say, "Are they good?Do you know any good websites on them?"
You say, "[IRL5] really likes them "
[GER11] says, "oh, you can try www.diefantastischenvier.de, I think it will fit"
[GER11] says, "I tried it, it works"
You say, "I've tried too.Thanks"
[GER11] says, "what was your last week like ?"
You say, "Have you no projects to do for this calss?"
You say, "Sorry,....class?"
[GER11] arrives from South Corridor
[GER11] says, "öhm, no"
[GER11] leaves for South Corridor
[GER11] says, "we just had to write a CV and a Covering Letter"
[GER11] says, "But I have a job at the FH here now"
You say, "Are you leaving to go somewhere else?"
[GER11] says, "What do you mean exactly"
[GER11] says, "sorry"
You say, "i don't understand you."
You say, "It doesn't matter"
[GER11] says, "considering the Internet offer of our Fachhochschule I have a job now"
You say, "Ahyway where is FH?What is it?"
[GER11] says, "FH just means Fachhochschule, it is just a short expression"
You say, "Ok,what do you have to do?"
You move to South Corridor
You view South Corridor...
Obvious exits: (North) to CLCS Foyer, [south] to The Yellow Room, (Brown, Cobb, & Eastgate) to
The Purple Room, [west] to The Crimson Room, [southeast] to The Maroon Room, [southwest] to The Chartreuse Room South Corridor

You enter a spacious auditorium with rows of chairs and a small platform stage. Type 'up' to enter the stage.

Obvious exits: (North) to CLCS Foyer, [south] to The Yellow Room, (Brown, Cobb, & Eastgate) to
The Purple Room, [west] to The Crimson Room, [southeast] to The Maroon Room, [southwest] to The Chartreuse Room
You move to CLCS Foyer
CLCS Foyer
You view CLCS Foyer...
You see Teacher's Desk, Big Table, Bulletin Board, and NEXT MEETING ON THURSDAY 19:00.
You see Peter and Klaus standing about.
You see News and Buffy.
Obvious exits: [in] to Helpdesk, (North) to North Corridor, [south] to South Corridor, [west] to West Corridor, (Brown, Cobb, & Eastgate) to East Corridor, [down] to The Student Lounge, [northwest] to Peter's Classroom, [northeast] to The AW Centre
[GER8] arrives from The Student Lounge
[GER8] leaves for North Corridor
You move to The Maroon Room
You view The Maroon Room...
Obvious exits: [northwest] to South Corridor
[GER11] says, "Then we have to edit the pages and sites and get them back on the server"
You say, "are you there?"
[GER11] says, "Well, I´m here"
You say, "VEry intersesting.Do you enjoy it?"
[GER11] says, "Who were you looking for"
[GER11] says, "I just started this week"
[GER11] says, "But I think it is a lot of fun"
You say, "Nobody ,just you."
[GER11] says, "oh, thanks"
[GER11] smiles
[GER11] says, "Did you get that silly questionnaire, too ?"
[IRL9] arrives from South Corridor
[IRL19] arrives from The Crimson Room
[IRL9] leaves for South Corridor
[IRL19] leaves for The Olive Room
You say, "Yeah,but I haven't filled it in yet"
[IRL18] arrives from South Corridor
[IRL18] leaves for South Corridor
You say, "Have you?"
[IRL19] arrives from The Chartreuse Room
[GER11] says, "I just received it 10 minutes ago, looks like work :-))"
Try this instead: I
[IRL19] leaves for The Crimson Room
You say, "I got it on Tuesday but I forgot"
[GER11] says, "I don´t have any time this weekend"

You say, “Yeah It lokks like alot of though has to go into it”
[GER11] says, “Until next Thursday we have to finish it, *urg*”
[GER11] says, “We have to write our first test next week, too”
You say, “I have another project to do for tomorrow. I will have to do it all night and all tomorrow”
You say, “what is your test on?”
[GER11] says, “at the subject “programming””
You say, “JAva!Sorting”
[GER11] says, “about binary trees and something like this”
You say, “How did you know?”
[GER11] says, “Yeah, keep it simple, we just started !!!!”
You say, “Not binary trees,but something like it”
[GER11] says, “No, it is just what our test is about”
[GER11] says, “I think you spoke of your own project, didn´t you”
[GER11] says, “so your project is about .. ?”
You say, “Sorry,yours is on Binary trees?”
[GER11] says, “yes, yours, too ?”
You say, “Mine is about Sorting Algorithms”
You say, “Wann must du es fertig?”
[GER11] says, “like binary sort and other sorting programs ?”
You say, “JA!”
[GER11] says, “Jetzt in Deutsch ?”
You say, “Wir haben nur 15 Minuten”
[GER11] says, “Ich habe nur kaum Zeit zu lernen, ich bin schließlich das ganze Wochenende weg”
[GER11] says, “Wieso ?”
You say, “Weil wir eine andere Klasse dann haben”
[GER11] says, “Du meinst “ein anderes Fach”, bis heute hattest Du aber immer bis 13:00 Uhr Zeit”
[GER11] says, “magst Du mich nicht mehr”
[IRL22] arrives from South Corridor
[IRL22] leaves for South Corridor
[IRL22] arrives from South Corridor
You say, “ich mag du.Aber es ist fast 12 uhr hier”
[IRL22] leaves for South Corridor
[GER11] smiles again
[GER11] says, “es heißt “ich mag Dich”, habt ihr eine andere Zeit als wir”
You say, “JA,wusstest du dass nicht?”
[GER11] says, “ups, nein, seit ihr eine Stunde zurück ?”
[GER11] says, “seid”
You say, “Wir sind ein Stunde fruher als du”
[GER11] says, “Oha, noch gar nicht zu Mittag gegessen heute ?”
You say, “Ich ahbe ein STunde frei nach meine FAch”
[GER11] says, “und welches Fach hast Du dann”
You say, “Computer Science...die Projekt an Sorting...”
[GER11] says, “aha, und wann fängt das an ? “

You say, “Machst du etwas jetzt?”
You say, “..oder die VErbindung ist sehr langsam”
[GER11] says, “Ich habe jetzt frei bis 15:30 Uhr, dann habe ich noch 1 1/2 Stunden Mathe und dann Wochenende”
You say, “Um eins Uhr”
[GER11] says, “habe morgen ja wieder frei :-))”
[GER11] says, “morgen um 13:00 Uhr geht dann die Fahrt los”
You say, “Icn bin um 4 Uhr fertig und morgen ich bin auch um 4 Uhe fertig.”
[GER11] says, “Was hast DU denn am Wochenende so vor ?”
You say, “Was bedeutet “geht dann dieFahrt los?”
[GER11] says, “Auch Party bis zum Umfallen”
[GER11] says, “the journey starts”
You say, “ich dachte das”
You say, “Ich gehe auch zur APrty am Freitag nacht”
You say, “..Party”
[GER11] says, “Wohin”
[GER11] says, “auch 3 Kästen Bier für 5 Leute :-))”
You say, “Wo ich komme von....Tullamore”
You say, “KAnn ich kommen??”
[GER11] says, “Nein, ich meinte, wo die Party ist ??”
[GER11] says, “of course I can help”
[GER11] says, “Na klar, ein Bett ist noch frei”
[GER11] says, “ansonsten machen wir uns ein wenig dünner, dann ist in einem von unseren Betten noch Platz für Dich :-))”
You say, “JA die PArty ist auch da.”
You say, “Mein Freund ist 21”
You say, “In seinenBetten?”
[GER11] says, “Wieso erwähnst Du jetzt Deinen Freund ? :-))”
[GER11] says, “es sind ja noch 5 andere Betten da, die schon “teilweise” belegt sind :-))”
You say, “Was ist erwahnst?”
[GER11] says, “it means “to mention””
You say, “Sorry,er ist nicht mein Freund(Boyfriend,just a friend)”
[GER11] says, “ach so, dann kann ich mir ja noch Hoffnungen machen, daß Du trotzdem vorbei kommst :-))”
You say, “Ich habe mit ihn die selbe Schule besucht”
[GER11] says, “das heißt ihr kennst Euch schon ziemlich lange ?”
You say, “Du weiss dass ich nicht kommen kann”
[GER11] says, “och bitte bitte bitte :-)))”
You say, “Ja,zehn Jahr oder mehr”
You say, “Hoffenlich spater kann ich du besuchen”
[GER11] says, “Gute Freunde sind sehr wichtig, besonders wenn man sich auf sie verlassen kann”
[GER11] says, “”Dich” besuchen”
You say, “Ja sehr richtig”

You say, “Sorry”
[GER11] says, “Es braucht Dir nicht Leid zu tun, das weißt Du doch”
You say, “Ok.”
[GER11] says, “Gibt es immer noch kein Foto von Dir ? Nicht, daß ich neugierig wäre”
You say, “Ich bin neu,und es gibt kein”
[GER11] says, “auch nicht privat, für Deine brandneue Homepage”
You say, “Ich habe blonde Haare, blaue Augen.Ich bin 5 ft 6”
[GER11] says, “Mist, weißt Du, wie man 5 ft 6 umrechnet”
You say, “Mist???”
[GER11] says, “Something like “Shit “”
You say, “umrechnet??”
[GER11] says, “what is it in meter and centimeter ??”
You say, “ich weiss nicht”
[GER11] says, “Gibt es bei Euch nur ft”
[GER11] says, “und inches oder sowas”
You say, “Wir mussen etwas in unsere Notebooks schrieben”
[GER11] says, “dummes Notebook, die letzten 2 Mal hat es auch nicht funktioniert”
You say, “es ist scheiss”
[GER11] laughs
You say, “ich weiss nicht was ich schreiben soll”
[GER11] says, “yeah, you´re right”
[GER11] says, “ich auch nicht, always something like: it was a nice conversation again”
You say, “ok i better go,I promiose i will e-mail you this week.just i hadn’t got time last wek,I’m a very busy person”
[GER11] says, “me, too and I look forward to it “
You say, “Yeah bla ...bla..bla”
[GER11] laughs again
You say, “Ok.Bis dann”
You say, “”Bye Bye!!Don’t forgwet to fill in your Questionnaire”
[GER11] gives [IRL16] a little kiss and embraces her
You say, “It will be so much fun,.....NOT!!”
[GER11] says, “Damn questionnaire :-))”
[GER11] says, “Bye”
You say, “I would kiss and hug you too but i forget how to.....on the computer !!”
You say, “BYE!!”
[GER11] says, “just the feeling as if.... it is quite nice”
You say, “BYE bye again!”
You say, “I’m definitely going now!”
Log Stopped: Thursday, November 18, 1999 11:53:49 am GMT

Appendix B
Tandem Booklets

TRINITY COLLEGE DUBLIN

ICT GERMAN

Guide to the Tandem E-mail & MOO Project between Fachhochschule Rhein-Sieg, Germany & Trinity College, Dublin, Ireland

Any queries regarding the Tandem Project please contact Klaus Schwienhorst **kschwien@tcd.ie**

TABLE OF CONTENTS:

The Rhein-Sieg/Dublin

Collaboration — The Rhein-Sieg/Dublin Tandem Project

During the Winter Semester this year, students will have the opportunity to take part in an Internet-based collaboration between learners of English from the Fachhochschule Rhein/Sieg (near Bonn), Germany and learners of German from Trinity College, Dublin, Ireland. Each student taking part in the project will receive the e-mail address(es) of their 'Tandem' partner(s) in the other country and vice versa.

Advantages of Internet collaboration

Tandem language learning via the Internet

This form of collaboration has a number of advantages if approached in the right way:

- your partner is a native speaker of your target language (English or German) and is thus an expert not only in the language but also in the culture of their country. This expertise means that your partner is able to say what is right and what is wrong (or what sounds more like a native speaker), but it does not necessarily mean s/he is able to explain why.
- your partner is also a learner of your native language (German or English) and thus in the same situation of learning a language (your native language in which you are an expert).
- you and your partner can decide what topics of mutual interest you want to talk about.

Tasks will also be set by the teachers of your language courses.

- you and your partner can decide what learning targets you want to achieve, what methods you want to use to achieve them, and what working arrangements you want to make.

Major principles of Tandem learning

Main Principles of Tandem learning

From these potential advantages evolve three major principles that should form the basis of Tandem learning:

- **reciprocity**: each student must benefit equally from the partnership, and can expect to receive as much help as s/he gives.
- **bilingualism**: each student should use both English and German for the same amount of time.
- **learner autonomy**: each student is responsible for his/her own learning process and must determine learning objectives and methods to achieve these. As you are in a partnership with your partner, there is also mutual responsibility to make the partnership work for your partner too.

What is required of you

There are two potential difficulties that may occur during the exchange:

- the partnership is a form of distance learning, your courses, teachers, environments, routines, facilities, term holidays etc. are different, so it requires some effort by both partners to make the partnership fruitful.
- the exchanges are in writing, and mostly in the form of (electronic) letters and exchanges in a MOO. Some students may thus mistake the Tandem partner for a pen-pal, work becomes unfocused, unbalanced, and trivial. Tandem learning, however, means much more commitment and discipline than that.

Tandem e-mail: first contact — Using e-mail in Tandem

Once you have received the name and e-mail address of your partner in Dublin, please write to make first contact.

If you have not received a reply from your partner within a week, contact:

Klaus Schwienhorst kschwien@tcd.ie

In the first message to your partner, you should include two parts:

- introduce yourself in your own language and explain in the target language how you want the Tandem partnership to work (what your expectations of your partner are, what you can deliver yourself, how you want to handle corrections, etc.).

Some Golden Rules!

- Write a mail or meet in the MOO at least once a week!
- Tell your partner if you cannot write or meet for any reason
- Write & communicate in both English AND German
- Correct each other (only a few corrections per mail)
- Ask your partner what he/she wants.
- If you have any problems with your partner tell Klaus at once!

What is a MOO? — Using the MOO

Multiple User Domain, Object-Oriented: A MOO is a text-based Multiple User Virtual Reality in which the participants can communicate with each other in real time by using the keyboard. You can also move around, create objects such as your own room to meet your partner in.

In this course you will be meeting your partner every week in the **CLCS CAMPUS MOO** which is a Virtual reality University and you will be expected to complete projects with your partner on-line and use the communication and projects to promote your language learning.

How to connect to a MOO

In order to access the **CLCS Campus MOO** you need a User ID and a password (from Klaus Schwienhorst)

Please send Klaus an e-mail at kschwien@tcd.ie

You can access the **CLCS Campus MOO** through NETSCAPE Communicator 4.08 or later or Microsoft® Internet Explorer 4.0 or later. Cookies, Java™ and JavaScript™ must be enabled.

type in the following address:
http://clcs072106.lcs.tcd.ie:8000/
You will then come to the log in page
Enter your User ID and your password and hit the login button.
You should now be in the FOYER of the **CLCS Campus.**

What to do once connected — Once connected there are a number of things which you can do in the MOO.

You can move around the MOO, communicate with people there and manipulate or create objects. You can make a 'date' and meet your Tandem partner in the MOO and complete the projects that you find there.

You do these things by entering commands in the field at the bottom of the left hand side of the screen or by clicking on the links in the right hand screen or the buttons in the menu bar at the top.
All MOO sessions are automatically logged and sent to your MOO-mail account. So: **do not log your own sessions: it happens automatically!**
Important MOO commands

Communicating in the MOO — Communication Commands:

To talk to people in the same room, type one of the two following lines:

say Hello
"Hello
Everybody in the room will see:'
Guest says, "Hello"
You will see:
You say, "Hello"

To talk to people in other rooms, type the following line:
-Margit Hello
You will see:
Quick Page successfully sent to Margit.

Margit will see:
Klaus pages, "Hello"

To communicate emotions (emote) in the same room, type in one of the following two lines: emote laughs.
:laughs.
Everybody in your room will see:
Guest laughs.
You will see:
You laugh.

To communicate emotes to somebody in a different room, type:
+Margit laughs.
You will see:
Emote successfully sent to Margit.
Margit will see:
[from Student Union] Guest laughs.

To send a private message to somebody in the same room:
whisper "Hello" to Margit
You will see:
You whisper, "Hello" to Margit.
Margit will see:
Guest whispers "Hello"

Navigating in the MOO — Navigation Commands:

To join somebody in another room (but page first and ask!), type:
@join Margit
You will see:
You join Margit in Margit's Study.
Margit will see:
Guest joins you in Margit's Study.

These are just some of the commands to get you started!

PROJECTS

You will all have a minimum of 4 projects to complete with your partner. Here is an outline of the tasks:

Project 1 Getting to know you......
AIM to get to know your partner
to talk about studying IT
to use the present, past and future

TIME 1–2 sessions

a Interview your partner
Why are you studying IT?
What did you enjoy/hate at school?
What do you want to do later when you have finished your studies?
What was your previous work experience?
What was the best/worst job you ever had?

b Find out the following information
Find out about studying IT in each other's colleges.
How long does it take?
What subjects are covered?
How are your studies financed?

Project 2 If looks could kill......

AIM to get to know your partner a bit better
to find out what your partner looks like
to express an opinion

TIME 1 session

Look at the photos of all the participants.
Guess which of the pictures is your partner.
Interview your partner and ask him/her for information about any of the following:
their appearance, likes, dislikes, hobbies,
Can you identify your partner now?

Project 3 Computer Developments

Aims: To discuss IT topics
To develop IT vocab
Use the past and present perfect

Time 1–2 Sessions

Discuss with your partner
What were the three most important developments in Information Technology and Computers in the past 40 years and why?
Look at the text on the MOO and answer the attached comprehension questions.

Project 4 Computers, Communication, Language

Aims: To discuss this type of learning
To do a web site analysis

Time 2–3 Sessions

Discuss with your partner:
What do you think about learning on-line?
Have you ever ddone an on-line course?
Do you think there will ever come a time when you don't have to come to college but will be doing all your studies from home via computer?
Do you have your own website?
Visit your partner's website if he/she has one.
Web Site Analysis
What makes a good web site?
Have a look at the following On-line Language Learning sites:
http://www.fh-rhein-sieg.de/spz/english/project/
OR
the language learning resources at:
http://www.tcd.ie/CLCS/languageresources.html
Do an analysis together with your partner of both your sites:
Think about the following:
Design — Navigation — Help — Index — Quantity and Quality of Info

Tandem work

Input

Language learner and language model — As we said in the introduction, you and your partner are both language learners and language models. There are a variety of means to improve your partnership and make it more effective.

- learn from the model of your partner. Read carefully through the German parts of your partner's e-mail; they provide you with a wealth of phrases and vocabulary in the right context.
- learn from the reformulation by your partner. Ask your partner how to say something particular in German. See how your partner reformulated whole phrases or paragraphs in your letters and compare them to your original effort. You may want to discuss various options and, for example, find out in what context some phrases are used and others are not.

Output

When you are writing in the foreign language it may well be that you find it more difficult than reading what you get from your partner.

- Try to write spontaneously without looking every word up in a dictionary. Try and think in the foreign language.
- Time yourself! Give yourself 20 minutes to write as much as possible in the foreign language; over a period of time you will see the amount and the quality improve.

On correction
Learn from corrections by your partner. Agree with your partner how to correct each other and how many errors should be corrected

Options for correction

So what is the ideal way to correct? As a rule of thumb, only **ten errors maximum** should be corrected in an e-mail (try to find a similar arrangement for the MOO) and make this focussed. You could, for instance, focus on verbs, only correcting wrong tenses or wrong conjugations or any other repeated mistake.

It may be helpful for your partner if you tell him

- what the most frequent errors were,
- what errors you want your partner **always** to correct,
- and maybe later you can comment more specifically on what errors your partner could have avoided.

Technically, always the best way to correct an e-mail from your partner is to use the **Reply** function and enclose the original e-mail.

Recycling material

Many students do not feed corrected errors back into their tandem work. However, you will notice that if you consciously try to recycle words, phrases or sentences, for instance by forming three sentences with the difficult expressions and asking your partner for help, you can learn to avoid errors and become more confident in the target language.

You should always print out the mails and MOO transcripts you receive and send, as well as any corrections and keep them in a folder. You may even want to include some of the material in the Language Portfolio.

This gives you the opportunity to be able to read through the exchanges again, use them to do work on grammar items which may have come up, learn vocabulary or use the information which your partner has sent you.

Tandem is an integral part of the course

Collaborative activities with your Tandem partner are part of this course. During the language courses, you are supposed to work closely with your partner, exchanging ideas, and exchanging cultural information.

Due to the different organisation of terms in Germany and Dublin, you will be able to collaborate only for a limited period of time, so make good use of it!

Tandem work and privacy

All exchanges that are collected with your permission will be treated confidentially and used only for research purposes by Jackie McPartland and Klaus Schwienhorst.

Useful Addresses

If you have any problems or queries about the Tandem project please contact:

Project Coordinator — Fachhochschule Rhein-Sieg Germany
Peter Kapec
peter.kapec@fh-rhein-sieg.de

Jackie McPartland
jacqueline.mcpartland@fh-rhein-sieg.de

Project Coordinator — Trinity College, Dublin Ireland
Klaus Schwienhorst
kschwien@tcd.ie

Appendix C
Tandem Questionnaire

TANDEM PROJECT QUESTIONNAIRE

You are taking part in an Internet-based collaboration between ICT students from Trinity College Dublin and the Fachhochschule Rhein-Sieg near Bonn. Your tandem partnership is a learning partnership. As with all forms of learning, it is important to reflect on what you do and evaluate what you have achieved, in order to gain the maximum personal benefit from your tandem partnership. The process of reflection, introspection and self-evaluation is in itself a very important support to your own learning.

To help you in this reflective process, we have provided a self-evaluation questionnaire for you to fill in (see below) and return to us as part of your learner dossier for your group work this year. It is essential that you take the time to reflect on the questions and write your responses.

Your responses will provide us with valuable feedback on the Dublin-Rhein-Sieg tandem project. If you have any suggestions or ideas for improving aspects of the tandem project, please feel free to add them below. As with your transcripts, **all student identities will remain anonymous** in our research reports. **You can answer in German or English.**

Your name:____________________________________

1. What kinds of topics have you discussed with your tandem partner?

____

____

____

2. What aspects of your tandem partner's English do you correct in the MOO, or help him/her with most?

____

____

____

3. What aspects of your German does your tandem partner correct in the MOO, or help you with most?

____

____

____

4. What did you do when you did not understand what your partner was saying in your **target** language, German?

	Frequency (1=very low, 5=very high)
change the subject	1 ☐ ☐ ☐ ☐ ☐ 5
ignore what s/he said	1 ☐ ☐ ☐ ☐ ☐ 5
guess the meaning	1 ☐ ☐ ☐ ☐ ☐ 5
ask partner to repeat	1 ☐ ☐ ☐ ☐ ☐ 5
ask partner to say it in other words	1 ☐ ☐ ☐ ☐ ☐ 5
ask partner for a translation	1 ☐ ☐ ☐ ☐ ☐ 5

Other/Comments:______________________________

____

____

5. What did you do when you did not understand what your partner was saying in your **native** language, English?

	Frequency (1=very low, 5= very high)
change the subject	1 ☐ ☐ ☐ ☐ ☐ 5
ignore what s/he said	1 ☐ ☐ ☐ ☐ ☐ 5
guess the meaning	1 ☐ ☐ ☐ ☐ ☐ 5
ask partner to repeat	1 ☐ ☐ ☐ ☐ ☐ 5
ask partner to say it in other words	1 ☐ ☐ ☐ ☐ ☐ 5
ask partner for a translation	1 ☐ ☐ ☐ ☐ ☐ 5

Other/Comments:______________________________

____

____

6. Do you think your tandem work in the MOO helps you in learning German? If so, how?

____

____

____

7. What insights into the target language (German) have you gained (if any) from reading and correcting your tandem partner's English?

____

____

____

8. What do you see as the main differences (if any) between tandem language learning in the MOO and other methods of language learning you have encountered?

____
____
____

9. Does tandem language learning in the MOO appeal to you? If so, why? Or, if not, why not?

____
____
____

10. Would you say that you have adapted the use of your native language (English) to your partner's level? If so, in what way(s)?

	Frequency (1=very low, 5= very high)
avoided certain words	1 ☐ ☐ ☐ ☐ ☐ 5
avoided idioms and colloquial phrases	1 ☐ ☐ ☐ ☐ ☐ 5
made sentences less complex	1 ☐ ☐ ☐ ☐ ☐ 5

Other/Comments:_______________________________
____
____

11. Would you say that your partner has adapted the use of his/her native language (German) to your level? If so, in what way(s) do you think he/she did?

	Frequency (1=very low, 5= very high)
avoided certain words	1 ☐ ☐ ☐ ☐ ☐ 5
avoided idioms and colloquial phrases	1 ☐ ☐ ☐ ☐ ☐ 5
made sentences less complex	1 ☐ ☐ ☐ ☐ ☐ 5

Other/Comments:_______________________________
____
____

12. Have you consciously reused words or phrases that your partner used?

☐ never ☐ rarely ☐ sometimes ☐ often ☐ whenever possible

If so, can you give examples?___________________________
____
____

13. Do you think the MOO work has helped you with your projects? If so, in what area(s):

    ☐ course topics ☐ written submissions ☐ oral presentations

    Comment:____

    ____

    ____

14. Do you think you were able to help your partners with their projects? If so, in what area(s):

    ☐ course topics ☐ written submissions ☐ oral presentations
    Comment:____

    ____

    ____

15. Finally, if you have any further reflections on your experience as a tandem learner, or any suggestions and ideas for improving aspects of the tandem project or the MOO environment, please add them below.

    ____

    ____

    ____

Appendix D
Interview questions

How does it feel to be back in the MOO?

How would or did you describe the MOO to others, such as friends or relatives?

Would you describe MOO language more like writing or speaking, or both? Why? What are the weaknesses/strengths of communicating like that for language learning?

Would you say your online character differed from the real-life character? If so, how?

Has the MOO exchange helped you in finding out where your own weaknesses and strengths in language learning are? Did your own opinion of your proficiency level change from what it was before the exchange, or through the exchange?

How important was it to have similar amounts of English and German in your exchanges?

How could the collaboration be made more effective?

Was there enough time in each session?

How much did you feel in control of the learning situation in the MOO, as compared to the classroom or a real face-to-face situation with a German speaker? (How would you compare that to other experiences you had with native speakers?) possible follow-up: how did you or could you make use of this control?)

When speaking German, did you perceive the MOO exchanges as a pressure or a challenge, as compared to classroom or other situations?

How much were you able to monitor your own and your partner's output when you compare it to face to face communication in German (for instance with the assistants)?

How much were you able to evaluate your own output when you compare it to face to face communication in German (for instance with the assistants)?

Is it important to keep track of your collaboration, such as re-reading transcripts or online notebook entries, etc.? How did you or could you use the session transcripts?

How do you rate the effectiveness of **improving** your German in the MOO, when compared to classroom work (with assistants) and face-to-face situations?

Finally, does the MOO help you more with fluency or accuracy?

Appendix E
Sample screen shots

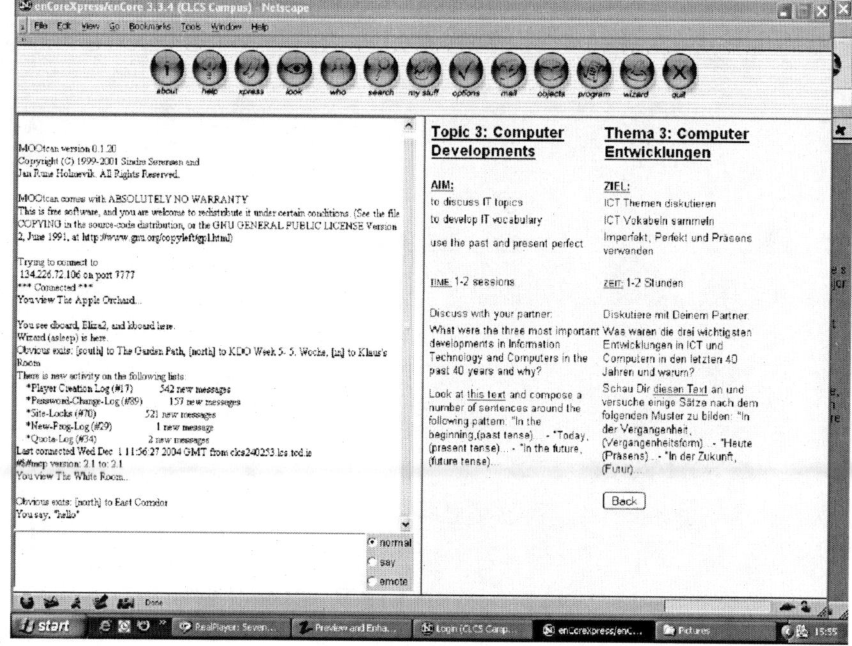

Figure E.1 Entry window to CLCS Campus

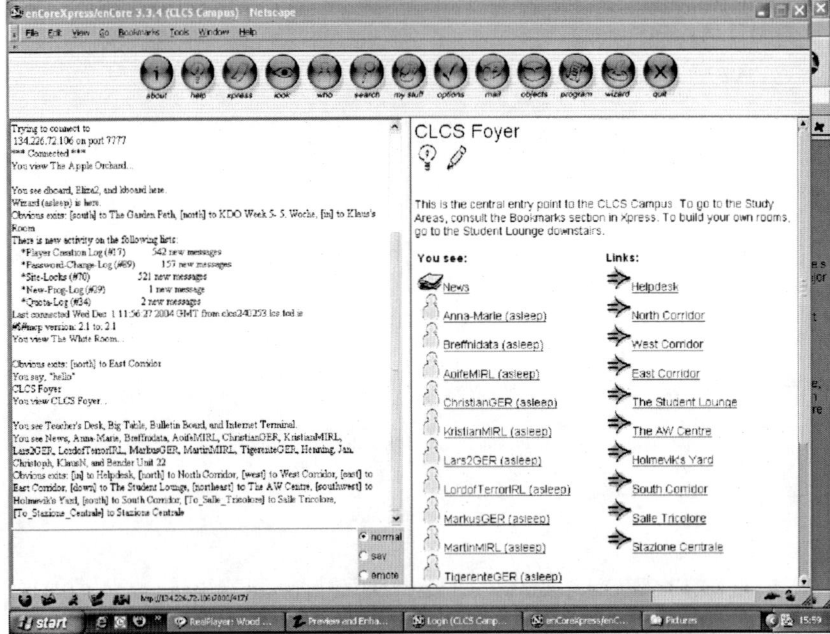

Figure E.2 Topic 3 in CLCS Campus

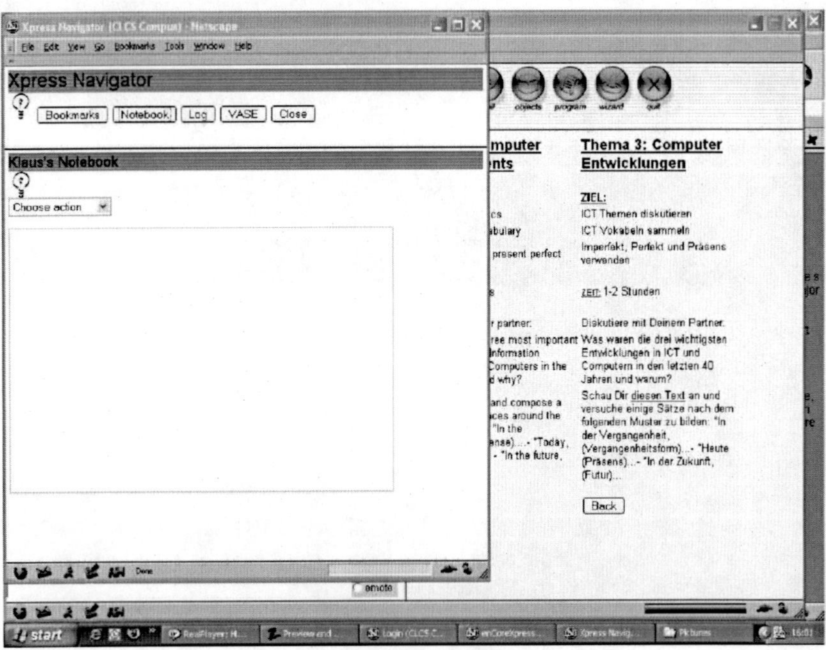

Figure E.3 Notebook function in CLCS Campus

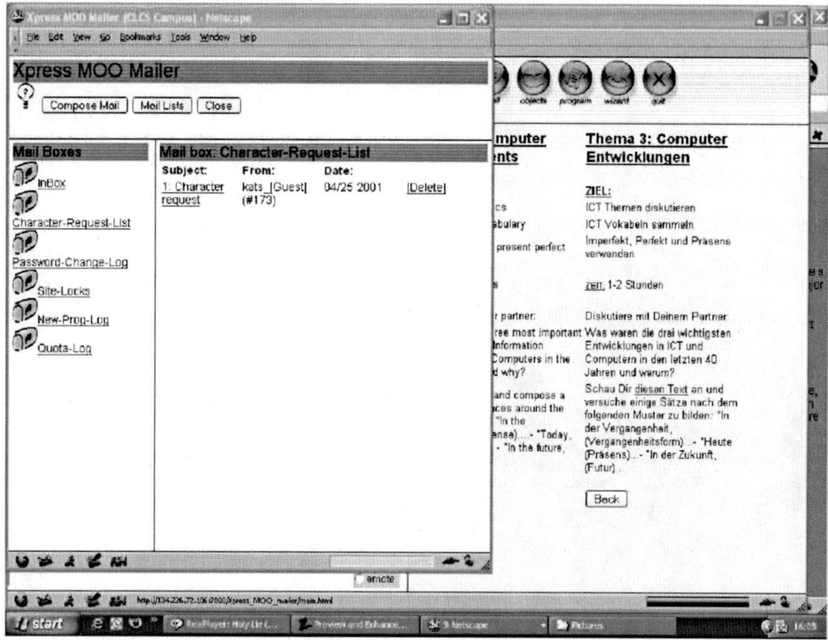

Figure E.4 MOO mail function in CLCS Campus

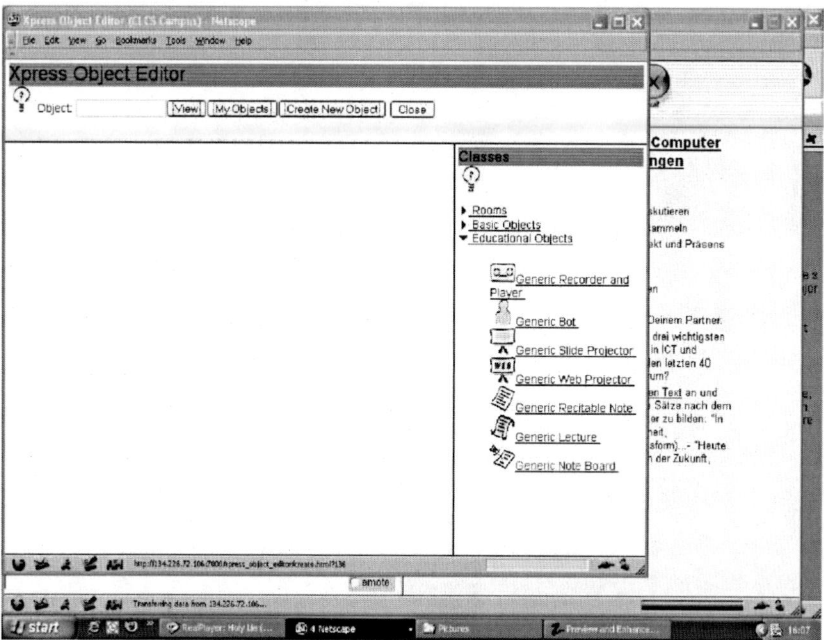

Figure E.5 Object editor in CLCS Campus

References

Aarseth, E. (1997). *Cybertext*. Baltimore: John Hopkins University Press.

Aarseth, E., & Jopp, C. (1998, 11 December). CALLMOO fase I - Sluttrapport. On-line. Retrieved 17 December, 2003, from http://cmc.hf.uib.no/dreistadt/eval/sluttrapp.html.

Aase, L., Fenner, A.-B., Little, D., & Trebbi, T. (2000). *Writing As Cultural Competence: A Study of the Relationship Between Mother Tongue and Foreign Language Learning Within a Framework of Learner Autonomy* (Vol. 56, CLCS Occasional Paper). Dublin: Trinity College, Centre for Language & Communication Studies.

Abrams, Z. I. (2001). Computer-mediated communication and group journals: expanding the repertoire of participant roles. *System*, 29(4), 489-503.

Advanced Network & Services Inc. (2004). Tele-Immersion. Retrieved 10 March, 2004, from http://www.advanced.org/teleimmersion.html.

Alcón Soler, E. (2002). Relationship between teacher-led versus learners' interaction and the development of pragmatics in the EFL classroom. *International Journal of Educational Research*, 37, 359–377. Retrieved 24 April, 2005, from http://www.sciencedirect.com/science?_ob=MImg&_imagekey=B6VDF-48Y0FV2-3-P&_cdi=5981&_user=103681&_orig=search&_coverDate=12%2F31%2F2002&_qd=1&_sk=999629996&view=c&wchp=dGLbVzb-zSkzS&md5=662159ebbb9eac0ca2a9797baf4ecc9b&ie=/sdarticle.pdf.

Appel, C., & Mullen, T. (2000). Pedagogical considerations for a web-based tandem language learning environment. *Computers and Education*, 34(3–4), 291-308.

Appel, M. C. (1997). Tandem Learning by E-mail: Some Psycholinguistic Issues and a Case Study. Unpublished M. Phil. thesis, University of Dublin, Trinity College, Dublin.

Appel, M. C. (1999). *Tandem Learning by E-mail: Some Basic Principles and a Case Study* (Vol. 54, CLCS Occasional Paper). Dublin: Trinity College, Centre for Language & Communication Studies.

Arneil, S., & Holmes, M. (1999). Juggling hot potatoes: Decisions and compromises in creating authoring tools for the web. *ReCALL*, 11(2), 12–19. Retrieved 24 April, 2005, from http://www.eurocall-languages.org/recall/rvol11no2.pdf

Aston, G. (1997). Involving learners in developing learning methods: Exploiting text corpora in self-access. In P. Benson & P. Voller (Eds.), *Autonomy and Independence in Language Learning* (pp. 204–214). London: Longman.

Baddeley, A., Gathercolea, S., & Papagno, C. (1998). The Phonological Loop as a Language Learning Device. *Psychological Review*, 105(1), 158-173. Retrieved 24 April, 2005, from http://www.sciencedirect.com/science?_ob=ArticleURL&_udi=B6X04-46P4NG3-7&_user=103681&_c

overDate=01%2F31%2F1998&_fmt=summary&_orig=search&_qd=1&_cdi=7204&view=c&_acct=C000007920&_version=1&_urlVersion=0&_userid=103681&md5=67f20eeb49848a59666a23f23fb4ddc2&ref=full.

Bailey, C. W., Jr. (1990). Intelligent multimedia computer systems: Emerging information resources in the network environment. *Library Hi Tech*, 8(1), 29–41.

Barnes, D. (1976). *From Communication to Curriculum*. Harmondsworth: Penguin.

Barrios, J. R., & Wilkes-Gibbs, D. (1998). How to MOO without making a sound. In C. Haynes & J. R. Holmevik (Eds.), *High Wired: On the Design, Use, and Theory of Educational MOOs* (pp. 45–87). Ann Arbor: University of Michigan Press.

Basturkmen, H., & Lewis, M. (2002). Learner perspectives of success in an EAP writing course. *Assessing Writing*, 8, 31–46.

Bates, J. (1994). The role of emotion in believable agents. *Communications from the ACM*, 37(7), 122–125.

Bauersfeld, H. (1988). Interaction, construction, and knowledge: Alternative perspectives for mathematics education. In T. Cooney & D. Grouws (Eds.), *Effective Mathematics Teaching* (pp. 27–46). Reston, VA: National Council of Teachers of Mathematics and Lawrence Erlbaum Associates.

Bax, S. (2003). CALL—past, present and future. *System*, 31(1), 13–28.

BBC. (1998). Results - The 'Turing Test'. On-line. Retrieved 31 March, 1998, from http://www.bbc.co.uk/tw/megalab/turing/turing_results.html.

BBC. (1999). Turing Test. On-line. Retrieved 1 September, 1999, from http://www.bbc.co.uk/tw/megalab/9903tur.shtml.

Beatty, K. (2003). *Teaching and Researching Computer-assisted Language Learning*. Harlow: Longman.

Bellamy, R. K. E. (1996). Designing educational technology: Computer-mediated change. In B. A. Nardi (Ed.), *Context and Consciousness: Activity Theory and Human-Computer Interaction* (pp. 123–146). Cambridge, MA: MIT Press.

Benson, P. (1997). The philosophy and politics of learner autonomy. In P. Benson & P. Voller (Eds.), *Autonomy and Independence in Language Learning* (pp. 18–34). London: Longman.

Benson, P. (2000). Autonomy as a learners' and teachers' right. In B. Sinclair, I. McGrath & T. Lamb (Eds.), *Learner Autonomy, Teacher Autonomy: Future Directions* (pp. 111–117). Harlow: Longman.

Benson, P. (2001). *Teaching and Researching Autonomy in Language Learning*. Harlow: Longman.

Bettelheim, B. (1987, March). The importance of play. *Atlantic Monthly*, 35–46.

Biocca, F. (1997). The cyborg's dilemma: progressive embodiment in virtual environments. Journal of Computer-Mediated Communication, 3(2). Retrieved 4 October, 1999, from http://www.ascusc.org/jcmc/vol3/issue2/biocca2.html.

Birdwhistell, R. L. (1970). *Kinesics and Context*. Philadelphia: Philadelphia University Press.

Blascovich, J. (2002). Social influence within immersive virtual environments. In R. Schroder (Ed.), *The Social Life of Avatars: Presence and Interaction in Shared Virtual Environments* (pp. 127–145). London: Springer Verlag.

Bødker, S. (1991). *Through the Interface-A Human Activity Approach to User Interface Design*. Hillsdale, NJ: Lawrence Erlbaum.

Boyle, R. (2000). Whatever happened to preference organisation? *Journal of Pragmatics*, 32(5), 583–604.

Braul, B. (2003, 7-10 May). A case study in asynchronous voice conferencing for language instruction. Paper presented at the WorldCall Conference, Banff, Canada.

Breen, M. P., & Candlin, C. (1980). The essentials of a communicative curriculum in language teaching. *Applied Linguistics*, 1(2), 89–112.

Brennan, S. E. (1990). Conversation as direct manipulation: an iconoclastic view. In B. Laurel (Ed.), *The Art of Human-Computer Interface Design* (pp. 393–404). Reading, MA: Addison-Wesley.

Brookfield, S. (1995). *Becoming a critically reflective teacher.* San Francisco: Jossey-Bass.

Brown, D. J., Cobb, S. V. G., & Eastgate, R. M. (1995). Learning in virtual environments (LIVE). In R. A. Earnshaw, J. A. Vince & H. Jones (Eds.), *Virtual Reality Applications* (pp. 245–252). London: Academic Press.

Brown, J. S. (1985). Process versus product: A perspective on tools for communal and informal electronic learning. *Journal of Educational Computing Research* (1), 179–201.

Brown, J. S., Collins, A., & Duguid, P. (1989). Situated cognition and the culture of learning. Educational Researcher, 18(1), 32–41. Retrieved 23 September, 1999, from http://www.ilt.columbia.edu/ilt/papers/JohnBrown.html.

Brown, J. S., Collins, A., & Duguid, P. (1996). Situated cognition and the culture of learning. In H. McLellan (Ed.), *Situated Learning Perspectives* (pp. 19–44). Englewood Cliffs, NJ: Educational Technology Publications.

Bruckman, A. (1992). Identity Workshop: Emergent Social and Psychological Phenomena in Text-based Virtual Reality. Retrieved 30 October, 2003, from ftp://ftp.cc.gatech.edu/pub/people/asb/papers/identity-workshop.rtf.

Bruckman, A. (1997). MOOSE Crossing: Construction, Community, and Learning in a Networked Virtual World for Kids. Unpublished PhD Dissertation, MIT, Boston, MA.

Bruckman, A., & Resnick, M. (1995). The MediaMOO Project: Constructionism and professional community. Convergence, 1(1). Retrieved 13 March, 1999, from http://www.cc.gatech.edu/~asb/convergence.html.

Bruner, J. (1966). *Towards a Theory of Instruction.* Cambridge MA: Harvard University Press.

Bruner, J. (1972). *The Relevance of Education.* Harmonsworth, Middlesex.

Bruner, J. (1986). *Actual Minds, Possible Worlds.* Cambridge, MA: Harvard University Press.

Bruner, J., & Ratner, N. (1978). Games, social exchange and the acquisition of language. *Journal of Child Language*, 5(1), 391–401.

Buckingham Shum, S., Marshall, S., Brier, J., & Evans, T. (2001, 22-24 March). Lyceum: Internet voice groupware for distance learning. Paper presented at the EURO-CSCL 2001: 1st European Conference on Computer-Supported Collaborative Learning, Maastricht, The Netherlands.

Busey, A. (1995). *Secrets of the MUD Wizards.* Indianapolis, IN: Sams Net Publ.

Byram, M. (1988). Foreign language education and cultural studies. *Language, Culture, and Curriculum*, 1(1), 15-31.

Cambourne, B. (1988). *The Whole Story: Natural Learning and the Acquisition of Literacy in the Classroom.* Gosford, New Zealand: Ashton Scholastic.

Carlstrom, E. (1992). Better living through language: The communicative implications of a text-only virtual environment, or, welcome to LambdaMOO. Retrieved 23 February, 2001, from http://tecfa.unige.ch/~jermann/communicative.txt.

Carr, A. A., Jonassen, D. H., Litzinger, M. E., & Marra, R. M. (1998, January/February). Good ideas to foment educational revolution: The role of systemic

change in advancing situated learning, constructivism, and feminist pedagogy. *Educational Technology*, 38, 5–15.
Carr, K. (1995). Introduction. In K. Carr & R. England (Eds.), *Simulated and Virtual Realities* (pp. 1–10). London: Taylor and Francis.
Cavnar, W. B., & Trenkle, J. M. (1994). N-gram-based text categorization. In Proceedings of Third Annual Symposium on Document Analysis and Information Retrieval (pp. 161–175). Las Vegas, NV: UNLV Publications/Reprographics.
Chan, M. (1996). No talking, please, just chatting: Collaborative writing with computers. Retrieved 30 October, 2003, from http://leahi.kcc.hawaii.edu/org/tcc_conf96/chan.html.
Chao, T., & Kabata, K. (2003, 7-10 May). Teaching Business Japanese with communication technology: Examination of face-to-face and online interaction. Paper presented at the WorldCall Conference, Banff, Canada.
Chapelle, C. (2001). *Computer Applications in Second Language Acquisition.* Cambridge: Cambridge University Press.
Chapelle, C. A. (1999). Theory and research: Investigation of 'authentic' language learning tasks. In J. Egbert & E. Hanson-Smith (Eds.), *Call Environments: Research, Practice, and Critical Issues* (pp. 101–115). Alexandria, VA: TESOL.
Cheng, W., Warren, M., & Xun-feng, X. (2003). The language learner as language researcher: putting corpus linguistics on the timetable. *System*, 31(2), 173–186.
Cherny, L. (1995). The MUD Register: Conversational Modes of Action in a Text-Based Virtual Reality. Unpublished PhD Dissertation, Stanford University.
Cherny, L. (1999). *Conversation and community: Discourse in a social MUD.* Cambridge: Cambridge University Press.
Christie, B. (1972). Report on series I experiments. Unpublished paper from New Rural Society Project, Fairfield University, Conn.
Chun, D. M., & Payne, J. S. (2004). What makes students click: working memory and look-up behavior. *System*, 32(4), 481-503. Retrieved 7 March, 2005, from http://www.sciencedirect.com/science?_ob=MImg&_imagekey=B6VCH-4DPGWG0-1-1&_cdi=5955&_user=103681&_orig=search&_coverDate=12%2F01%2F2004&_qd=1&_sk=999679995&view=c&wchp=dGLbVtb-zSkzV&md5=cba6a410fc9bc7e1fa454c01c0329d20&ie=/sdarticle.pdf.
Clark, A. (1998). Magic words: How language augments human computation. In P. Carruthers & J. Boucher (Eds.), (pp. 162–183).
Cobb, P., Yackel, E., & Wood, T. (1992). Interaction and learning in mathematics classroom situations. *Educational Studies in Mathematics*, 23, 99–122.
Cobb, T. (1997). Is there any measurable learning from hands-on concordancing? *System*, 25(3), 301–315.
Cobb, T. (1999). Breadth and depth of lexical acquisition with hands-on concordancing. *Computer-Assisted Language Learning*, 12(4), 345–360.
Cognition and Technology Group at Vanderbilt. (1993). Anchored instruction and situated cognition. *Educational Technology*, 33, 52–70.
Cognition and Technology Group at Vanderbilt. (1996). Anchored instruction and situated cognition revisited. In H. McLellan (Ed.), *Situated Learning Perspectives* (pp. 123–154). Englewood Cliffs, NJ: Educational Technology Publications.
Collins, A., Brown, J. S., & Newman, S. E. (1989). Cognitive apprenticeship: Teaching the crafts of reading, writing, and mathematics. In L. B. Resnick (Ed.), *Knowing, learning, and instruction* (pp. 453–494). Hillsdale, NJ: Lawrence Erlbaum.

Colomb, G. G., & Simutis, J. A. (1996). Visible conversation and academic inquiry: CMC in a culturally diverse classroom. In S. Herring (Ed.), *Computer-Mediated Communication: Linguistic, Social, and Cross-Cultural Perspectives* (pp. 203–222). Amsterdam: John Benjamins.

Costa, D. (2003). Virtual worlds. PC Magazine, 22(19). Retrieved 3 May, 2004, from http://www.pcmag.com/print_article/0,3048,a=108534,00.asp.

Council of Europe. (2001). *Common European Framework of Reference for Languages: Leaning, Teaching, Assessment.* Cambridge: Cambridge University Press.

Cowan, R., Choi, H. E., & Kim, D. H. (2003). Four questions for error diagnosis and correction in CALL. *CALICO Journal*, 20(3), 451–463.

Csikszentmihalyi, M. (1978). Intrinsic rewards and emergent motivation. In M. Lepper & D. Greene (Eds.), *The Hidden Costs or Reward: New Perspectives on the Psychology of Human Motivatio*n (pp. 205–216). Hillsdale, NJ: Lawrence Erlbaum Associates.

Csikszentmihalyi, M. (Ed.). (1991). *Flow: The Psychology of Optimal Experience.* New York: HarperCollins.

Csikszentmihalyi, M., & Csikszentmihalyi, I. S. (Eds.). (1988). *Optimal Experience: Psychological Studies of Flow in Consciousness.* Cambridge: Cambridge University Press.

Curtis, P. (1997, March). LambdaMOO Programmer's Manual For LambdaMOO Version 1.8.0p6, May 1997. On-line. Retrieved 10 December, 2003, from http://cmc.uib.no/moo/docs/manuals/formatted/html/ProgrammersManual.html.

Cziko, G. A., & Park, S. (2003). Internet audio communication for second language learning: A comparative review of six programs. *Language Learning & Technology*, 7(1), 15–27. Retrieved 5 April, 2004, from http://llt.msu.edu/vol7num1/pdf/review1.pdf.

Daft, R. L., & Lengel, R. H. (1984). Information richness: A new approach to managerial behavior and organization design. In B. M. Staw & L. L. Cummings (Eds.), *Research in Organizational Behavior* (Vol. 6, pp. 191-233). Greenwich, CT: JAL.

Dalwood, M. (1977). The reciprocal language course. *Audio Visual Language Journal*, 15, 73–80.

Dam, L. (1990). Developing learner autonomy in a school context- what about the teacher? In R. Duda & P. Riley (Eds.), *Learning Styles* (pp. 189–197). Nancy: Presses Universitaires de Nancy.

Dam, L. (1995). *Learner Autonomy 3: From Theory to Classroom Practice.* Dublin: Authentik.

Dam, L. (2000). Why focus on learning rather than teaching? From theory to practice. In D. Little, L. Dam & J. Timmer (Eds.), *Focus On Learning Rather Than Teaching: Why and How?* (pp. 18–37). Dublin: CLCS.

Dam, L., Legenhausen, L., & Wolff, D. (1990). Text production in the foreign language classroom and the word processor. *System*, 18(3), 325–334.

Darhower, M. (2002). Interactional features of synchronous computer-mediated communication in the intermediate L2 class: A sociocultural case study. *CALICO Journal*, 19(2), 249–277.

Dautenhahn, K., Ogden, B., & Quick, T. (2002). From embodied to socially embedded agents – Implications for interaction-aware robots. *Cognitive Systems Research*, 3(3), 397–428.

Day, M., Crump, E., & Ricky, R. (1996). Creating a virtual academic community: scholarship and community in wide-area multiple-user synchronous discussions. In T. M. Harrison & T. Stephen (Eds.), *Computer Networking and Scholarly Communication in the Twenty-First-Century University* (pp. 291–311). Albany, NY: State University of New York Press.

Debski, R. (2003). Technology and second language learning through socialization. In S. Naidu (Ed.), *Learning and Teaching with Technology* (pp. 129–145). London and Sterling, VA: Kogan Page.

Devitt, S. (1986). *Learning a Foreign Language Through the Media* (Vol. 18, CLCS Occasional Paper). Dublin: Trinity College, Centre for Language & Communication Studies.

Devitt, S. (1989). *Classroom Discourse: Its Nature and Its Potential for Language Learning* (Vol. 21, CLCS Occasional Paper). Dublin: Trinity College, Centre for Language & Communication Studies.

Dickinson, L. (1987). *Self-instruction in Language Learning.* Cambridge: Cambridge University Press.

Dickinson, L. (1992). *Learner Autonomy 2: Learner Training for Language Learning.* Dublin: Authentik.

Dieberger, A., & Tromp, J. (1995). The Information City Project- A virtual reality user interface for navigation in information spaces. User Experience Review, 11(January/February).

DiMatteo, A. (1990). Under erasure: A theory for interactive writing in real time. *Computers and Composition*, 7, 71–84.

DiMatteo, A. (1991). Communication, writing, learning: An anti-instrumentalist view of network writing. *Computers and Composition*, 8(3), 5–19.

Donaldson, R. P., & Kötter, M. (1999). Language learning in cyberspace: Teleporting the classroom into the target culture. *Calico*, 16(4), 531–557.

Dubrovsky, V. J., Kiesler, S., & Sethna, B. N. (1991). The equalization phenomenon: Status effects in computer-mediated and face-to-face decision-making groups. *Human Computer Interaction*, 6, 119–146.

Ebbrell, D. (1998, 13 September 2001). WIDA Authoring Suite: Review. Retrieved 16 January, 2002, from http://www.lang.ltsn.ac.uk/cit/reviews/wida.htm.

Eck, A., Legenhausen, L., & Wolff, D. (1994). Der Einsatz der Telekommunikation in einem lernerorientierten Fremdsprachenunterricht. In W. Gienow & K. Hellwig (Eds.), *Interkulturelle Kommunikation und prozeßorienterte Medienpraxis im Fremdsprachenunterricht: Grundlagen, Realisierung, Wirksamkeit* (pp. 43–57). Seelze: Friedrich Verlag.

Edelsky, C. (1993). Who's got the floor? In D. Tannen (Ed.), *Gender and Conversational Interaction* (pp. 189–230). New York: Oxford University Press.

Egbert, J., Chao, C.-c., & Hanson-Smith, E. (1999). Computer-enhanced language learning environments: An overview. In J. Egbert & E. Hanson-Smith (Eds.), *Call Environments: Research, Practice, and Critical Issues* (pp. 1–13). Alexandria, VA: TESOL.

Egbert, J., & Hanson-Smith, E. (1999). Preface. In J. Egbert & E. Hanson-Smith (Eds.), *Call Environments: Research, Practice, and Critical Issues* (pp. ix–x). Alexandria, VA: TESOL.

Egido, C. (1988). Videoconferencing as a technology to support group work: A review of its failures. Paper presented at the CSCW '88.

Ellis, G., & Sinclair, B. (1989). *Learning to Learn English: A Course in Learner Training.* Cambridge: Cambridge University Press.

Ellis, R. (1985). *Understanding Second Language Acquisition.* London: Oxford University Press.

Engeström, Y. (1991). Activity theory and individual and social transformation. Multidisciplinary *Newsletter for Activity Theory*, 7/8, 6–17.

Entwistle, N. (1987). A model of the teaching-learning process. In J. T. E. Richardson, M. W. Eysenck & D. W. Piper (Eds.), *Student Learning: Research in*

Education and Cognitive Psychology (pp. 13–28). Milton Keynes: Society for Research into Higher Education/ Open University Press.

Esch, E. (1996). Promoting learner autonomy: Criteria for the selection of appropriate methods. In R. Pemberton, E. S. L. Li, W. W. F. Or & H. D. Pierson (Eds.), *Taking Control: Autonomy in Language Learning* (pp. 35–48). Hong Kong: Hong Kong University Press.

Esch, E. (1997). Learner training for autonomous language learning. In P. Benson & P. Voller (Eds.), *Autonomy and Independence in Language Learning* (pp. 164–175). London: Longman.

Eurydice. (2005). *Key Data on Teaching Languages at Schools in Europe*. Brussels: Eurydice European Unit.

Evard, R. (1993). Collaborative networked communication: MUDs as systems tools. Paper presented at the Seventh Systems Administration Conference (LISA VII), Monterey, CA. Retrieved 12 April, 2000, from ftp://ftp.lambda.moo.mud.org/pub/MOO/papers/Evard.ps.

Ewing, J. M., Dowling, J. D., & Coutts, N. (1999). Learning using the World Wide Web: A collaborative learning event. *Journal of Educational Multimedia and Hypermedia*, 8(1), 3–22.

Fakespace Systems Inc. (2005). Fakespace Systems. Retrieved 3 October, 2005, from http://www.fakespacesystems.com/.

Falbel, A. (1989). Friskolen 70: An Ethnographically Informed Inquiry Into the Social Context of Learning. Unpublished Thesis in partial fulfillment for the degree of Doctor of Philosophy, Massachusetts Institute of Technology, Boston MA.

Falsetti, J., & Schweitzer, E. (1995). SchMOOze University: A MOO for ESL/EFL students. In M. Warschauer (Ed.), *Virtual Connections: On-line Activities and Projects for Networking Language Learners* (pp. 231–232). Honolulu, HI: University of Hawai'i, Second Language Teaching and Curriculum Center.

Felix, U. (2003a). An orchestrated vision of language learning online. In U. Felix (Ed.), *Language Learning Online: Towards Best Practice* (pp. 7–18). Lisse: Swets & Zeitlinger.

Felix, U. (2003b). Pedagogy on the line: Identifying and closing the missing links. In U. Felix (Ed.), *Language Learning Online: Towards Best Practice* (pp. 147–170). Lisse: Swets & Zeitlinger.

Foner, L. (1993). What's an Agent Anyway? Retrieved 7 October, 1999, from http://lucien.berkeley.edu/MOO/Agents-Julia.ps.

Fontaine, G. (1993). The experience of a sense of presence in intercultural and international encounters. *Presence: Teleoperators and Virtual Environments,* 1(4), 1–9.

Fosnot, C. T. (1996a). Constructivism: A psychological theory of learning. In C. T. Fosnot (Ed.), *Constructivism: Theory, Perspectives, and Practice* (pp. 8–33). New York: Teachers College Press.

Fosnot, C. T. (1996b). Preface. In C. T. Fosnot (Ed.), *Constructivism: Theory, Perspectives, and Practice* (pp. ix–xi). New York: Teachers College Press.

Frei, C., Dixon, E., & Van Deusen-Scholl, N. (2003, 20–24 May). On slate: Create uses of Blackboard in and outside the classroom. Paper presented at the Calico Conference, Ottawa, Canada.

Garrett, N. (1997). Where do research and practice meet? Developing a discipline. *ReCALL*, 10(1), 7–12.

Gass, S. M., & Varonis, E. M. (1991). Miscommunication in nonnative speaker discourse. In N. Coupland, H. Giles & J. M. Wiemann (Eds.), *Miscommunication and Problematic Talk* (pp. 121–145). Newbury Park: Sage Publications.

Gerhard, M., Moore, D., & Hobbs, D. (2004). Embodiment and copresence in collaborative interfaces. International *Journal of Human-Computer Studies*, 61(4), 453–480.

Gibson, J. J. (1966). *The Senses Considered as Perceptual Systems*. Boston, MA: Houghton Mifflin.

Gibson, J. J. (1979). *The Ecological Approach to Visual Perception*. Boston, MA: Houghton Mifflin.

Gibson, W. (1984). *Neuromancer*. London: Harper Collins.

Gnutzmann, C. (1997). Language awareness: Progress in language learning and language education, or reformulation of old ideas? *Language Awareness*, 6(2–3), 65–74.

Godwin-Jones, R. (2003). Optimising web course design for language learners. In U. Felix (Ed.), *Language Learning Online: Towards Best Practice* (pp. 43–56). Lisse: Swets & Zeitlinger.

Goldman-Segall, R. (1992). Collaborative virtual communities: Using Learning Constellations, a multimedia ethnographic research tool. In E. Barrett (Ed.), *Sociomedia* (pp. 257–296). Cambridge, MA: MIT Press.

Granger, S. (1998). *Learner English on Computer*. London & New York: Addison Wesley Longman.

Granger, S. (2002). A bird's-eye view of learner corpus research. In S. Granger, J. Hung & S. Petch-Tyson (Eds.), *Computer learner corpora, second language acquisition and foreign language teaching* (pp. 3–33). Amsterdam/Philadelphia: John Benjamins.

Granger, S. (2003). Error-tagged learner corpora and CALL: A promising synergy. *CALICO Journal*, 20(3), 465--480.

Granger, S., Hung, J., & Petch-Tyson, S. (Eds.). (2002). *Computer learner corpora, second language acquisition and foreign language teaching*. Amsterdam/Philadelphia: John Benjamins.

Greeno, J. G. (1991). Number sense as situated knowing in a conceptual domain. *Journal for Research in Mathematics Education*, 22, 170–218.

Gremmo, M.-J., & Riley, P. (1995). Autonomy, self-direction and self access in language teaching and learning: The history of an idea. *System*, 23(2), 151–164.

Gumperz, J. (1982). *Discourse Strategies*. Cambridge: Cambridge University Press.

Gunawardena, C. N. (1995). Social presence theory and implications for interaction and collaborative learning in computer conferences. *Journal of Educational Telecommunications*, 1(2/3), 147–166.

Gygi, K. (1990). Recognizing the symptoms of hypertext...and what to do about it. In B. Laurel (Ed.), *The Art of Human-Computer Interface Design* (pp. 279–288). Reading, MA: Addison-Wesley.

Halliday, M. A. K. (1978). *Language As Social Semiotic*. London: Edward Arnold.

Hamburger, H. (1995). Tutorial tools for language learning by two-medium dialogue. In V. M. Holland, J. D. Kaplan & M. R. Sams (Eds.), *Intelligent Language Tutors: Theory Shaping Technology* (pp. 183–199). Mahwah, NJ: Lawrence Erlbaum Publ.

Hamburger, H., & Hashim, R. (1992). Foreign language tutoring and learning environment. In M. L. Swartz & M. Yazdani (Eds.), *Intelligent Tutoring Systems for Foreign Language Learning* (pp. 201–218). Berlin: Springer Verlag.

Hampel, R. (2003, 7-10 May). "Virtual encounters": Integrating theory and practice in the design, implementation and evaluation of audio-graphic online tuition. Paper presented at the WorldCall Conference, Banff, Canada.

Hampel, R., & Barber, E. (2003). Using internet-based audio-graphic and video conferencing for language teaching and learning. In U. Felix (Ed.), *Language Learning Online: Towards Best Practice* (pp. 171–191). Lisse: Swets & Zeitlinger.

Hanson-Smith, E. (1999). Classroom practice: Using multimedia for input and interaction in CALL environments. In J. Egbert & E. Hanson-Smith (Eds.), *Call Environments: Research, Practice, and Critical Issues* (pp. 189–215). Alexandria, VA: TESOL.

Hay, K. E. (1996a). Legitimate peripheral participation, instructionism, and constructivism: Whose situation is it anyway? In H. McLellan (Ed.), *Situated Learning Perspectives* (pp. 89–99). Englewood Cliffs, NJ: Educational Technology Publications.

Hay, K. E. (1996b). The three activities of a student: A reply to Tripp. In H. McLellan (Ed.), *Situated Learning Perspectives* (pp. 201–212). Englewood Cliffs, NJ: Educational Technology Publications.

Hayashi, R. (1991). Floor structure of English and Japanese conversation. *Journal of Pragmatics*, 16, 1–30.

Haynes, C. (1998). Help! There is a MOO in this class! In C. Haynes & J. R. Holmevik (Eds.), *High Wired: On the Design, Use, and Theory of Educational MOOs* (pp. 161–176). Ann Arbor: University of Michigan Press.

Haynes, C., & Holmevik, J. R. (Eds.). (1998). *High Wired: On the Design, Use, and Theory of Educational MOOs*. Ann Arbor: University of Michigan Press.

Heath, C., & Luff, P. (1991). Disembodied conduct: Communication through video on a multi-media office environment. Paper presented at the CHI '91.

Heeter, C. (1991, Fall). The look and feel of direct manipulation. *Hypernexus: Journal of Hypermedia and Multimedia Studies.*

Hegelheimer, V., & Tower, D. (2004). Using CALL in the classroom: Analyzing student interactions in an authentic classroom. *System*, 32, 185-205. Retrieved 20 December, 2004, from http://www.sciencedirect.com/science?_ob=MImg&_imagekey=B6VCH-4C2NHTX-1-3&_cdi=5955&_user=103681&_orig=search&_coverDate=06%2F30%2F2004&_qd=1&_sk=999679997&view=c&wchp=dGLbVzz-zSkWA&md5=c53e04148442706b8e5af871e06a4e42&ie=/sdarticle.pdf.

Heift, T. (2001). Error-specific and individualised feedback in a Web-based language tutoring system: Do they read it? *ReCALL*, 13(1), 99–109.

Heift, T. (2002). Learner control and error correction in ICALL: Browsers, peekers and adamants. *CALICO Journal*, 19(3), 295–313.

Heift, T. (2003). Multiple learner errors and meaningful feedback: A challenge for ICALL systems. *CALICO Journal*, 20(3), 533–548.

Heift, T., & Schulze, M. (2003). Error diagnosis and error correction in CALL. *CALICO Journal*, 20(3), 433–436.

Hendricks, H. (2003a, 7-10 May). Interactive video through Internet-controlled DVD. Paper presented at the WorldCALL Conference, Banff, Canada.

Hendricks, H. (2003b, 20-24 May). Interactive Video with WebDVD- An update. Paper presented at the Calico Conference, Ottawa, Canada.

Henner-Stanchina, C. (1985). Two years of autonomy: Practice and outlook. In P. Riley (Ed.), *Discourse and Learning* (pp. 191–205). London: Longman.

Henning, E., & Van der Westhuizen, D. (2004). Crossing the digital divide safely and trustingly: how ecologies of learning scaffold the journey. *Computers & Education*, 42(4), 333–352.

Herring, S. (1999). Interactional coherence in CMC. Journal of Computer-Mediated Communication, 4(4). Retrieved 22 August, 2000, from http://www.ascusc.org/jcmc/vol4/issue4/herring.html.

Hiltz, S. R., & Turoff, M. (1981). The evolution of user behavior in a computerized conference system. *Communications of the ACM*, 24, 739–751.

HIPERNET. (1995). *Report on System Integration and Installation* (No. RACE 2115; HIPERNET Identifier D6181). Cambridge: HIPERNET consortium.

Holec, H. (1979). Autonomy in Foreign Language Learning. Strasbourg: Council of Europe.

Holec, H. (1985). On autonomy: some elementary concepts. In P. Riley (Ed.), *Discourse and Learning* (pp. 173--190). London: Longman.

Holland, V. M., Kaplan, J. D., & Sabol, M. A. (1999). Preliminary tests of language learning in a speech-interactive graphics microworld. *CALICO Journal*, 16(3), 339–359.

Holmevik, J. R., & Blanchard, M. (1998). Taking the MOO by the horns. In C. Haynes & J. R. Holmevik (Eds.), *High Wired: On the Design, Use, and Theory of Educational MOOs* (pp. 107–147). Ann Arbor: University of Michigan Press.

Holmevik, J. R., & Haynes, C. (2000). *MOOniversity*. Boston: Allyn & Bacon.

Hughes, C., & Hewson, L. (1998, July/August). Online interactions: Developing a neglected aspect of the virtual classroom. *Educational Technology*, 38, 48-55.

Hung, D. W. L., & Wong, A. F. L. (2000, March-April). Activity theory as a framework for project work in learning environments. *Educational Technology*, 40, 33-37.

Hutchins, E. L., Hollan, J. D., & Norman, D. A. (1986). Direct manipulation interfaces. In S. W. Draper & D. A. Norman (Eds.), *User Centered Design*. Hillsdale, NJ: Lawrence Erlbaum Associates.

Hyltenstam, K., & Pienemann, M. (Eds.). (1985). *Modelling and Assessing Second Language Acquisition*. Clevedon, Avon: Multilingual Matters.

ISOC/Socrates. (2006). LOLIPOP - Language On-line Portofolio Project. Retrieved 4 October, 2006, from http://www.isoc.siu.no/isocii.nsf/projectlist/116998.

Jacobson, D. (1996). Contexts and cues in cyberspace: The pragmatics of naming in text-based virtual realities. *Journal of Anthropological Research*, 52, 461–479.

Jefferies, E., Ralph, M. A. L., & Baddeley, A. D. (2004). Automatic and controlled processing in sentence recall: The role of long-term and working memory. *Journal of Memory and Language*, 51(4), 623–643. Retrieved 10 March, 2005, from http://www.sciencedirect.com/science?_ob=MImg&_imagekey=B6WK4-4D7CCX6-2-7&_cdi=6896&_user=103681&_orig=search&_coverDate=11%2F01%2F2004&_qd=1&_sk=999489995&view=c&wchp=dGLbVzb-zSkzk&md5=c829d6b87049b22b7216624d589c0a9c&ie=/sdarticle.pdf

Johns, T. (1988). Whence and whither classroom concordancing? In T. Boengaerts, T. v. Els & H. Wekker (Eds.), *Computer Applications in Language Learning* (pp. 9–33). Dordrecht: Foris.

Johns, T. (1991). Should you be persuaded: Two examples of data-driven learning. In T. Johns & P. King (Eds.), *Classroom Concordancing* (pp. 1–16). Birmingham: Centre for English Language Studies.

Johnston, B. (1999). Theory and research: Audience, language use, and language learning. In J. Egbert & E. Hanson-Smith (Eds.), *Call Environments: Research, Practice, and Critical Issues* (pp. 55–64). Alexandria, VA: TESOL.

Johnston, J. (2003, 2 March). Teachers call for urgent action as pupils write essays in text-speak. *Sunday Herald* [London and Edinburgh]. from http://www.sundayherald.com/print31826.

Jones, C. (n.d.). Wida's Authoring Suite. Retrieved 8 January, 2002, from http://www.wida.co.uk.

Kapec, P. (2004). Autonomous language learning in a MOO environment: Theory and practice in a tandem project between the Bonn-Rhein-Sieg University of Applied Sciences and Trinity College Dublin. Unpublished MA ELT thesis, University of Nottingham, UK.

Kapec, P., & Schwienhorst, K. (2005). In two minds? Learner attitudes to bilingualism and the Bilingual Tandem Analyser. *ReCALL*, 17(2), 254–268.

Kaplan, J. D., & Holland, V. M. (1995). Application of learning principles to the design of a second language tutor. In V. M. Holland, J. D. Kaplan & M. R. Sams (Eds.), *Intelligent Language Tutors: Theory Shaping Technology* (pp. 273–287). Mahwah, NJ: Lawrence Erlbaum Publ.

Kaplan, J. D., Sabol, M., Wisher, R., & Seidel, R. (1998). The Military Language Tutor (MILT) program: An advanced authoring system. *Computer-Assisted Language Learning,* 11(3), 265–287.

Kaptelinin, V. (1996). Computer-mediated activity: Functional organs in social and developmental contexts. In B. A. Nardi (Ed.), *Context and Consciousness: Activity Theory and Human-Computer Interaction* (pp. 45–68). Cambridge, MA: MIT Press.

Kelly, G. (1955, repr. 1991). *The Psychology of Personal Constructs* (Vol. 1). London: Routledge.

Kelly, R. (1996). Language counselling for learner autonomy: The skilled helper in self-access language learning. In R. Pemberton, E. S. L. Li, W. W. F. Or & H. D. Pierson (Eds.), *Taking Control: Autonomy in Language Learning* (pp. 93–113). Hong Kong: Hong Kong University Press.

Kern, R., & Warschauer, M. (2000). Introduction: Theory and practice of network-based language teaching. In M. Warschauer & R. Kern (Eds.), *Network-based Language Teaching: Concepts and Practice.* New York: Cambridge University Press. Retrieved 16 February, 2001, from http://www.lll.hawaii.edu/web/faculty/markw/nbl-intro.html.

Klein, J. T. (1999). Computer Response to User Frustration (Technical Report No. TR#480). Boston, MA: MIT Media Laboratory Vision and Modeling Group. Retrieved 9 February, 2000, from http://vismod.media.mit.edu/pub/tech-reports/TR-480.pdf.

Kötter, M. (2001). Developing distance language learners' interactive competence-can synchronous audio do the trick? *Journal of Educational Telecommunications*, 7(4), 327–353.

Kötter, M. (2002). *Tandem Learning on the Internet.* Frankfurt: Peter Lang.

Kötter, M. (2003). Negotiation of meaning and codeswitching in online tandems. *Language Learning & Technology*, 7(2), 145–172. Retrieved 5 December, 2003, from http://llt.msu.edu/vo7num2/kotter/.

Kötter, M., & Shield, L. (2000). Teacher and learner roles: Same or different in a 24/7 real-time audio-conferencing environment? C@lling Japan, 9(2). Retrieved 4 November 2000, from http://jaltcall.org/cjo/10_00/kotter_shield.html.

Kötter, M., Shield, L., & Stevens, A. (1999). Real-time audio and e-mail for fluency: Promoting distance language learners oral skills via the Internet. *ReCALL*, 11(2), 55–60.

Kramsch, C. (1998). *Language and Culture.* Oxford: Oxford University Press.

Kramsch, C., A'Ness, F., & Lam, W. S. E. (2000). Authenticity and authorship in the computer-mediated acquisition of L2 literacy. *Language Learning and Technology*, 4(2), 78–104.

Krashen, S. (1981). *Second Language Acquisition and Second Language Learning.* Oxford: Pergamon.

Kreeft Peyton, J. (1999). Theory and research: Interaction via computers. In J. Egbert & E. Hanson-Smith (Eds.), *Call Environments: Research, Practice, and Critical Issues* (pp. 17–26). Alexandria, VA: TESOL.

L'haire, S., & Vandeventer Faltin, A. (2003). Error diagnosis in the Free Text Project. *CALICO Journal*, 20(3), 481–495.

Lafford, P. A. (2003, 20–24 May). Collaborative CALL the Wimba way. Paper presented at the Calico Conference, Ottawa, Canada.

Lamy, M.-N. (2003, 7–10 May). Redefining fluency: Discourse competence in synchronous learning online. Paper presented at the WorldCall Conference, Banff, Canada.

Lamy, M.-N., & Goodfellow, R. (1999). "Reflective conversation" in the virtual language classroom. *Language Learning and Technology*, 2(2), 43-61. Retrieved 21 October 2000, from http://llt.msu.edu/vol2num2/article2/index.html.

Lave, J. (1991). Situated learning in communities of practice. In L. B. Resnick, J. M. Levine & S. D. Teasley (Eds.), *Perspectives on socially shared cognition.* Washington, DC: American Psychological Association.

Lave, J., & Wenger, E. (1991). *Situated Learning: Legitimate Peripheral Participation.* Cambridge: Cambridge University Press.

Lee, J. (2002, 19 September). I Think, Therefore IM. *New York Times.* Retrieved 5 October, 2002, from http://www.nytimes.com/learning/teachers/featured_articles/20020919thursday.html.

Lee, L. (2004). Learners' perspectives on networked collaborative interaction with native speakers of Spanish in the US. *Language Learning and Technology*, 8(1), 83–100.

Lee, W. (1996). The role of materials in the development of autonomous learning. In R. Pemberton, E. S. L. Li, W. W. F. Or & H. D. Pierson (Eds.), *Taking Control: Autonomy in Language Learning* (pp. 167–184). Hong Kong: Hong Kong University Press.

Leont'ev, A. N. (1978). *Activity, Consciousness, and Personality.* Englewood Cliffs, NJ: Prentice-Hall.

Leont'ev, A. N. (1981). *Problems of the Development of the Mind.* Moscow: Progress.

Levi-Strauss, C. (1968). *The Savage Mind.* Chicago: University of Chicago Press.

Levy, M. (1997). *Computer-Assisted Language Learning.* Oxford: Clarendon Press.

Little, D. (1988). Autonomy and self-directed learning: An Irish experiment. In H. Holec (Ed.), *Autonomy and Self-Directed Learning: Present Fields of Application* (pp. 77–84). Strasbourg: Council of Europe.

Little, D. (1989). *Self-access Systems for Language Learning.* Dublin: Authentik.

Little, D. (1991). *Learner Autonomy 1: Definitions, Issues, and Problems.* Dublin: Authentik.

Little, D. (1994). Words and their properties: arguments for a lexical approach to pedagogical grammar. In T. Odlin (Ed.), *Perspectives on Pedagogical Grammar* (pp. 99–122). Cambridge: Cambridge University Press.

Little, D. (1995). Learning as dialogue: the dependence of learner autonomy on teacher autonomy. *System*, 23(2), 175–181.

Little, D. (1996). Freedom to learn and compulsion to interact: Promoting learner autonomy through the use of information systems and information technologies. In R. Pemberton, E. S. L. Li, W. W. F. Or & H. D. Pierson (Eds.), *Taking Control: Autonomy in Language Learning* (pp. 203–218). Hong Kong: Hong Kong University Press.

Little, D. (1997a). Language awareness and the autonomous language learner. *Language Awareness*, 6(2–3), 93–104.

Little, D. (1997b). Responding authentically to authentic texts: A problem for self-access language learning? In P. Benson & P. Voller (Eds.), *Autonomy and Independence in Language Learning* (pp. 225–236). London: Longman.

Little, D. (1997c). The role of writing in second language learning: some neo-Vygotskian reflections. In R. Kupetz (Ed.), *Vom Gelenkten zum freien Schreiben im Fremdsprachenunterricht* (pp. 117–128). Frankfurt am Main: Peter Lang.

Little, D. (1997d). Seminar on research in CALL. *ReCALL*, 10(1), 127–128.

Little, D. (1998). Learning and teaching languages at distance: Problems and possibilities. In L. Jottini (Ed.), *Le Attività dei Centri Linguistici in una Dimensione Europea* (pp. 57–67). Cagliari: Cooperativa Universitaria Editrice Cagliaritana.

Little, D. (1999). Developing learner autonomy in the foreign language classroom: A social-interactive view of learning and three fundamental pedagogical principles. *Revista Canaria de Estudios Ingleses*, 38, 77–88.

Little, D. (2001). Learner autonomy and the challenge of tandem language learning via the Internet. In A. Chambers & G. Davies (Eds.), *Information and Communications Technologies and Language Learning: A European Perspective* (pp. 29–38). Lisse: Swets and Zeltlinger.

Little, D. (2003). The European Language Portfolio, reflective language learning and the assessment of communicative proficiency. In R. Ahrens (Ed.), *Europäische Sprachenpolitik- European Language Policy* (pp. 291–302). Heidelberg: Universitätsverlag Winter.

Little, D. (2005). The Common European Framework and the European Language Portfolio: Involving learners and their judgements in the assessment process. *Language Testing*, 22(3), 321–336.

Little, D., Devitt, S., & Singleton, D. (1989). *Learning Foreign Languages from Authentic Texts*. Dublin: Authentik.

Little, D., & Perclová, R. (2001). *The European Language Portfolio: A Guide for Teachers and Teacher Trainers*. Strasbourg: Council of Europe, Modern Languages Division.

Little, D., & Ushioda, E. (1997). Designing, implementing and evaluating a project in tandem language learning via e-mail. *ReCALL*, 10(1), 95–101.

Little, D., & Ushioda, E. (1998). *Institution-Wide Language Programmes*. London: Centre for Information on Language Teaching and Research.

Little, D., Ushioda, E., Appel, M. C., Moran, J., O'Rourke, B., & Schwienhorst, K. (1999). *Evaluating Tandem Language Learning by E-Mail: Report on a Bilateral Project* (Vol. 55, CLCS Occasional Paper). Dublin: Trinity College, Centre for Language & Communication Studies.

Little, D. G., & Grant, A. J. (1986). *Learning German Without a Teacher: Report on a Self-Instructional Programme for Undergraduate Students of Engineering Science at Trinity College, Dublin, 1982–84* (Vol. 14, CLCS Occasional Paper). Dublin: Trinity College, Centre for Language & Communication Studies.

Little, D. G., & Singleton, D. M. (1988). *Authentic Materials and the Role of Fixed Support in Language Teaching: Towards a Manual for Language Learners*

(Vol. 20, CLCS Occasional Paper). Dublin: Trinity College, Centre for Language & Communication Studies.

Littlejohn, A. (1997). Self-access work and curriculum ideologies. In P. Benson & P. Voller (Eds.), *Autonomy and Independence in Language Learning* (pp. 181–191). London: Longman.

Lombard, M., & Ditton, T. (1997). At the heart of it all: The concept of presence. Journal of Computer-Mediated Communication, 3(2). Retrieved 4 March, 1998, from http://www.ascusc.org/jcmc/vol3/issue2/lombard.html.

Long, M. H. (1981). Questions in foreigner talk discourse. *Language Learning*, 31, 135–157.

Long, M. H. (1983). Native-speaker/ non-native speaker conversations and the negotiation of comprehensible input. *Applied Linguistics*, 4, 126–141.

Lotman, Y. M. (1988). Text within a text. *Soviet Psychology*, 26, 32–51.

Malone, T. W., Lepper, M., Miyake, N., & Cohen, M. (1987). Making learning fun: A taxonomy of intrinsic motivations for learning. In R. E. Snow & M. J. Farr (Eds.), *Aptitude, Learning, and Instruction: III. Conative and Affective Process Analyses* (pp. 223–253). Hillsdale NJ: Erlbaum.

Manning, C. (2004, 14 February). Kirrkirr: software for the exploration of indigenous language dictionaries. On-line. Retrieved 10 March, 2004, from http://www-nlp.stanford.edu/kirrkirr/.

Manning, C., & Parton, K. (2001). What's needed for lexical databases? Experiences with Kirrkirr. In Proceedings of the IRCS Workshop on Linguistic Databases (pp. 167–173). Philadelphia: University of Pennsylvania.

Masny, D. (1997). Linguistic awareness and writing: Exploring the relationship with language awareness. *Language Awareness*, 6(2–3), 105–118.

McGarry, D. (1995). *Learner Autonomy 4: The Role of Authentic Texts*. Dublin: Authentik.

McGrath, I. (2000). Teacher autonomy. In B. Sinclair, I. McGrath & T. Lamb (Eds.), *Learner Autonomy, Teacher Autonomy: Future Directions* (pp. 100–110). Harlow: Longman.

McIntosh, S., Braul, B., & Chao, T. (2003). A case study in asynchronous voice conferencing for language instruction. *Educational Media International*, 40(1–2), 63–74. Retrieved 5 December, 2003, from http://taylorandfrancis.metapress.com/index/HERMVHU7YVJJ6R3Q.pdf.

McLellan, H. (1996). Situated learning: Multiple perspectives. In H. McLellan (Ed.), *Situated Learning Perspectives* (pp. 5–18). Englewood Cliffs, NJ: Educational Technology Publications.

Meskill, C. (1990). Where in the world of English is Carmen Sandiego? *Simulation & Gaming*, 21(4), 457–460.

Mezirow, J. (1985). A critical theory of self-directed learning. In S. Brookfield (Ed.), *Self-Directed Learning: From Theory to Practice* (pp. 17–30). San Francisco: Jossey-Bass.

Miller, G. A., & Gildea, P. M. (1987). How children learn words. *Scientific American*, 257(3), 94–99.

Milroy, L. (1984). Comprehension and context: Successful communication and communicative breakdown. In P. Trudgill (Ed.), *Applied Sociolinguistics* (pp. 7–31). London: Academic Press.

Milton, J., Smallwood, I., & Purchase, J. (1996). From word processing to text processing. In R. Pemberton, E. S. L. Li, W. W. F. Or & H. D. Pierson (Eds.), *Taking Control: Autonomy in Language Learning* (pp. 233–248). Hong Kong: Hong Kong University Press.

Müller, M., Schneider, G., & Wertenschlag, L. (1988). Apprentissage autodirigé en tandem à l'Université. In H. Holec (Ed.), *Autonomy and Self-Directed*

Learning: Present Fields of Application (pp. 65–76). Strasbourg: Council of Europe.

Murphey, T. (1987). *Teaching One to One*. Harlow: Longman.

Murray, D. E. (1985). Conversation for Action: The Computer Terminal as Medium of Communication. Unpublished PhD Dissertation, Stanford University.

Murray, D. E. (1992). Collaborative writing as a literacy event: implications for ESL instruction. In D. Nunan (Ed.), *Collaborative Language Learning and Teaching* (pp. 100–117). Cambridge: Cambridge University Press.

Murray, D. E. (2000). Protean communication: The language of computer-mediated communication. *TESOL Quarterly*, 34(3), 397–421.

Murray, J. H. (1997). *Hamlet on the Holodeck*. New York: The Free Press.

Mynatt, E. D., O'Day, V., Adler, A., & Ito, M. (1998). Network communities: Something old, something new, something borrowed... *Computer Supported Cooperative Work: The Journal of Collaborative Computing*(7), 123–156.

n.a. (2003, 4 March). SMS essay rings alarm bells for youth literacy. Sydney Morning Herald. from www.smh.com.au/articles/2003/03/03/1046540139361.html.

Nardi, B. A. (1996a). Activity theory and human-computer interaction. In B. A. Nardi (Ed.), *Context and Consciousness: Activity Theory and Human-Computer Interaction* (pp. 7–16). Cambridge, MA: MIT Press.

Nardi, B. A. (1996b). Preface. In B. A. Nardi (Ed.), *Context and Consciousness: Activity Theory and Human-Computer Interaction* (pp. xi–xiii). Cambridge, MA: MIT Press.

Nardi, B. A. (1996c). Studying context: A comparison of activity theory, situated action models, and distributed cognition. In B. A. Nardi (Ed.), *Context and Consciousness: Activity Theory and Human-Computer Interaction* (pp. 69–102). Cambridge, MA: MIT Press.

Neisser, U. (1976). *Cognition and Reality*. San Francisco, CA: Freeman.

Nelson, T. H. (1965). A file structure for the complex, the changing, and the indeterminate. Paper presented at the 20th National Conference of the ACM.

Newell, A. (1990). *Unified Theories of Cognition*. Cambridge, MA: Harvard University Press.

Ninio, A., & Bruner, J. (1978). The achievement and antecedents of labelling. *Journal of Child Language*, 5(1), 1–15.

no author. (n.d.). MAELC Access for External Users. On-line. Retrieved 3 March, 2004, from http://www.labschool.pdx.edu/maelc_access.html.

North, S. M. (1996, Winter). Effectiveness of virtual reality in the motivation processes of learners. *International Journal of Virtual Reality*, 2.

Nunan, D. (1992). Introduction. In D. Nunan (Ed.), *Collaborative Language Learning and Teaching* (pp. 1–10). Cambridge: Cambridge University Press.

O'Day, V., Bobrow, D., Bobrow, K., Shirley, M., Hughes, B., & Walters, J. (1998). Moving practice: From classrooms to MOO rooms. *Computer Supported Cooperative Work: The Journal of Collaborative Computing*(7), 9–45.

O'Rourke, B. (1998). A network-based tool for organizing second-language vocabulary. In T. Ottmann & I. Tomek (Eds.), *Proceedings of ED-Media/ED-Telecom '98*. Charlottesville, VA: Association for the Advancement of Computing in Education.

O'Rourke, B. (2002). Metalinguistic Knowledge in Instructed Second Language Acquisition: a Theoretical Model and its Pedagogical Application in Computer-Mediated Communication. Unpublished PhD Thesis, Trinity College, Dublin.

O'Rourke, B. (2005). Form-focused interaction in online tandem learning. *CALICO Journal*, 22(3), 433–467.

O'Rourke, B., & Schwienhorst, K. (2000). Learner databases and virtual worlds-Using computers to create collaborative learning environments. In M. Ruane & D. P. Ó. Baoill (Eds.), *Integrating Theory and Practice in LSP and LAP* (pp. 123–132). Dublin: ALC & IRAAL.

O'Rourke, B., & Schwienhorst, K. (2003). Talking text: reflections on reflection in computer-mediated communication. In D. Little, J. Ridley & E. Ushioda (Eds.), *Learner Autonomy in the Foreign Language Classroom: Teacher, Learner, Curriculum and Assessment* (pp. 47–60). Dublin: Authentik.

Olson, D. R. (1991). Literacy as metalinguistics. In D. R. Olson & N. Torrance (Eds.), *Literacy and Orality* (pp. 251–270). Cambridge: Cambridge University Press.

Oviatt, S., & Cohen, P. (1988). *Discourse structure and performance efficiency in interactive and noninteractive spoken modalities* (Tech Report No. 454). Menlo Park, CA: SRI International.

Oxford, R. L. (1995). Linking theories of learning with intelligent computer-assisted language learning (ICALL). In V. M. Holland, J. D. Kaplan & M. R. Sams (Eds.), *Intelligent Language Tutors: Theory Shaping Technology* (pp. 359–369). Mahwah, NJ: Lawrence Erlbaum Publ.

Oxford, R. L. (2003). Toward a more systematic model of L2 learner autonomy. In D. Palfreyman & R. C. Smith (Eds.), *Learner Autonomy Across Cultures: Language Education Perspectives* (pp. 75–91). London: Palgrave Macmillan.

Palfreyman, D., & Smith, R. C. (Eds.). (2003). *Learner Autonomy Across Cultures: Language Education Perspectives*. London: Palgrave Macmillan.

Palmer, M. L. (1995). Interpersonal communication and virtual reality: Mediating interpersonal relationships. In F. Biocca & M. R. Levy (Eds.), *Communication in the Age of Virtual Reality* (pp. 277–299). Hillsdale, NJ: Lawrence Erlbaum.

Pantelidis, V. (1993, April). Virtual reality in the classroom. *Educational Technology*, 33, 23–27.

Papert, S. (1990). Constructionism versus Instructionism. Paper presented at the Annual Meeting of the American Educational Research Association, Boston, April.

Papert, S. (1991). Situating constructionism. In I. Harel & S. Papert (Eds.), *Constructionism* (pp. 1–12). Norwood, NJ: Ablex Publishing. Retrieved 4 June, 2000, from http://www.papert.org/articles/SituatingConstructionism.html.

Papert, S. (1993). *The Children's Machine: Rethinking School in the Age of the Computer*. New York: Basic Books.

Papert, S. (1999). Ghost in the Machine: Seymour Papert on How Computers Fundamentally Change the Way Kids Learn. Interview of Seymour Papert by Dan Schwartz. Retrieved 8 July, 2000, from http://www.papert.org/articles/GhostInTheMachine.html.

Parks, M. R., & Floyd, K. (1996). Making friends in cyberspace. *Journal of Computer-Mediated Communication*, 1(4). Retrieved 21 June, 1998, from http://www.ascusc.org/jcmc/vol1/issue4/parks.html.

Parks, M. R., & Roberts, L. D. (1997). "Making MOOsic": The development of personal relationships on-line and a comparison to their off-line counterparts. Paper presented at the Annual Conference of the Western Speech Communication Association, Monterey, California. Retrieved 4 July, 1998, from http://www.geser.net/moo.htm.

Pellettieri, J. (2000). Negotiation in cyberspace: The role of chatting in the development of grammatical competence. In M. Warschauer & R. Kern (Eds.),

Network-based Language Teaching: Concepts and Practice (pp. 59–86). Cambridge: Cambridge University Press.

Perani, D. (2005). The neural basis of language talent in bilinguals. *Trends in Cognitive Sciences*, 9(5), 211–213. Retrieved 6 October, 2005, from http://www.sciencedirect.com/science?_ob=MImg&_imagekey=B6VH9-4FNTHDR-1-1&_cdi=6061&_user=103681&_orig=search&_coverDate=05%2F31%2F2005&_qd=1&_sk=999909994&view=c&wchp=dGLbVlz-zSkWW&md5=94878733ab9bc27afd20796a78801d4e&ie=/sdarticle.pdf.

Perry, J. (1979). The problem of the essential indexical. *Nous,* 13, 3–21.

Piaget, J. (1950). *The Psychology of Intelligence.* London: Routledge.

Piaget, J. (1952). *The Origins of Intelligence in Children.* New York: International University Press.

Piaget, J. (1977). *The Development of Thought: Equilibration of Cognitive Structures.* New York: Viking Press.

Picard, R. W., & Klein, J. (2002). Computers that recognise and respond to user emotion: theoretical and practical implications. *Interacting with Computers*, 14(2), 141–169.

Pinto, D. (1996). What does 'schMOOze' mean? Non-native speaker interactions on the Internet. In M. Warschauer (Ed.), *Telecollaboration in Foreign Language Learning* (pp. 165–184). Honolulu, HI: University of Hawai'i, Second Language Teaching and Curriculum Center.

Pujolà, J.-T. (2001). Did CALL feedback feed back? Researching learners' use of feedback. *ReCALL*, 13(1), 79–99.

Quarrick, G. (1989). *Our Sweetest Hours: Recreation and the Mental State of Absorption.* Jefferson, NC: McFarland.

Raeithel, A., & Velichkovsky, B. M. (1996). Joint attention and co-construction: New ways to foster user-designer collaboration. In B. A. Nardi (Ed.), *Context and Consciousness: Activity Theory and Human-Computer Interaction* (pp. 199–233). Cambridge, MA: MIT Press.

Rapanotti, L., & Hall, J. G. (2000, 23–25 August). Lyceum: Audio visual conferencing in distance education. Paper presented at the LTSN-ICS 1st Annual Conference, Heriot-Watt University Edinburgh. Retrieved 7 November, 2002, from http://www.ics.ltsn.ac.uk/pub/conf2000/Papers/Rapoanotti.pdf.

Rautenhaus, H. (Ed.). (1996). *Authentische Texte und Konkordanzprogramme im Englischunterricht.* Oldenburg: Carl v. Ossietzky Universität.

Reder, S., Harris, K., & Setzler, K. (2003). The Multimedia Adult ESL Learner Corpus. *TESOL Quarterly*, 37(3), 546–557.

Reinman, S. (1995). Electronic mail: Where does it fall in the oral/literate continuum? Unpublished draft.

Resnick, M. (1991). Xylophones, hamsters, and fireworks: The role of diversity in constructionist activities. In I. Harel & S. Papert (Eds.), *Constructionism.* Norwood, NJ: Ablex. Retrieved 12 April, 1998, from http://llk.media.mit.edu/papers/archive/XH.html.

Rézeau, J. (2001). Concordances in the classroom: The evidence of the data. In A. Chambers & G. Davies (Eds.), *Information and Communications Technologies and Language Learning: A European Perspective* (pp. 147–166). Lisse: Swets and Zeltlinger.

Rice, R. E., & Love, G. (1987). Electronic emotion: Socioemotional content in a computer-mediated network. *Communication Research*, 14, 85–108.

Ridley, J. (1997). *Reflection and Strategies in Foreign Language Learning.* Frankfurt am Main: Peter Lang.

Roberts, L., Smith, L. M., & Pollock, C. (1996a). Exploring virtuality: Telepresence in text-based virtual environments. Paper presented at the Cybermind

Conference, Curtin University of Technology, Perth, Western Australia. Retrieved 14 April, 1997, from http://www.nicoladoering.net/Hogrefe/roberts.htm.

Roberts, L. D., Smith, L. M., & Pollock, C. (1996b). MOOing till the cows come home: The search for sense of community in virtual environments. Paper presented at the 6th National Australian and New Zealand Community Psychology Conference: Promoting Action Research and Social Justice, Toodyay, Western Australia, 7–9 June.

Roberts, L. D., Smith, L. M., & Pollock, C. (1997). "u r a lot bolder on the net": The social use of text-based virtual environments by shy individuals. Paper presented at the International Conference on Shyness and Self-Consciousness, Cardiff, July 14–17.

Rose, H. (1996). Design and Construction of a Virtual Environment for Japanese Language Instruction. Unpublished Masters thesis, University of Washington, Seattle.

Rose, H., & Billinghurst, M. (1995). Zengo Sayu: an immersive educational environment for learning japanese (Technical Report No. 4-95). Seattle: Human Interface Technology Laboratory, University of Washington. Retrieved 14 April, 1997, from http://www.hitl.washington.edu/publications/r-95-4.html.

Rubin, A. (1980). A theoretical taxonomy of the differences between oral and written language. In R. J. Spiro, B. C. Bruce & W. F. Brewer (Eds.), *Theoretical Issues in Reading Comprehension* (pp. 411–438). Hillsdale, NJ: Lawrence Erlbaum Associates.

Ryan, J. (1995). A uses and gratifications study of the Internet social interaction site LambdaMOO: Talking with the 'Dinos'. Unpublished Master of Arts thesis, Ball State University, Muncie, Indiana.

Ryan, S. M. (1997). Preparing learners for independence: Resources beyond the classroom. In P. Benson & P. Voller (Eds.), *Autonomy and Independence in Language Learning* (pp. 215–224). London: Longman.

Sams, M. R. (1995). Advanced technologies for language learning: The BRIDGE Project within the ARI language tutor program. In V. M. Holland, J. D. Kaplan & M. R. Sams (Eds.), *Intelligent Language Tutors: Theory Shaping Technology* (pp. 7–21). Mahwah, NJ: Lawrence Erlbaum Publ.

Sanchez, B. (1995). MOO-la-la: Conversing in virtual Paris. In M. Warschauer (Ed.), *Virtual Connections: On-line Activities and Projects for Networking Language Learners* (pp. 229–230). Honolulu, HI: University of Hawai'i, Second Language Teaching and Curriculum Center.

Sanchez, B. (1996). MOOving to a new frontier in language teaching. In M. Warschauer (Ed.), *Telecollaboration in Foreign Language Learning* (pp. 145–164). Honolulu, HI: University of Hawai'i, Second Language Teaching and Curriculum Center.

Scharle, Á., & Szabó, A. (2000). *Learner autonomy : a guide to developing learner responsibility*. Cambridge ; New York: Cambridge University Press.

Schiano, D. J., & White, S. (1998). The first noble truth of cyberspace: People are people (even when they MOO). Paper presented at the CHI '98, 18-23 April, Los Angeles, CA.

Schmidt, R. (1990). The role of consciousness in second language learning. *Applied Linguistics,* 11, 129–158.

Schoelles, M., & Hamburger, H. (1996). Cognitive tools for language pedagogy. *Computer-Assisted Language Learning*, 9(2–3), 213–234.

Schoenfeld, A. H. (1987). What's all the fuss about metacognition? In A. H. Schoenfeld (Ed.), *Cognitive Science and Mathematics Education* (pp. 189–216). Hillsdale, NJ: Erlbaum.

Scholes, R. J., & Willis, B. J. (1991). Linguistics, literacy, and the intensionality of Marshall McLuhan's Western man. In D. R. Olson & N. Torrance (Eds.), *Literacy and Orality* (pp. 215–235). Cambridge: Cambridge University Press.

Schön, D. A. (1987). Teaching artistry through reflection-in-action. In D. A. Schön (Ed.), *Educating the Reflective Practitioner* (pp. 22–40). San Francisco, CA: Jossey-Bass Publishers.

Schroeder, R. (Ed.). (2002). *The Social Life of Avatars: Presence and Interaction in Shared Virtual Environments*. London: Springer Verlag.

Schweller, K. (1998). MOO educational tools. In C. Haynes & J. R. Holmevik (Eds.), *High Wired: On the Design, Use, and Theory of Educational MOOs* (pp. 88–106). Ann Arbor: University of Michigan Press.

Schwienhorst, K. (1998). The "third place"- virtual reality applications for second language learning. *ReCALL*, 10(1), 118–126.

Schwienhorst, K. (2000a). Telecommunications projects in language learning: Organisation, facilitation, evaluation. In E. Brown (Ed.), *Improving Student Performance in Language Learning Through ICT* (pp. 29–31). London: CILT.

Schwienhorst, K. (2000b). Virtual reality and learner autonomy in second language acquisition. Unpublished PhD thesis, Trinity College Dublin, Dublin.

Schwienhorst, K. (2002a). Evaluating tandem language learning in the MOO : Discourse repair strategies in a bilingual Internet project. *Computer Assisted Language Learning*, 15(2), 135–146.

Schwienhorst, K. (2002b). Pressures, potentials, and affordances: The role of tools in CALL environments. *Communication & Cognition - Artificial Intelligence*, 19(3-4), 133–149.

Schwienhorst, K. (2002c). The state of VR: A meta-analysis of virtual reality tools in second language acquisition. *Computer-Assisted Language Learning*, 15(3), 221–239.

Schwienhorst, K. (2002d). Why virtual, why environments? Implementing virtual reality concepts in computer-assisted language learning. *Simulation & Gaming*, 33(2), 196–209.

Schwienhorst, K. (2003). Neither here nor there? Learner autonomy and intercultural factors in CALL environments. In D. Palfreyman & R. C. Smith (Eds.), *Learner Autonomy Across Cultures: Language Education Perspectives* (pp. 164–180). London: Palgrave Macmillan.

Schwienhorst, K. (2004a). Detachment and reflection: Awareness and presence in a synchronous text-based environment. In R. Satchell & N. Chenik (Eds.), *University Language Centres : Forging the Learning Environments of the Future* (pp. 43–62). Paris: CercleS.

Schwienhorst, K. (2004b). Native-speaker/non native-speaker discourse in the MOO: Topic negotiation and initiation in a synchronous text-based environment. *Computer-Assisted Language Learning*, 17(1), 35–50.

Schwienhorst, K., & Borgia, A. (2006). Monitoring bilingualism: Pedagogical implications of the Bilingual Tandem Analyser. *CALICO Journal*, 23(2), 349–362.

Sharwood Smith, M. (1996). The Garden of Eden and Beyond: On Second Language Processing (Vol. 44, CLCS Occasional Paper). Dublin: Trinity College, Centre for Language & Communication Studies.

Shield, L., Davies, L. B., & Weininger, M. J. (2000). Fostering (pro)active language learning through MOO. *ReCALL*, 12(1), 35–48.

Shield, L., & Weininger, M. J. (1999). Collaboration in a virtual world- Groupwork and the distance language learner. In R. Debski & M. Levy (Eds.), *WorldCall: Global Perspectives on Computer Assisted Language Learning*.

Amsterdam: Swets & Zeitlinger. Retrieved 14 April, 2000, from http://www.cce.ufsc.br/lle/alemao/markus/VirtualWorld.html.

Shneiderman, B. (1982). The future of interactive systems and the emergence of direct manipulation. *Behaviour and Information Technology*, 1, 237–256.

Short, J., Williams, E., & Christie, B. (1976). *The Social Psychology of Telecommunications*. London: Wiley.

Shultz, J. J., Florio, S., & Erickson, F. (1982). Where's the floor? Aspects of the cultural organization of social relationships in communication at home and in school. In P. Gilmore & A. A. Glatthorn (Eds.), *Children In and Out of School* (pp. 88–123). Washington, D.C.: Center for Applied Linguistics.

Slatin, J. M. (1992). Is there a class in this text? Creating knowledge in the electronic classroom. In E. Barrett (Ed.), *Sociomedia* (pp. 27–51). Cambridge, MA: MIT Press.

Smets, J. F., Stappers, P. J., Overbeeke, K. J., & Mast, C. v. d. (1995). Designing in virtual reality: perception-action coupling and affordances. In K. Carr & R. England (Eds.), *Simulated and Virtual Realities* (pp. 189–208). London: Taylor and Francis.

Squires, D. (1999, May-June). Educational software for constructivist learning environments: Subversive use and volatile design. *Educational Technology*, 39, 48–54.

St. John, E. (2001). A case for using a parallel corpus and concordancer for beginners of a foreign language. *Language Learning & Technology*, 5(3), 185–203. Retrieved 30 October, 2001, from http://llt.msu.edu/vol5num3/stjohn/

Stone, A. R. (1995). *The War of Desire and Technology at the Close of the Mechanical Age*. Cambridge, MA: The MIT Press.

Sturtridge, G. (1982). Individualised learning: What are the options for the classroom teacher? In M. Geddes & G. Sturtridge (Eds.), *Individualisation* (pp. 8–14). London: Modern English Publications.

Svensson, P. (2003). Virtual worlds as arenas for language learning. In U. Felix (Ed.), *Language Learning Online: Towards Best Practice* (pp. 123–143). Lisse: Swets & Zeitlinger.

Swain, M. (1985). Communicative competence: some roles of comprehensible input and comprehensible output in its development. In S. Gass & C. Madden (Eds.), *Input in Second Language Acquisition*. Rowley, MA: Newbury House.

Tammelin, M. (1998). From telepresence to social presence: The role of presence in a network-based learning environment. In S. Tella (Ed.), *Aspects of Media Education: Strategic Imperatives in the Information Age* (pp. 219–232). Helsinki: Media Education Centre, Department of Teacher Education, University of Helsinki. Retrieved 14 April, 1999, from http://www.edu.helsinki.fi/media/mep8/tammelin.pdf.

Tammelin, M. (2003, 3-6 September). Anybody out there? The roles of presence and community in network-based learning environments. Paper presented at the EUROCALL Conference, Limerick, Ireland.

Taylor, M. (1990). Simulations and adventure games in CALL. *Simulation & Gaming*, 21(4), 461–466.

Tennison, J., & Shadbolt, N. R. (1998). APECKS: A Tool to Support Living Ontologies. Retrieved 3 January, 1999, from http://ksi.cpsc.ucalgary.ca/KAW/KAW98/tennison/.

Tharp, R., & Gallimore, R. (1988). *Rousing Minds to Life: Teaching, Learning, and Schooling in a Social Context*. Cambridge: Cambridge University Press.

Thomsen, H. (2000). Learners' favoured activities in the autonomous classroom. In D. Little, L. Dam & J. Timmer (Eds.), *Focus On Learning Rather Than Teaching: Why and How?* (pp. 71–86). Dublin: CLCS.

Thomsen, H., & Gabrielsen, G. (1991). *New Classroom Practices in Foreign Language Teaching: Co-operative Teaching-Learning.* Copenhagen: Danmarks Lærerhøjskole.

Tort-Moloney, D. (1997). Teacher Autonomy: A Vygotskian Theoretical Framework (Vol. 48, CLCS Occasional Paper). Dublin: Trinity College, Centre for Language & Communication Studies.

Towell, J., & Towell, E. (1997). Presence in text-based networked virtual environments or "MUDs". *Presence: Teleoperators and Virtual Environments,* 6(5), 590–595. Retrieved 23 March, 1998, from http://www.fragment.nl/mirror/various/Towell_et_al.1997.Presence_in_MUDs.htm,

Toyoda, E., & Harrison, R. (2002). Categorization of text chat communication between learners and native speakers of Japanese. *Language Learning and Technology,* 6(1), 82–99. Retrieved 30 March, 2003, from http://llt.msu.edu/vol6num1/toyoda/.

Tractinsky, N. (2004). Tools over solutions? comments on Interacting with Computers special issue on affective computing. *Interacting with Computers,* 16(4), 751–757.

Trebbi, T., Jopp, C., & Coco, M. (2003, 16–18 October). Didaktisk rollespill i en MOO: Er læringen satt på spill? Paper presented at the Digital Dannelse Conference, Oslo.

Tromp, J. G., & Dieberger, A. (1995). MUDs as text-based spatial user interfaces and research tools. *Journal of Intelligent Systems,* 5(2–4), 179–202.

Trueman, B. (1996). QuickTime VR and English as a second language. *Virtual Reality in the Schools,* 1(4).

Tudini, V. (2003). Using native speakers in chat. *Language Learning and Technology,* 7(3), 141–159. Retrieved 20 May, 2004, from http://llt.msu.edu/vol7num3/tudini/.

Turbee, L. (1995). MundoHipano: A text-based virtual environment for learners and native speakers of Spanish. In M. Warschauer (Ed.), *Virtual Connections: On-line Activities and Projects for Networking Language Learners* (pp. 233–234). Honolulu, HI: University of Hawai'i, Second Language Teaching and Curriculum Center.

Turkle, S. (1995). *Life on the Screen.* New York: Simon & Schuster.

Turner, J. (1995). A virtual treasure hunt: Exploring the three-dimensional aspect of MOOs. In M. Warschauer (Ed.), *Virtual Connections: On-line Activities and Projects for Networking Language Learners* (pp. 242–244). Honolulu, HI: University of Hawai'i, Second Language Teaching and Curriculum Center.

Ushioda, E. (1996). *Learner Autonomy 5: The Role of Motivation.* Dublin: Authentik.

Van der Linden, E. (1993). Does feedback enhance computer-assisted language learning. *Computers & Education,* 21(1–2), 61–65.

van Lier, L. (2000). From input to affordance: Social -interactive learning from an ecological perspective. In J. Lantolf (Ed.), *Sociocultural theory and Second Language Learning* (pp. 245–260). Oxford: Oxford University Press.

Vaughan, N., & Garrison, D. R. (2005). Creating cognitive presence in a blended faculty development community. *The Internet and Higher Education,* 8(1), 1–12.

Vilmi, R. (1999). CALL issues: Language learning over distance. In J. Egbert & E. Hanson-Smith (Eds.), *Call Environments: Research, Practice, and Critical Issues* (pp. 427–441). Alexandria, VA: TESOL.

Voller, P. (1997). Does the teacher have a role in autonomous language learning? In P. Benson & P. Voller (Eds.), *Autonomy and Independence in Language Learning* (pp. 98–113). London: Longman.

von Glasersfeld, E. (1984). An introduction to radical constructivism. In P. Watzlawick (Ed.), *The Invented Reality*. New York: Norton.

von Glasersfeld, E. (1987). Learning as a constructive activity. In C. Janvier (Ed.), *Problems of Representation in the Teaching and Learning of Mathematics* (pp. 3–18). Hillsdale, NJ: Erlbaum.

von Glasersfeld, E. (1989). Constructivism. In T. Husen & T. N. Postlethwaite (Eds.), *The International Encyclopedia of Education* (1st ed., Vol. 1, pp. 162–163). Oxford: Pergamon.

von Glasersfeld, E. (1996). Introduction: Aspects of constructivism. In C. T. Fosnot (Ed.), *Constructivism: Theory, Perspectives, and Practice* (pp. 3–7). New York: Teachers College Press.

Vygotsky, L. S. (1978). *Mind in society*. Cambridge, MA: Harvard University Press.

Vygotsky, L. S. (1986). *Thought and Language*. Cambridge, MA: MIT Press.

Wachman, R. (1999). Classroom practice: Autonomy through authoring software. In J. Egbert & E. Hanson-Smith (Eds.), *Call Environments: Research, Practice, and Critical Issues* (pp. 403–426). Alexandria, VA: TESOL.

Walther, J. B. (1992). Interpersonal effects in computer-mediated interaction: A relational perspective. *Communication Research*, 19(1), 52–90.

Walther, J. B. (1996). Computer-mediated communication: Impersonal, interpersonal, and hyperpersonal interaction. *Communication Research*, 23(1), 3–43.

Walther, J. B. (1997). Group and interpersonal effects in international computer-mediated collaboration. *Human Communication Research*, 23(3), 342–369.

Walther, J. B., Anderson, J. F., & Park, D. W. (1994). Interpersonal effects in computer-mediated interaction: A meta-analysis of social and antisocial communication. *Communication Research*, 21(4), 460–487.

Wang, Y. (2004). Supporting synchronous distance language learning with desktop videoconferencing. *Language Learning & Technology*, 8(3), 90–121. Retrieved 14 June, 2005, from http://llt.msu.edu/vol8num3/pdf/wang.pdf.

Warschauer, M. (1996a). Comparing face-to-face and electronic discussion in the second language classroom. *Calico Journal*, 13(2), 7–26.

Warschauer, M. (1996b). Computer-assisted language learning: an introduction. In S. Fotos (Ed.), *Multimedia Language Teaching* (pp. 3–20). Tokyo: Logos International. Retrieved 5 May, 1998, from http://www.gse.uci.edu/markw/call.html.

Warschauer, M. (1996c). Computer-mediated collaborative learning: Theory and practice. Honolulu, HI: University of Hawai'i, Second Language Teaching and Curriculum Center. from http://www.gse.uci.edu/markw/cmc1.html.

Warschauer, M. (2000). The death of cyberspace and the rebirth of CALL. *English Teachers' Journal*, 53, 61–67. Retrieved 5 June, 2001, from http://www.gse.uci.edu/markw/cyberspace.html.

Warschauer, M. (Ed.). (1995). *Virtual Connections: On-line Activities and Projects for Networking Language Learners*. Honolulu, HI: University of Hawai'i, Second Language Teaching and Curriculum Center.

Warschauer, M. (Ed.). (1996d). *Telecollaboration in Foreign Language Learning*. Honolulu, HI: University of Hawai'i, Second Language Teaching and Curriculum Center.

Warschauer, M., & Healey, D. (1998). Computers and language learning: An overview. *Language Teaching*, 31, 57–71. Retrieved 5 June, 1999, from http://www.gse.uci.edu/markw/overview.html

Weijdema, W. (2000, 31 August–2 September). Using a web-based portfolio for improving language competencies. Paper presented at the EUROCALL Conference, Dundee. Retrieved 11 March, 2001, from http://www.efa.nl/publicaties/docs.pf-taal.doc.

Wells, G. (1981a). Introduction. In G. Wells (Ed.), *Learning through Interaction* (pp. 1–21). Cambridge: Cambridge University Press.

Wells, G. (1981b). Language as interaction. In G. Wells (Ed.), *Learning through Interaction* (pp. 22–72). Cambridge: Cambridge University Press.

Wells, G. (1981c). Language, literacy and education. In G. Wells (Ed.), *Learning Through Interaction* (pp. 240–276). Cambridge: Cambridge University Press.

Wells, G., & Chang-Wells, G. L. (1992). *Constructing knowledge together*. Portsmouth, NH: Heinemann.

Wertsch, J. (1981). The concept of activity in Soviet psychology: An introduction. In J. Wertsch (Ed.), *The Concept of Actvity in Soviet Psychology*. Armonk, NY: M.E. Sharpe.

Wilkins, H. (1991). Computer Talk. *Written Communication*, 8(1), 56–78.

Willis, J. (2000, January-February). The maturing of constructivist instructional design: Some basic principles that can guide practice. *Educational Technology*, 40, 5–16.

Winke, P., & MacGregor, D. (2001). Review of Hot Potatoes. *Language Learning & Technology*, 5(2), 28–33.

Wolff, D. (1994). *New Approaches to Language Teaching: An Overview* (Vol. 39, CLCS Occasional Paper). Dublin: Trinity College, Centre for Language & Communication Studies.

Wolff, D. (2000). Second language writing: a few remarks on psycholinguistic and instructional issues. *Learning and Instruction*, 10(1), 107–112.

Wright, T. (1987). *Roles of Teachers and Learners*. Oxford: Oxford University Press.

Yuan, Y. (2003). The use of chat rooms in an ESL setting. *Computers and Composition*, 20(2), 194–206.

Zhang, S., & Fulford, C. P. (1994, July-August). Are interaction time and psychological interactivity the same thing in the distance learning television classroom? *Educational Technology*, 34, 58–64.

Zohrab, P. (1996). Virtual language and culture reality (VLCR). *Virtual Reality in the Schools*, 1(4). Retrieved 4 May, 1997, from http://www.coe.ecu.edu/vr/vrits/1-4zohra.htm.

Index